Handbook of Organizational Health Psychology

Programs to Make the Workplace Healthier

edited by

SAM KLARREICH, Ph.D.

PSYCHOSOCIAL PRESS
Madison   Connecticut

Copyright © 1998, Psychosocial Press

PSYCHOSOCIAL PRESS® and PSP (& design)® are registered trademarks of International Universities Press, Inc.

All rights reserved. No part of this book may be reproduced by any means, nor translated into a machine language, without the written permission of the publisher.

Library of Congress Cataloging-in-Publication Data

Handbook of organizational health psychology : programs to make the
  workplace healthier / edited by Sam Klarreich.
    p.   cm.
  Includes bibliographical references and index.
  ISBN 1-887841-17-2
  1. Industrial psychiatry.   2. Psychology, Industrial.
3. Employees—Mental health.   I. Klarreich, Samuel H.
RC967.5.H36   1998
658.3'82—dc21   98-22824
                                                                   CIP

Manufactured in the United States of America

Contents

Contributors		vii
Preface		xi
Introduction	A Bright Future for Organizational Health Psychology—Sam Klarreich	xv

Part I: Interventions to Promote Organizational Health — 1

Chapter 1.	How to Evaluate People for Small- to Medium-Sized Growth Companies—William Knaus	5
Chapter 2.	Attitudinal Differentiation: Corporate Belief System Analysis and Employee Performance Expectations—D. Keith Ferrell and Ann Marie Kopec	23
Chapter 3.	Why Computerized Life-Style Assessment Is Good for Business—Steven J. Stein and Harvey A. Skinner	35
Chapter 4.	How to Gain Access to a Company as a Consultant—John Gallup	43
Chapter 5.	Reducing Procrastination in the Workplace—Hank Robb	55
Chapter 6.	Creating the Family Friendly Workplace: Barriers and Solutions—Mark Frankel	79
Chapter 7.	How to Prevent Job Burnout in the Workplace—Diana R. Richman	101
Chapter 8.	A Cognitive Perspective on Absenteeism—Nancy Haberstroh Knaus	125
Chapter 9.	Changing People from Tender-Minded to Tough-Minded: A PATHWAY for Dealing with Chronic Pain—G. Barry Morris	139
Chapter 10.	How to Master Workplace Stress—Albert Ellis and Jack Gordon	157
✓Chapter 11.	Wellness in the Workplace: A Fourfold Path—F. Michler Bishop	173

v

Part II: Programs for Organizational Renewal in a Changing Environment — 199

Chapter 12. Change at Work: Why It Hurts and What Employers Can Do about It—Thomas E. Backer and John Porterfield — 203

Chapter 13. Resiliency: The Skills Needed to Move Forward in a Changing Environment—Sam Klarreich — 219

Chapter 14. Experiential Training for Organizational Transformation—Tim Dixon — 239

Chapter 15. Organizational Renewal: Outcome Management—The Other Side of Process Management—John F. C. McLachlan — 261

Name Index — 275
Subject Index — 285

Contributors

Thomas E. Backer, Ph.D., is president, Human Interaction Research Institute, a Los Angeles based nonprofit center for research and technical assistance on innovation and change, and an associate clinical professor of medical psychology, UCLA Medical School.

F. Michler Bishop, Ph.D., CAS, is director of alcohol and substance abuse services for the Institute for Rational–Emotive Therapy in New York, where he supervises training activities for the treatment of addictions using an integrated cognitive, emotive, and behavioral approach. He is also an associate professor at S.U.N.Y. College at Old Westbury. He has presented or copresented over 50 workshops and training sessions in this country and around the world, including two continuing education workshops at the recent American Psychological Association's Annual Convention.

Tim Dixon is the director of Brock University's Corporate Adventure Training Institute (CATI). In addition to providing adventure and experiential training and development opportunities for organizations, he coordinates CATI research studies on the transfer of training to a work setting. His involvement within the community of practitioners using experiential methods includes serving since 1993 as chair of the international professional group, Experience Based Training and Development, as well as co-authoring *Safety Practices in Adventure Programming* under the auspices of the Association for Experiential Education.

Albert Ellis, Ph.D., founder of rational–emotive behavior therapy and the president of The Institute for Rational–Emotive Therapy in New York, has shaped the field of counseling/psychotherapy and is recognized around the globe for his remarkable contributions. He has more than 65 books and monographs to his credit, and has written over 700 articles.

D. Keith Ferrell is a licensed psychologist and certified addictions counselor in private practice and president of the Pennsylvania Institute for Rational–Emotive Therapy and Ferrell and Associates Inc., Wilkes-Barre, Pennsylvania. He is an associate fellow of the Institute for Rational–Emotive Therapy, New York, and an accredited supervisor in rational–emotive methods.

Mark Frankel, Ph.D., is founder and president of Microchip Human Services Inc., a leading provider of child and elder care information and referral services in Canada since 1988. In 1991, the organization launched *TakingCare,* North America's first fully automated referral service based on interactive voice response and fax-on-demand technology. *TakingCare* now supplies more than 40 corporations across Canada with comprehensive child and elder care assistance. He has worked for more than 20 years in the fields of family and community mental health. He is the co-author of *Treating the Multiproblem Family: A Casebook.* He has also authored both articles and research studies concerned with the work–family interface.

John Gallup headed an enormously successful medium-sized growth company. During his tenure, he moved it from an 18 to a 34% market share. He accomplished this result in a highly competitive fine paper products market. He understood that his products had to be exceptional to compete, but that he had to market them effectively to gain market share.

Jack Gordon practices rational–emotive behavior therapy.

Sam Klarreich, Ph.D., C.Psych., is president of The Berkeley Centre for Effectiveness and The Centre for Rational–Emotive Therapy (Toronto), and has a distinguished career that spans more than 20 years as a psychologist, author, advisor, and senior level consultant. He has written numerous professional papers, five books, and many articles on a variety of health related topics.

Nancy Haberstroh Knaus, Ph.D., M.B.A., is the director of psychological services for the Monson Developmental Center. She has participated in major assessment center programs, conducted marketing research, and devised programs for assisting mentally retarded people to live a less restricted existence. Her training and experience is both in psychology and business.

William Knaus, Ph.D., is a pioneer in the cognitive revolution in psychotherapy. He wrote the seminal works on procrastination, has published 10 self-help books, and numerous articles on how to take charge of your life, and currently has 3 new books in process, one of which is to help job hunters. He devised an original cognitive-skills development school mental health program for children that has enjoyed 25 years of positive research.

Ann Marie Kopec is a licensed clinical social worker and certified addictions counselor in private practice and the executive director of the Pennsylvania Institute for Rational–Emotive Therapy, Wilkes-Barre, Pennsylvania. She is a fellow of the Institute for

Rational-Emotive Therapy, New York, and an accredited supervisor in rational–emotive methods. She has lectured internationally on the topics of victimization and posttraumatic stress disorder, and is the author of several journal articles in the area of rational–emotive behavior therapy.

John F. C. McLachlan, Ph.D., has conducted outcome studies for the government and private sectors. He designed and implemented a series of outcome projects as director of outcome management at Peel Memorial Hospital. His publications have been in the general area of assessment, evaluation of treatment, and quality achievement. He is a Toronto based psychologist in private practice.

G. Barry Morris, Ph.D., is a registered psychologist, director of the Canadian Institute for Rational–Emotive Therapy, president of Rational Alternatives Consulting Ltd., and a professor at the University of Saskatchewan. Rational Alternatives Consulting operates as an assessment referral service for numerous employee and family assistance programs in Saskatoon and the surrounding area and offers a pain management program to the Saskatchewan government insurance and the Saskatchewan Worker's Compensation Board for individuals suffering from chronic pain and chronic stress syndromes. He provides an anger management program to inmates at the Saskatchewan Correctional Institute and the Regional Psychiatric Centre and conducts numerous workshops on stress, leadership, and work related issues with both business and educational groups.

John Porterfield, M.A., is a counselor and consultant in private practice.

Diana R. Richman, Ph.D., licensed clinical psychologist and organizational consultant, serves as director, clinical supervisor at A.P.P.L.E. Inc., Queens and Long Island, New York, where she supervises and trains mental health practitioners in the treatment of alcohol and substance disorders. She is senior supervisor and coordinates the career counseling programs at the Institute for Rational–Emotive Therapy in New York. She consults with major corporations in the areas of job burnout, stress management, career and management development, interpersonal communication, and assertiveness skills. She has authored numerous publications on the application of cognitive behavioral and rational–emotive behavioral techniques to work related issues.

Hank Robb, Ph.D., A.B.P.P., C.A.S., received his doctorate in counseling psychology from the University of Nebraska, Lincoln, in

1978. He is a Diplomate of the American Board of Professional Psychology in both Counseling Psychology and Behavioral Psychology, a Certified Addictions Specialist of the American Academy of Health Care Providers in the Addictive Disorders, and an Associate Fellow of the Institute for Rational-Emotive Therapy, New York.

Harvey A. Skinner, Ph.D., is Professor and Chair of the Department of Behavioural Science, Faculty of Medicine, University of Toronto; and also is a Senior Scientist at the Addiction Research Foundation of Ontario. Dr. Skinner has published widely on the use of computer technology and has developed a number of assessment instruments (e.g., Family Assessment Measure).

Steven J. Stein, Ph.D., is president of Multi-Health Systems, a leading test publishing company and holds an appointment of assistant professor in the Department of Psychiatry at the University of Toronto. He received his Ph.D. in clinical psychology from the University of Ottawa and was previously the director of research at Thistletown Regional Centre, a large child and adolescent treatment center in Toronto.

Preface

SAM KLARREICH, Ph.D.

It is no surprise to find companies wrestling with organizational changes such as restructurings, downsizings, realignments, mergers, rightsizings, and eventual "reinvention." Whatever the phenomenon, companies struggle to find that proper mix of the right people with the right systems and processes to move forward, remain competitive, and improve the bottom-line.

Unique opportunities may become available for organizational psychologists, if they are able to meet the needs of these changing organizations and offer valuable and value-added services.

In the process of change, a multitude of issues arise. Because companies are whittling away at the number of overall employees (and middle managers in particular), the workload has increased for those left behind to pick up the pieces. Although everyone is attempting to work "smarter," they are nonetheless working significantly harder. This has translated into increased anger, frustration, impatience, and a significant rise in interpersonal conflicts. People seem to be running flat out in an attempt to do their work, keep their jobs, and "look good" in the process. Yet there are breakdowns and people react with intense emotion and accompanying increases in stress reactions.

Because of the marked changes in organizations and their people, families have been profoundly impacted. Dual career families seem to be the norm. Both partners feel the need to work to maintain a reasonable standard of living. However, when they come home exhausted, irritable, and stressed, the possibility of tempers running high increases. In fact marital and family problems have escalated. The incidence of child abuse, spousal abuse, and parental abuse has increased. Sexual inactivity and intimacy problems between partners have increased.

With the rise of domestic and workplace pressures, substance abuse disorders have increased. People resort to alcohol or both prescripton and illegal drugs in order to be able to come to grips with the ever-changing realities of living. With this increased reliance on mood altering substances come more profound problems on the home front and more serious problems on the job.

In an attempt to look for quick-fix solutions, organizational leaders have focused their attention on improving technical efficiency. Thus companies have invested tremendous amounts of money in new or improved technology. All the while, employees are scratching their heads wondering why training and development dollars have been slashed, why health care benefits have been restricted. If companies are to move forward and stay competitive and even leading edge, it is critical that energy, resources, and funds be devoted to the people side of the equation.

To compound matters, the health care system has experienced its own restructuring and reinvention. Managed care, with its apparent shortcomings, has become the order of the day. There have been employee complaints about the lack of quality care and service. Quality seems to have been replaced by efficiency, cost-effectiveness, and making a profit through the provision of rapid assessments and short-term interventions.

No doubt escalating costs have badly hurt organizations and the health care system. But have the present answers provided solutions or created more problems? If employees are seriously stressed on the job and suffering, and are faced with reduced health care benefits at work and a health care system that doesn't seem to care, no wonder a few do the unspeakable and in a fit of anger and rage take out their frustrations on their employer or society. They might destroy company property, or sabotage the computer system, or steal valuable and proprietary information. In the worst case scenario, they may arm themselves with a gun or rifle, walk into the office, and start shooting, taking the lives of others and eventually perhaps their own. Although, this might sound overly dramatic, such events have already taken place!

There is clearly a pressing need for organizational health psychology, given what is transpiring in the workplace and in the health care system. Organizational health psychologists and practitioners need to instruct organizations and their leaders through a variety of services and programs to become more "psychologically minded." This means teaching the leaders-managers to know their people on many levels in order to motivate, help, and inspire them to move forward, while the tides of change continue. Organizational health psychology can help through a variety of channels, namely:

- Consulting
- Coaching
- Counseling
- Skills training
- Experiential learning

Working with employees certainly cannot be overlooked. Organizational health psychologists and practitioners need to teach employees to be more resilient and *engage* change rather than avoid or deny it.

Once organizations and their leaders-managers and employees experience the benefits of organizational health psychology, people are likely to feel better and perhaps rely less upon the health care system and utilize company benefits less often. When this happens, everyone wins: The health care system is less burdened, corporate benefit costs are no longer spiraling, and employees are healthier and more productive!

Introduction: A Bright Future for Organizational Health Psychology

SAM KLARREICH, Ph.D.

It has become blatantly obvious that change as we know it will not cease. It is being driven and will continue to be driven by technological advancement, global competition, corporate reengineering efforts, and the prevailing desire to do things better and more efficiently, with a look to improving that sacred bottom line. Greater accountability, working harder and smarter, place unrelenting pressure on management and employees.

As companies forge new directions in attempts to continue to be competitive and efficient, they will also look for ways to do things better with fewer resources. In the process, they will need to be mindful of the health and well-being of their people, otherwise serious health and morale problems will abound. Companies will need to demonstrate that they care and are concerned about their people. A way to achieve this will be to deliver services and programs that are offered by organizational health psychologists and practitioners. Indeed organizational health psychology has a bright future and will become a necessary part of the fabric and the dynamic of companies.

The nature of what is meant by a "job" will continue to change. Already people are encouraged to job share, to consider working part-time or as a "temp." Doing jobs "on contract" is a growing reality. There are many people who have been encouraged to leave a company with the offer to be brought back on contract. This way the organization can trim its fixed costs and the person still has work to do. However, once the job is completed, there is no assurance of anything else. So the person then needs to find other contract work either with the same organization or another one. Early retirement packages are an ongoing phenomenon and will continue to be a viable option for companies looking to cut their numbers. The big question remains, "Where do all these people go?" These job changes will continue to place a heavy burden on those who are losing their regular jobs as well as those who are still employed.

Organizational health psychologists will play a key role in assisting people to adjust to their job changes and teach them to redefine work altogether. They will assist the survivors to make the necessary adjustments to continue performing productively while preparing for another possible restructuring in the future. Beliefs about job stability, security, and predictability will need to be permanently altered and replaced with a new worldview of what a "job" truly is. It is employing one's skills, abilities, and resources to perform a needed task or series of tasks for someone who requires your services, without the guarantee that those services will again be required once the tasks are completed. It will then be the responsibility of the individual to uncover the next job opportunity either with the same organization or another one. It sounds like a risky proposition, but it is one that is already taking shape.

Changes in the concept of the workplace will continue. No longer are people required to be at the workplace to get the job done. Home offices are springing up everywhere and this trend will continue at a rapid pace. The workplace is also taking on a global perspective. People can communicate worldwide through electronic mail. An office in Asia can rapidly relay messages to an office in Europe. People in different offices all over the world can have lengthy, stimulating meetings without ever facing one another in person, via satellite communication and teleconferencing. Because of its heavy reliance on technological advancements, the workplace will support less interpersonal contact and meetings in favor of electronic communication, as a way to heighten efficiency. This may spawn a decline in interpersonal involvement that may present its own set of problems. Because of a declining interest in the interpersonal nature of work, i.e., relating to and talking with others, special attention may need to be directed to these very important issues.

Organizational health psychologists will play a key role in helping people to adjust to new working conditions as well as helping them to improve on underutilized interpersonal skills.

Career development will continue to become more the responsibility of the employee than management. The employee will need to ensure that he or she is ready, prepared, and able to move forward inside an organization with new and improved skills or move out of the organization with the skills needed to make a smooth transition.

Organizational health psychologists will have an opportunity to assist people to improve their career skill sets and make it possible for them to be more confident and able to become more mobile inside an organization or make the transition to another company should the need arise.

Health and well-being of people will continue to be assaulted by numerous workplace stressors, pressures, and the ever-present mandate of doing more with less. Added to this will be the pressing need to balance company demands against family demands for equal time and energy.

Organizational health professionals will play a leading role in helping people deal with the real urgencies of balancing work and family without "going crazy" in the process. In fact professionals will need to make certain that they are themselves living examples of this essential flexibility and are practicing what they preach.

In conclusion it is possible that companies, in the future, will have on their staff, either as a contract consultant or as a salaried specialist, an organizational health psychologist, to advise, consult, and offer programs. This professional will provide unique and needed services to help the organization and its people deal with the sequelae of change and their impact on jobs, the workplace, career development, health, and family. As traditional notions of job security, stability, and predictability erode and are replaced with new and ever growing notions that espouse flexibility, mobility, job impermanence, and a stronger reliance on personal skills, competencies, and commitments, organizational health psychologists should have a long and interesting future ahead helping people make the transition.

Part I

Interventions to Promote Organizational Health

This section describes a variety of interventions that promote organizational health through the enhancement of employee health, well-being, and productivity.

In chapter 1 Knaus indicates that the health of a workplace begins with the strengths and capabilities of the people who provide the services, produce the products, and support the organization. Small- to medium-sized growth companies face special challenges because their personnel requirements are often intense as the organization "upsizes" and requires more specialized talent. It is here that modern prescreening strategies can pay significant dividends both in supporting the growth of the organization and in furthering its general health. This chapter describes what to do to support the efforts of small- to medium-sized growth companies through helping management find the best people available for key jobs that support the growth of the operation.

Ferrell and Kopec point out that individuals and organizations as well as employees and employers interact so as to satisfy mutually exclusive goals. When goals are readily identifiable and congruent, individuals and organizations are typically able to work in harmony in order to satisfy their goals. When goal incongruity is manifested overtly or covertly, neither entity is able to readily satisfy its needs or attain its goals. This chapter explores attitudinal and value differences between organizations and individuals, role and performance expectations, and an intervention approach which is designed to reduce conflict and enhance employee performance through a better understanding of inherent belief systems.

Stein and Skinner indicate that many organizations are pressed to justify increased expenditures in health benefits, employee assistance programs, and health promotion. However, the costs of absenteeism due to illness, stress, and burnout are overwhelming. Because business leaders have difficulty in connecting soft measures of human performance to the bottom line, little progress has been made in dealing with employee life-style issues. Their chapter describes a program that can be most useful to organizations. This program, the Computerized Lifestyle Assessment (CLA), provides awareness and early intervention. It is designed to provide a simple and comprehensive technique for routine case identification, allowing for early recognition of problems in a variety of settings.

Gallup's chapter deals with the importance of people in furthering the growth of a highly successful medium-sized growth company. He describes how to develop a consulting relationship with a growth company and the ways in which mental health consultants can contribute to an organization. He advises establishing prescreening personnel assessment systems, cross-transfer programs, staff development programs, mental health interventions, market research programs, employee conference programs, outplacement services, and career counseling. He sees that psychologists can visibly contribute their skills to further the health of an organization, its people, and the community in which it operates.

Robb's chapter points out that procrastination at work is quite often a chronic condition. Whether chronic or transitory, the treatment must include first recognizing what is deeply important in an individual's life so as to then effectively prioritize, plan, and follow through. Procrastinators tend to both underpredict the amount of time necessary to complete a task and overpredict the time available. They can also anticipate problems in tolerating the necessity of working even when they do not feel like it. Both planning and follow-through can be enhanced and anxiety and depression reduced, by systematically countering tendencies to: (1) demand that self, others, and the world change because it would be preferable if they were different; (2) act as if unpleasant realities are either worse than they can possibly be or at least worse than they actually are; and (3) rate one's personhood based on performance. He presents a variety of methods for overcoming these problems.

Frankel in his chapter addresses the issue that employers have been slow to adopt family friendly programs and policies. Despite some notable exceptions and a substantial body of evidence supporting family-responsive programming, most workplaces have resisted change. Powerful barriers exist to both adoption and usage of such programs. Further progress depends upon a frank recognition of these difficulties and a willingness to consider new and enhanced approaches to the issue. He presents recent systems based research that offers insights into the work–family relationship and a basis for a more effective conceptual framework for tackling work–family problems. More realistic and pragmatic marketing approaches are also offered.

Richman indicates that throughout the fluctuating economic and career development cycle, job burnout has continued to pervade the workplace. Employees experience debilitating symptoms that result in problems for individuals and their organizations. Many recommendations for preventing and treating job burnout emphasize behavioral and situational change. However, helping employees to deal with uncontrollable work-related events when desired external workplace conditions are unrealistic needs to be addressed. Her chapter suggests that individuals can learn to identify and modify their internal cognitions when unexpected stressful workplace events occur. A cognitive–behavioral approach is presented for preventing and treating the job burnout syndrome. Five cognitive themes associated with job burnout are described, with burnout beliefs within each theme delineated.

Knaus points out that voluntary absenteeism in the workplace adds to the high cost of doing business. Investigators, however, have derived little agreement in defining terms, developing sound research methodologies, and gaining conclusive empirical results about this important area. Empirical studies have conclusively found zero to weak correlations between attitudes of job satisfaction, job involvement, and absenteeism. These results partially flow from inconsistently defined concepts of job dissatisfaction and involvement and loosely defined mechanisms for voluntary absent behavior. Her chapter describes these issues and provides cognitive mechanisms for voluntary absence behavior that define a direction for future research.

Morris notes that chronic pain is of growing importance in the North American workplace. Traditionally chronic pain has been defined and treated within a biomedical framework. More recently, the biopsychosocial model has emerged as the most useful approach to understanding and managing chronic pain syndromes. In his chapter he identifies the critical components of a biopsychosocial approach to pain management, in which the psychosocial component is based on rational–emotive behavior therapy. These components constitute a seven-step pathway to a psychologically healthy orientation to chronic pain that empowers clients to regain and maintain control of this aspect of their lives.

Ellis and Gordon indicate that in today's rapidly changing work environment, many kinds of stressors confront working people and significantly contribute to various stress-related, unhealthy, psychological, and physiological symptoms and problems. In their chapter, they discuss the rational–emotive behavior therapy approach to stress-related disorders. Rational–emotive behavior therapists show people who work in highly stressful conditions how they can minimize needless distress and learn to accept and cope successfully with stressors in the immediate future that they cannot eliminate. Typical stressors in the working environment which contribute to stress-related symptoms are discussed and rational–emotive behavioral treatments are detailed and explained.

Finally, Bishop details in his chapter how mental health professionals can help people maintain and improve their physical and psychological wellness by teaching and learning a combination of cognitive, emotive and behavioral techniques, thereby honoring the interactiveness of our thinking, emotions, and behaviors. Spiritual techniques may also be useful, as they combine cognitive, emotive, and behavioral approaches, albeit with a different meaning. Hence, his chapter focuses on how individuals may work on themselves in four interconnected ways. However, as the U.S. culture often overemphasizes the role of the individual, powerful social, economic, and political factors beyond the individual's control which strongly affect wellness should not be ignored.

1.

How to Evaluate People for Small- to Medium-Sized Growth Companies

WILLIAM KNAUS, Ph.D.

An assistant personnel director presents a candidate for evaluation and prefaces her statement with, "Our search firm has great confidence that Joe will be the next purchasing manager." A review of the person's resume shows that he had 12-year tenure with his last employer where he served two of those years as purchasing manager.

The assistant personnel director reported that the candidate was "outplaced" because the company downsized and eliminated his position. The candidate has been out of work for 3 years. You ask how the candidate explains this employment gap? The personnel worker says that the candidate reports that he owned his own business for a year. He said that the economy went sour in his geographic region, and so he dissolved the company. He then consulted for a time. The candidate now seeks a challenging position in a growth company where he can put his entrepreneurial and consultant skills to good use.

In an assessment center evaluation, the candidate adequately solved 3 of 10 basic problems related to the purchasing manager position. The assessment center procedure relies on multiple measures, multiple criteria, multiple observers, and job specific simulations (see "Selecting People for Growing Companies" on pages 15–17 for a description of this method). He provided substandard solutions to the other seven simulated problem conditions. In a problem solving group simulation, he was unable to coordinate the group effort to produce a productive outcome. In a role-playing situation, with a company employee playing the part of a company "vendor," the candidate concluded a deal that would have proved disadvantageous to the company.

The candidate's performances across simulation conditions were rated by a team of five trained assessors using five operationally defined management dimensions. These dimensions were problem analysis, planning, organizing, coordinating, and evaluation. Four of the raters were company employees, and the fifth was the author. In this phase of the evaluation, each member of the assessment team independently judged the candidate as a below average performer.

Later, in an "informal" luncheon interview, the candidate volunteered that he had spent the previous evening at a bar. He reported that he recognized that he had done poorly in the simulations, and offered the explanation that he was fatigued from staying up too late. Asked for details about his business, he reported that the company he incorporated did not go beyond the planning stage. Although he did groundwork for his consulting business, and presented brochures and other support materials, he had one consulting arrangement that lasted for 5 weeks. He presented a dysphoric mood as he voluntarily spoke of his efforts to stay sober.

During a final review of this candidate's application, one member of the personnel staff argued that if management hired him, the candidate would be grateful to the company and would be so eager to work that he would do an outstanding job. He reasoned that the candidate had 3 years of pent-up work energy ready to be unleashed and was ready to turn his life around. Other personnel workers held that the assessment center data made a compelling argument for declining to pursue the candidate's application.

To resolve the conflict between the assessment results and one personnel staff's predictions, the chief executive officer (CEO) followed up and obtained opinions from several of his company's vendors who had supplied the candidate's former employer. The response he received was consistent with assessment center findings. The CEO also discovered that the candidate's former employer not only did not downsize the company, but acquired an additional organization to support the business. Because of his evaluation and assessment center data, the CEO declined to hire the candidate.

Personnel are at greater risk of workplace stress under conditions where an operation is inadequately managed or staffed with too many difficult people. At the extreme, such conditions can significantly decrease morale and increase the risk of turnover, but also evoke symptoms of stress among some employees that include burnout, depression, anxiety, substance abuse disorders, procrastination, and physical illness. Such conditions weigh against efficiency and productivity and argue for valid prescreening selection systems that can reduce such risks and increase the probability of good selections.

Many top managers hold to the belief that people with positive dispositions are more productive than their more melancholic peers. Straw and Barsade (1993) have challenged this view. While admitting that such beliefs may not be fundamentally wrong, they assert that the beliefs are compromised by personal and situational work conditions. However, most would agree that personnel who function responsibly, show integrity, display tolerance, and exhibit sound work values and skills normally help strengthen the organization. Promoting conditions to make the workplace healthier starts with selecting people for positions of responsibility who can efficiently and effectively add to the growth and health of the organization.

THE CHALLENGE

This chapter is for organizational psychologists who are interested in working with managers who want to know more about how to use modern personnel selection technology to strengthen their growth organizations. It is also for other specialists who are professionally trained in assessment methodology, who want to establish consulting relationships with small- and medium-sized growth companies where they can apply their training and where they can make objective contributions to a growth company's means of selecting and retaining top performers.

Small- to medium-sized growth companies may infrequently use human resources strategies and practices (Terpstra, 1994). Such practices, however, can give them a competitive edge in a changing local, national, and global environment. Thus, knowledgeable decision makers and organizational psychologists may find many opportunities to collaborate on devising productive human resources selection strategies. There are sound reasons for this collaboration.

- Many small- to medium-sized growth organizations rely on interview methods, reference checks, resumé reviews, and home-grown paper-and-pencil inventory methods. Many of these methods lack adequate levels of objectivity, reliability, validity, sensitivity, and utility. In some cases, this is like putting on a set of translucent lenses and using a rubber yardstick to build a house. The picture is rarely very clear and

the measure can change from day to day. Psychologists, and other specialists qualified in the use of restricted psychological measures, can provide substantive selection instruments that rely on empirical research and standardization procedures and "expert" interpretations. Although there will be variances and imperfections in such measures, empirically supported yardsticks will normally provide a truer picture of a candidate's capabilities for a position. Thus, many candidates would be hired who would otherwise have been denied consideration. Poor hires are less likely, but will still occur.
- Empirically valid assessment methods can benefit companies which wish to incorporate technologically sophisticated selection methods into their hiring practices. Measures, as obtained through assessment centers, provide management with screened candidates with demonstrated capabilities to do key parts of the job. Although most candidates are considered within the context of trade-offs (strengths, weaknesses, limitations, special considerations, salary requirements, and so forth), under the assessment center scenario, there should be a lower selection error rate.
- By virtue of their specialized training as scientist/practitioners, organizational psychologists are highly qualified to administer, monitor, evaluate, and upgrade employee selection measures. They are routinely informed by their professional organizations, through newsletters, conferences, and professional journals on issues such as within-group norming, the 1991 Civil Rights Act, testing standards, and new trends in measurements and assessments.
- The small- to medium-sized growth company market is fragmented. Historically such markets have provided unusual opportunities for those who can devise and sell a service that proves more cost effective and valuable than existing methods.

THE FOUNDATIONS FOR CONSULTING

The selection of competent people to support a growth company's mission significantly decides the future of an organization. Companies where the balance shifts toward the hiring of above average performers for positions that require strong talent, will eventually gain market share advantage over competitors of similar size who do not take advantage of modern personnel assessment strategies.

The selection of candidates with demonstrated competency helps the organization in at least four additional ways. Executive management will normally (1) pay out fewer training dollars and get more benefit from training expenditures; (2) have less turnover due to poor selections and placements; (3) expend less time in direct supervision because above-average performers are more likely to recognize and solve problems more efficiently and effectively; (4) profit from having key people with above average planning, organizing, coordinating, and evaluative skills. Competent performers may also support the company's mission and objectives by studying and reporting on new initiatives that will enable the operation to grow.

Assuming that a company can achieve competitive advantages as a result of superior hiring and promotional practices, these major and minor premises form the platform for this chapter: (1) Organizational psychologists who are trained to pursue the challenge of supporting a company's growth can apply expert experience and technical knowledge to the task of picking the right person for a job; (2) they rely on research, expert experience, and reliable and valid selection methods to increase the probability that the hired person will function with reasonable effectiveness.

The major and minor premise supports this conclusion: As a group, trained, competent organizational psychologists are likely to produce selection programs that can help separate above average performers from average or substandard performers. It also follows, as a logical extension, that the most valid measures for personnel selection—assessment centers, job simulations, biographical inventories, and other standardized inventories—are typically designed and evaluated by organizational psychologists. As these procedures also are normally evaluated by the professional community of organizational psychologists, the consumer has an added layer of protection.

There is substantial evidence to support the two premises, the conclusion, and the logical extension. These components differentiate people who have formal training in the construction, administration, or evaluation of personnel selection measures and tools, from many nonpsychologically trained competitors who normally rely on poorly validated, home-grown tests and programs to support their selection business.

In the next section, I will describe arguments for the inclusion of organizational psychologists, and other professionally trained measurement professionals, in the small- and medium-sized company personnel selection market.

SELECTION COST FACTORS

People selection is an important phase of running a growth company. New positions open, there will be a normal turnover. Without an ongoing strong presence of competent staff in an organization, a business can lose ground to the competition.

Picking the right people will normally translate into cost savings and increased profits. The savings can be found in reduced recruitment costs, training costs, worker's compensation costs, employee turnover costs, and outplacement costs. The profits are found in the results of the performance of people who have higher level problem-solving skills.

Top performers predictably get the job done more effectively and often require less supporting staff. This translates into productivity advantages, and, predictably, a healthier workplace environment as people who are challenged by their work will have less time to waste in unproductive pursuits—busywork. Thus, the company that has the technology to routinely recruit and select above average performers for key positions should be in a better position to outperform competition that relies on less valid selection methods including the "throw bodies into the job until one sticks" approach.

Whether an assessment center prescreening system is utilized will significantly depend on payback factors. There is a growing trend for companies to look at their human resources functions to find ways to make them profitable. O'Connell (1995) notes that two years is a reasonable time for new human services systems to pay for themselves in cost savings and productivity improvements. Odon (1995) suggests additional categories where preemployment screening efforts can save their organizations the costs of "poor hires" that might result in negligence lawsuits, workplace violence, disruptive quirky performances, and unpredictable behavior. Compared with costs associated with relocations, bonuses, profit sharing, and "perks," carefully conducted selection assessments promise to be a valuable bargain. However, if there is always going to be one candidate for a job—a most unlikely occurrence—then selection systems don't pay. In cases where there are multiple applicants, and management prefers to hire the best all-round candidate for a complex job, modern assessment center technologies can help pay for themselves by significantly improving the probability of identifying the "best" candidate from a pool of candidates.

Assessment center costs are normally quite nominal relative to their return. They may range between $500 to $2,000 per evaluation in consultant costs. The costs would depend on the complexity of the assessment and the comprehensiveness of an accompanying report. The recruitment costs for external candidates, on the other hand, may involve about 50% of, say, a hired executive's annual salary plus the search firm's administrative costs. Selection errors at the executive level can total around $300,000. A poor hire may cost between $20,000 to $40,000 at the supervisory level. Although assessment center type evaluations involve variances and errors, over a reasonable period of time there should be fewer hiring mistakes.

ASSESSMENT ISSUES

The following sections on competitive and in-house issues extends the argument that supports the use of psychological prescreening selection services in small- and medium-sized growth companies.

Competitive Issues

Because of both the costs and importance of prescreening people for the job, there is an industry that provides consultation and testing services to help large companies, and small businesses, select the right people for their organization.

The managers of small- to medium-sized growth companies can identify "providers" who have prescreening selection programs with acceptable construct and predictive validity by their answer to this fundamental question: Where is the evidence to support the test's (program's) reliability and validity? When you hear anecdotal stories and glowing testimonials, you can suspect that the method is without demonstrated validity. Narratives about single subject successes carry very little weight in the scientific community, also in the courts. They normally do more to mislead than to elucidate. For example, the testimonials may come from the "test maker's" golfing partners. Those who use scientifically validated assessment procedures will provide data that show the reliability and predictive validity for the system, and how these numbers were obtained.

Search firms provide a valuable contribution to the recruiting–selection process. For example, management may have a job filled that they do not want to advertise. They may want the search to be confidential because of potential embarrassment to the person who currently holds the position. Under other circumstances, they may want a person with some rather unique skills and qualifications that they do not have either the time or the experience to find or recruit.

The search firm is in business to find candidates. Their advantages lie in their staff's experience in identifying people who can fill a job. The better firms will find replacements if the recommended candidate does not work out within a prescribed time period. This relationship saves management considerable time finding and pre-screening candidates.

Search firm personnel typically rely on "research" that involves networking, background checking, and interviewing methods. While search firm staff are normally objective in reporting educational background, work history, and job progression, some may unconsciously bias their descriptions through errors of omission and errors of commission in developing their candidates' "personality profile." Moreover, search firms are normally challenged to extrapolate from how a person is presumed to have performed at one level in a particular environment to how they are likely to perform at the "new" company. Search firm visits to the company to examine the environment do not assume a correspondence between a candidate's competencies and the demands of the job.

When a skilled organizational psychologist provides oversight to this phase of the selection process, search firm people may have an added incentive to stretch their resources to assure that their candidates are going to be favorably reviewed, by identifying better candidates. For example, I found that such oversight, in the case of one company, changed the ratio of successful to unsuccessful search firm candidates from 1:5 to 1:2.

Sometimes the more challenging part of building a valid selection system involves overcoming myths. Although the interview is the most widely used method in personnel selection, statistics consistently have shown that interviews are quite variable in predicting performance and sometimes have inadequate reliability and validity for use in personnel selection.

Data from various studies show that interview results are highly inconsistent. A sampling of studies showed interviews attaining zero correlation (Zedeck, Tziner, & Middlestadt, 1983), .22 (Motowidlo, Carter, Dunnette, & Tippins, 1992), and .46 (Weekley & Gier, 1987) against work performance. The format of the interview, however, influences predictive efficacy. The more formally structured interviews consistently show efficacy over the less structured methods (McDaniel, Whetzel, Schmidt, & Maurer, 1994; Wiesner & Cronshaw, 1988; Wright, Lichtenfels, & Pursell, 1989).

Despite their unpredictable results, the interview has value when it provides information related to background, educational level, goals, previous work functions, and other factual data. The interview process also can be used to screen out clearly unqualified candidates.

Interview systems have limitations in predicting job effectiveness because: (1) The skills that go into responding to interview questions and in performing job functions are not necessarily related. (2) Political initiatives can shape interview results. (3) Interview systems invite illusions of insight and validity that represent distorted judgments as when interviewers come to believe that their gut feelings are both accurate and predictive (Knaus & Hendricks, 1986). However, carefully constructed formal interviews where the interviewer asks the candidate to spell out the processes through which he or she achieves results may add to an interview's predictive validity. These interview process responses can later be compared to the actual responses the candidate makes in work related simulations in the assessment center process.

Another issue relates to change. Sometimes seemingly minor changes, say to supplement the interview with a job simulation, can meet resistance. Thus, some company people will need time to think out the pros and cons of new assessment procedures, and to go through a process of change including testing them before accepting them. Knaus (1982, 1994) and Prochaska, DiClemente, and Norcross (1992) describe stages of change models that illustrate the processes people go through when undergoing change.

In-House Issues

Promoting from within the organization helps improve employee morale, serves as an incentive for tenure, and can dramatically reduce costs associated with an external candidate search. However, experience and time of tenure at one job level does not assure competency at the next level. Thus, decision makers can benefit from assessment center data that can improve their predictive judgments on the reassignments, transfers, and promotions of internal candidates. It does a lot of good when a capable employee performs as expected at a higher level of responsibility.

Operating within this in-house system, the organizational psychologist works to help shape selection judgments through exercising an objective, empirical bias. This effort often involves the strong support of both human resources management and the CEO.

SELECTING PEOPLE FOR GROWING COMPANIES

People with higher level work competencies will tend to find more efficient ways to do the job, and will normally require less management support than their less competent peers. Thus, the growth oriented company will gain advantages through hiring employees who want to stretch and grow and who have the proficiency to achieve their ambitions. When above average performers become the dominating group managing the more complex functions of the organization, they will tend to promote a healthy and productive workplace because they can work more effectively under such conditions.

An important psychological axiom is that we can best understand the person within the situation in which he or she will operate. Within that situation, there are many variables and variances. The assessment center approach is an important procedure for applying that axiom.

For more than 50 years, the assessment center concept has been reasonably consistent in showing predictive validity across varying methods and conditions. The preponderance of the evidence favors this method, particularly in management selection. Recent research continues to support the efficacy of the system (Bray, 1982; Feltham, 1988; Gaugler, Rosenthal, Thornton, & Bentson, 1987; Maukisch, 1986; McEvoy & Beatty, 1989; Ritchie & Moses, 1983; Thornton & Cleveland, 1990; Tziner, Ronen, & Hacohen, 1993; Tziner, Meir, Dahan, & Birate, 1994). However, while the evidence favors the efficacy of the assessment center procedure, some investigators have pointed to its limitations (Joyce, Thayer, & Pond, 1994).

Because of the assessment center's demonstrated validity and utility, I will highlight this method as a tested framework that can be (1) adapted to small- and medium-sized growth company settings, and (2) implemented on an "as needed" basis.

The assessment center is a process, not a place. It is a process where one can use multiple measures, multiple criteria, and multiple assessors. At least one of these measures involves observing a candidate in a job related situation or simulation, then measuring the efficacy of the candidate's performance against job relevant criteria (Knaus 1989a, 1989b; Knaus & Gaiennie, 1978; Moses & Byham, 1977).

The heart of the assessment process is in the job relevant evaluation dimensions. These dimensions are operationally defined and can include such factors as communications skills, cognitive flexibility, and organizing skills.

The assessment center concept is logical. Suppose that you are a football coach. You have lost your quarterback. If you were in this situation, would you review the resumés of candidates and interview them and then base your decision on interview results and recommendations, or would you base your decision on observed performances? Would you have certain actions you would look for, such as scampering skills, passing skills, play making skills, or leadership skills? Such criteria would be the evaluation dimensions for judging your quarterback candidates. In a similar fashion, the assessment center gives top management a chance to sample a candidate's performance prior to a hiring decision.

Such procedures not only help companies identify capable candidates, they also may serve as a job preview for the candidate. Indeed, some candidates appreciate the assessment center process because it helps them decide whether the job functions are to their liking. Moreover, Rynes and Connerley (1993) have found that when employment screening systems have high face and content validity, candidates tend to view them as equitable.

In examining the performance of different candidates, assessment center personnel can, for example, help answer such questions as these: Who can analyze important problems and devise effective solutions? Who can plan a course of action that leads to a productive result? Who can best organize resources to support the plan? Who is best able to interact with people, communicate effectively, motivate them, and guide them in accomplishing the plan? What candidates are quick to alter their plans when they run up against immovable roadblocks? If you were a human resources manager, or a CEO, would you not want to have this information?

The assessment center process is not without some irregularities. Companies vary in their culture, direction, products, competitive strategies, and productivity. The method is likely to interact with changing conditions. Some members of an assessment center team may engage in a joint enterprise to collectively bias the outcome of the measure to support their prejudgments. Because of these, and other factors, it normally requires time to adapt assessment center systems to an organization's varying and developing demands, and to provide safeguards to assure its continued validity.

Those who design their systems so that they are simple, cost effective, and can be implemented on short notice will normally have an advantage over both competitors with cumbersome, often unwieldy, large-scale assessment center systems and competitors with homegrown prescreening programs. Indeed, small, rapid mobilization programs may significantly outperform the larger programs.

Careful modifications to enhance the system's flexibility can yield a double dividend in cost-effectiveness and increased validity (Adler, 1987). Knaus's work (1992) supports this conclusion. Over 12 years, he obtained a 91.8% accuracy rating for a brief, flexible, intensive, rapidly mobilized, assessment center approach. The system was designed to evaluate single candidates for management, sales, staff, and other key functions using multiple tasks, multiple raters, and proprietary evaluation dimensions.

ESTABLISHING A DIRECTION

Managements of small- and medium-sized growth companies will differ in their philosophies about whether or not to use assessment center technology. Among those who see merit in this approach, some will want to control the process using only company people as system administrators. Others will prefer to refer their people to an external service. The third group will prefer to work in tandem with a qualified psychological or measurement consultant because of these advantages:

- Compared to external referrals, it is less costly to the organization when management can free subordinates for brief periods of time to serve as role-players and evaluators.
- The process allows people within the system to contribute their knowledge about the company in determining whether the candidate would fit within the organization.
- The process supports cross-company views when people from different levels and areas of an organization participate in the process.
- The various simulations and evaluative procedures yield training opportunities for participating staff without additional cost. In this environment, employees can both learn and contribute. They also can work to improve their performances by testing new ways of operating within the context of their participation in select problem solving simulations.
- Management has opportunities to see how their own people perform when they participate in simulations and when they render judgments about the performances of external job candidates. Thus, the system provides preview opportunities for management to identify their more capable people, including their "diamonds in the rough," for future job considerations.
- The system's objectivity and training opportunities convey the message that selection decisions are equitable. This can have a constructive effect on morale.
- The process extends the concept of participatory management where internal "assessors" do have the opportunity to influence decisions that relate to the company's health and growth.

In this "cooperative" environment, personnel staffs continue to perform many of the screening functions they previously conducted, including prescreening interviews, resumé reviews, identification of potential candidates, and so forth. The psychological consultant's role in this environment becomes one of coach, objective outside assessor, and product developer to streamline and strengthen this process.

DEVELOPING A PROGRAM

The development and implementation of an assessment center break out into different phases, each of which provides opportunities to structure the assessment center program with objective measures and to assess the predictive powers of such measures. Some of this challenging work is best done with the organizational psychologist, or measurement expert, working with company people. For example, in-basket tasks are normally developed in tandem with knowledgeable company people.

The evolution of an assessment center may include, but is not limited to, this developmental process:

- Conceptual and behavioral objectives are devised for the jobs where candidates are to be assessed.
- Guidelines and cross-validation strategies are created for reviewing resumés that include evaluative dimensions that are relevant to such assessments.
- Standardized formal telephone interview inventories are developed that may also be used for screening candidates through Internet communications. Concomitantly, rating systems are devised based on evaluation dimensions suitable for assessing the results of such interviews.
- Standardized formal interviews are produced that include problem-solving questions, process questions, and job function questions. Simulations are included that link directly to job functions that can be rated using task relevant evaluation dimensions.
- Objective prescreening strategies are devised that help identify internal candidates who might qualify for specific positions. This procedure helps increase the chances that a proposed candidate has the required attributes to perform effectively in a new role without first having to prematurely subject the individual to formal screening procedures.
- Biographical forms are created that show the relevance of experience and background factors to the targeted job. This form also can provide cross-validation for resumé and interview data. Some items can be designed to tap the process by which the candidate had solved job related problems.

- In-basket problem simulations are produced that can be assessed with evaluation dimensions and rating scales.
- Simulations are designed to evoke the candidate's characteristic approach to supervising "crews" or groups for management and leadership positions. Depending upon the job requirements, simulations for professional presentation are created. Task appropriate and job related evaluation dimensions are used to assess attributes required for competent job performance.
- Psychometric inventories are identified that have predictive validity for specific job relevant functions, attributes, or skills.
- Staff will be identified, trained, and supervised to assist in the implementation of the assessment center procedures. Included in this training are recording and rating observations, and how to maintain confidentiality.
- Evaluation procedures are devised for measuring candidates' responses during company tours. Such measures can relate to style, approach, quality of questions asked, observation skills, "change ideas," and so forth.
- When feasible, real-life problem-solving conditions are provided. For example, one of the assessment strategies used to identify effective salespeople was to have the candidate visit a store that sold the company's product, evaluate the company's position in the store, "informally" talk to store clerks about the company's product, and afterwards, devise a competitive strategy to increase sales in that particular store. This strategy provides opportunities for candidates to demonstrate marketing and merchandizing skills, people communications skills, analytic skills, planning skills, organizing skills, and general style and approach on a sales call.

The developmental process may appear complex; however, it is readily accomplished by specialists experienced in this area. The assessment center involves a fluid process that occurs in a context where one may routinely modify and upgrade the system to meet new challenges. For example, the types of employees required may vary with economic and market changes. New technology can be added as it becomes available. The predicted outcomes can be continuously monitored and measured in a reasonable manner through process-outcome research (Knaus, 1992).

In cases where small- to medium-sized growth companies do not have dollar resources readily available to fund the developmental costs of this program, and where management is serious about using this procedure, the organization might contract with an entrepreneurial psychologist to design a proprietary system without billing the company for this phase of the process. The professional retains the ownership of the system. This developmental phase would include familiarization with the company, its products, markets, production procedures, and people as well as producing the system. The organizational psychologist's contract for operating the proprietary system would involve implementing the assessment technology on a case-by-case basis for a predetermined price that is acceptable to both the professional and company management. It may also involve a specific contract for a yearly retainer. This arrangement may appeal to some professionals who find that contributing to a small- to medium-sized growth company's prosperity can be challenging and rewarding.

Although this entrepreneurial effort involves some risk, assessment center designs that competently support the company's growth can lead to other opportunities for the organizational psychologist or measurement specialist, such as contributing to the organization through designing and implementing customer surveys or conducting marketing research.

A healthy workplace does not normally happen by accident, and there also is no guarantee that this outcome can happen by design. Nevertheless, organizational psychologists, consulting professionals, and managers who work together to employ modern assessment center prescreening personnel selection systems load the dice in favor of a healthier, more prosperous growth operation.

REFERENCES

Adler, S. (1987). Toward the more effective use of assessment center technology in personnel selection. *Journal of Business and Psychology, 2*(1), 74–83.

Bray, D. W. (1982). The assessment center and the study of lives. *American Psychologist, 37*(2), 180–189.

Feltham, R. (1988). Validity of a police assessment centre: A 19-year follow-up. *Journal of Occupational Psychology, 61*(2), 129–144.

Gaugler, B. B., Rosenthal, D. B., Thornton, G. C., & Bentson, C. (1987). Meta-analysis of assessment center validity. *Journal of Applied Psychology Monograph, 72*(3), 493–511.

Joyce, L. W., Thayer, P. W., & Pond, S. B. (1994). Managerial functions: An alternative to traditional assessment center dimensions? *Personnel Psychology, 47*(1), 109–121.

Knaus, W. J. (1982). *How to conquer your frustrations.* Englewood Cliffs, NJ: Prentice Hall.

Knaus, W. J. (1989a). How to build a top-notch service team. Interview with Robert Hard. *Customer Service Manager's Letter, 1*(9), 67–68.

Knaus, W. J. (1989b). Sizing up job applicants. Interview with Barry Lenson. *Executive Strategies, 4*(11), 2–3.

Knaus, W. J. (1992). A cognitive perspective on organizational change. *Journal of Cognitive Psychotherapy, 6*(4), 277–294.

Knaus, W. J. (1994). *Change your life now: Powerful techniques for positive change.* New York: Wiley.

Knaus, W. J., & Gaiennie, L. R. (1978, April). Selecting key personnel: The assessment center way. *Commerce,* 33–36.

Knaus, W. J., & Hendricks, C. (1986). *The illusion trap.* New York: World Almanac.

Maukisch, H. (1986). Measures of success of assessment center systems: A research review. *Psychologie und Praxis, 30*(2), 86–91.

McDaniel, M. A., Whetzel, D. L., Schmidt, F. L., & Maurer, S. D. (1994). The validity of employment interviews: A comprehensive review and meta-analysis. *Journal of Applied Psychology, 79*(4), 599–616.

McEvoy, G. M., & Beatty, W. (1989). Assessment centers and subordinate appraisals of managers: a seven year examination of predictive validity. *Personnel Psychology, 42*(1), 37–52.

Moses, J. L., & Byham, W. C. (1977). *Applying the assessment center method.* New York: Pergamon.

Motowidlo, S. J., Carter, G. W., Dunnette, M. D., & Tippins, N. (1992). Studies of the structured behavioral interview. *Journal of Applied Psychology, 77*(5), 571–587.

Odon, C. R. (1995). Candid candidates. *Security Management, 39*(5), 66–70.

O'Connell, S. E. (1995). Calculate the return on your investment for better budgeting. *Human Resources Magazine, 40*(10), 39–43.

Prochaska, J. O., DiClemente, C. C., & Norcross, J. C. (1992). In search of how people change: Applications to addictive behaviors. *American Psychologist, 47*(9), 1102–1114.

Ritchie, R. J., & Moses, J. L. (1983). Assessment center correlates of women's advancement into middle management: A 7-year longitudinal analysis. *Journal of Applied Psychology, 68*(2), 227–231.

Rynes, S. L., & Connerley, M. L. (1993). Applicant reactions to alternative selection procedures. *Journal of Business & Psychology, 7*(3), 261–277.

Straw, B. M., & Barsade, S. G. (1993). Affect and managerial performance: A test of the sadder but wiser vs. happier-and-smarter hypothesis. *Administrative Science Quarterly, 38*(2), 304–331.

Terpstra, D. E (1994). HRM: A key to competitiveness. *Management Decision, 32*(9), 10–14.

Thornton, G. C., & Cleveland, J. N. (1990). Developing management talent through simulation. *American Psychologist, 45*(2), 190–199.

Tziner, A., Ronen, S., & Hacohen, D. (1993). A four-year validation study of an assessment center in a financial corporation. *Journal of Organizational Behavior, 14*(3), 225–237.

Tziner, A., Meir, E. I., Dahan, M., & Birati, A. (1994). An investigation of the predictive validity and economic utility of the assessment center for the high management level. *Canadian Journal of Behavioral Science, 26*(2), 228–245.

Weekley, J. A., & Gier, J. A. (1987). Reliability and validity of the situational interview for a sales position. *Journal of Applied Psychology, 72*(3), 484–487.

Wiesner, W. H., & Cronshaw, S. F. (1988). A meta-analytic investigation of the impact of interview format and degree of structure on the validity of the employment interview. *Journal of Occupational Psychology, 61*(4), 275–290.

Wright, P. M., Lichtenfels, P. A., & Pursell, E. D. (1989). The structured interview: Additional studies and a meta-analysis. *Journal of Occupational Psychology, 62*(3), 191–199.

Zedeck, S., Tziner, A., & Middlestadt, S. E. (1983). Interviewer validity and reliability: An individual analysis approach. *Personnel Psychology, 36*(2), 355–370.

2.

Attitudinal Differentiation: Corporate Belief System Analysis and Employee Performance Expectations

D. KEITH FERRELL and ANN MARIE KOPEC

Over the years the authors have counseled many individuals who were either referred by their employer or self-referred for job related stress or performance deficiencies. During the course of their treatment it became apparent that many employees typically entertain the notion that their employers' expectation of their performance is unreasonable or that the needs of the employer were dissimilar or incongruent with those of the employee.

Richman (1992) suggests that employees and employers are not dissimilar to marital partners with regard to their identified problems, and that many organizations maintain a bureaucratic and cognitive structure which reflects the belief or attitude that problems are caused by the employee's failure to comply with the organization's expectations.

Lachman and Aranya (1986) add support to the premise that incongruent or noncomplementary belief systems between organizations and their employees is a major contributing factor with regard to job dissatisfaction and turnover. They suggest that bureaucratic–organizational value systems emphasize hierarchical control and authority, conformity to organizational goals, norms and regulations, and organizational loyalty. Unless this value system is shared by the employee, assuming that it is clearly conveyed to the employee at the time of employment, conflict is sure to develop, resulting in a decrease in productivity or an increase in turnover rate.

Richman (1992) believes that the first step in resolving employee–employer issues or conflicts is to acknowledge that a problem exists. She further notes that employees and employers often deny their dual responsibility for problem identification or solving. When employee belief systems are congruent with employer or organization belief systems, job satisfaction and enhanced performance is likely to follow (Maccoby, 1988; McGregor, 1960; Schein, 1978).

It is the authors' premise that in many cases the belief systems of both employees and employers are irrational and incongruent with their stated goals or objectives. The belief systems of organizations and individuals resemble the irrational thoughts underlying emotional disturbance as promulgated by rational–emotive behavior theory (Ellis, 1962, 1971, 1991).

Through the examination of the aims of organizations and individuals, employee and employer role differentiation, and belief system identification, the authors hope to offer a schema for the examination and elimination of belief system incongruities, which lead to untenable employee performance expectations and the deterioration of the organizational–individual partnership.

CHARACTERISTICS OF CORPORATIONS AND INDIVIDUALS

As Cangemi and Mitchell (1975) so aptly note, the basic aim of business is profit and materialism. Lachman and Aranya (1986) point out that organization and employee value systems are incompatible and often lead to different role orientations; the aims of employees differ and are often incongruent with that of business. The employee belief system emphasizes such notions as conformity to individual goals and standards, autonomy, self-control, and loyalty, in contrast to an organizational value system that emphasizes conformity and fidelity. When these two sets of values or belief systems are not consistent, commitment to both may constitute a problem for the organization and the individual, oftentimes leading to job dissatisfaction and turnover (Bartol, 1994; Engel, 1970).

The study of work adjustment by Lofquist and Dawis (1969) led to the conclusion that work adjustment was based on the concept of correspondence between the individual and environment. They reported that correspondence (agreement with one another) involves harmony between the employee and work environment, suitability of the employee and the work setting, and a complementary relationship between the employee and the environment. They also state that into this relationship the individual brings his or her requirements of the environment; the environment likewise has its own requirements of the individual.

The "theory of work adjustment" further postulates that each individual has a work personality consisting of structure and style. The work environment is defined in terms of particular skill requirements and need reinforcers. Work adjustment can be predicted from the correspondence between work personality and work environment (Lofquist and Dawis, 1969). We suggest that a work personality is a compilation of work–vocation based beliefs and a work environment, a set of complex reinforcers defined by organizational mission and purpose that interact and contribute to an individual's ability to achieve job satisfaction. Dawis and Lofquist (1984) state there are four adjustment styles that are basic to achieving and maintaining an adaptive relationship between the individual and their work environment: flexibility, activeness, reactiveness, and perseverance. They note that activeness and reactiveness may be thought of as adjustment modes, with flexibility determining when adjustment modes are to be used and perseverance determining the length of time they would be used. The authors suggest, however, that adaptiveness must be defined by the degree of attitudinal congruity inherent and implied in the aforementioned styles of work adjustment.

Like employees, organizations can either be healthy or unhealthy. Cangemi and Mitchell (1975) suggest that the following behavioral indicators might be suggestive of a corporation that is experiencing difficulties: friction; internal strife; disagreement concerning goals; lack of clear-cut commitment on the part of both management and employees; interpersonal rivalries; decreasing initiative; inability to exchange views without conflict; no faith in the leadership; and limited insight into the needs and desires of its subordinates. These behavioral indicators are just a sampling of symptoms that interfere with any organization's ability to meet its goals. The authors agree with Cangemi and Mitchell (1975) when they suggest that:

> Organizations must build and maintain a sense of positive personal worth and importance for the people that work within them. The most important principle here is the relationships in the organization, particularly the relationships between superiors and subordinates. These relationships must be supportive and egobuilding. (p. 46)

Before an organization can fulfill its objectives, it must have a "sense" of its personnel. Abraham Maslow in *Eupsychian Management* (1965) outlined a multitude of inferences organizations can make about their employees in order to assist in its goal actualization. The following is a list of those inferences that the authors believe are most important: (1) employees are to be kept informed as completely as possible; (2) employees are psychologically adaptive; (3) employees are predisposed to be self-actualizing; (4) employees are resilient; (5) employees can improve, but cannot be perfect; (6) employees would prefer to feel respected and important; (7) employees are predisposed to improve upon things; (8) employees prefer meaningful work to meaningless work; and (9) employees have the efficacy of self-choice. A successful organization is one that has adopted a healthy, rational leadership style and helps its people attain their goals, desires, and needs while at the same time being able to facilitate its own growth through management by objectives.

Kozak and Cangemi (1977) describe a corporation as "a legal person which directs through management the use of capital, machines, and people in accomplishing certain objectives" (p. 33). They note that the primary goal of all corporations is their self-perpetuation. Present in some form or fashion according to Scott (1962) are four major objectives: profit, service, social, and personal. Each corporation will prioritize these objectives differently. Historically, corporations have operated from the premise that their employees were motivated primarily by a desire to maximize their economic gains (McDermid, 1960). Monetary compensation is not the only objective that motivates.

Regardless of one's view of human motivation, a hierarchy of needs does exist in all individuals and is the basis for goal-directed behavior. The type of behavior an individual will exhibit will depend upon a variety of extrinsic and intrinsic factors including his or her belief system. According to Sayles (1965), healthy, adaptive individuals within a work environment strive to satisfy a higher level of need, that includes such aspirations as forming strong social groups, becoming independent and creative, exercising autonomy and discretion to express their individual personalities without fear of reprisal. He notes that formal organizations, on the other hand, seek to program individual behavior by demanding conformity, obedience, and dependence and by establishing a strictly defined division of work and rigid rules of formal organizational structure and behavior.

Although organizational theory has advanced, the management practices of most corporations have not changed dramatically over time. The longer corporations avoid recognizing the human needs of their employees, the more frustrated and disturbed they will become, which will affect their ability to satisfy objectives.

BELIEF SYSTEM IDENTIFICATION IN THE WORKPLACE

The identification of beliefs and their specific relationship to emotions and behavior is typically reserved for counselors in counseling settings, not within the confines of the workplace. The authors believe that the identification of specific beliefs of employees in any work setting needs to begin with an analysis of expectations or unmet expectations. Porter and Steers (1973) suggest that the concept of unmet expectations may be viewed as the discrepancy between what an employee encounters on the job in the way of positive and negative experiences and what he or she expected to encounter. Wanous, Poland, Premack, and Davis (1992) note that unmet expectations cause a variety of potential adjustment problems (i.e., low job satisfaction and early turnover). They further note that organizations can increase employee performance if job previews are realistic and contain information that clarifies the employee's role expectation. How are expectations identified within a corporate or work setting? Porter and Steers (1973) suggest that job newcomers be asked a single simple question after they enter an organization: "Consider what you expected to experience in this organization and compare it to what you now experience, and rate the degree of consistency between the two." Although a single question might be an oversimplification of what is inherently a complex personnel process, the identification of belief states and their relationship to performance might very well begin with the asking of such a simple question by management. It is recognized that the initial contact between an organization and its prospective members is very often a frustrating experience. Both the employer and the employee need to gather accurate information about the other in order to reach a decision. However, both have a need to look attractive to the other. This increases the possibility of biasing the information exchanged (Porter, Lawler, & Hackman, 1975). If organizations avoided the tendency to present themselves in an unrealistically positive light, voluntary employee turnover in addition to attitudinal incongruity would be reduced.

One method readily available to corporations that would facilitate the identification and sharing of beliefs and/or expectations is commonly known as the Realistic Job Preview (RJP; Wanous, 1973). If employees are made aware of problems and difficulties to be faced on the job, they will cope better when they arise, either because they are less disturbed by problems about which they were warned or because they may rehearse methods of handling these types of problems. For the employee, a realistic job preview conveys, indirectly, a message of openness and honesty. Dugoni and Ilgen (1981) report that employees who receive a realistic job preview are more likely to believe that the organization will deal with them in an open and honest fashion.

Another method available to management as a means by which to identify beliefs or expectations that either will promote job satisfaction and productivity, or reduce them, is the performance evaluation. Murphy and Cleveland (1991) report that there is little information available as to how organizations set performance standards, and whether inappropriate standards lead to maladaptive behavior and outcomes. They further note that organizations are more concerned with the evaluative purpose of performance standards, rather than with the effect of the standards on those to whom they apply. Bobko and Colella (1994) believe that if organizations set standards without considering their possible translation into individual performance goals, individuals may adopt minimal-level standards as their personal goals, and consequently both motivation and subsequent performance may be lower than had more difficult personal goals been set.

Klimoski and Hayes (1980) conclude that when goals and expectations are explicit and when organizations are consistent with their demands, yet supportive, job satisfaction will follow. Also employee involvement in goal-setting and performance evaluation is very important for enhanced job performance.

The identification of a corporate belief system and its relationship to employee performance appears limited to specific methodologies intended to measure an employee's performance or to appraise one of its expectations. While the results of current research seem to promote the view that the employee is most important in any organization, it would seem most appropriate that a method exist whereby attitudinal incongruency can either be eliminated or dealt with more effectively so as to facilitate goal attainment by both employer and employee.

According to Morris (1993) a higher degree of congruency and increased effectiveness would be attained if the psychological model of the employee–organization relationship focused directly on the employee's self-defeating beliefs. The same can be said about the identification of the organization's self-defeating beliefs and of its willingness to invest the time and energy in facilitating a process whereby an employee in concert with management could identify self- and corporation-defeating beliefs as a means by which to enhance their relationship.

Morris (1993) points out that there is a similarity between the common irrational thoughts that underlie emotional and behavioral maladaption and Senge's (1990) seven self-defeating beliefs maintained by employees about ineffective organizations. Irrational concepts such as demandingness, self-rating, low frustration tolerance, as advanced by rational–emotive behavior theory (REBT; Ellis, 1962, 1971, 1985, 1991) appear to be evidenced in employees of ineffective organizations. As Morris (1993) so aptly points out, "the successful organization meets the needs of the people and, in turn, the people meet the needs of the organization. In other words, the organization attempts to meet the personal goals of the employee, the employee seeks to achieve the goals of the organization" (p. 36).

Ellis (1991) postulates that the primary goals of human beings are to be happy with themselves and with others educationally, vocationally, economically, and recreationally. Once these goals have been satisfied, with help from the employer, the employee is in a much better position to make work contributions.

Current research and theories point to the fact that it is inherently in the best interest of both the individual and the corporation to identify their specific goals and expectations, and to recognize, identify, and modify any belief states that might well interfere with goal attainment or performance. The authors believe that REBT and methodology (Ellis, 1962, 1971) is a model that can be effectively employed to eliminate corporate–individual belief state incongruity.

BELIEF SYSTEM INCONGRUITY: AN INTERVENTION APPROACH

Rational–Emotive Behavior Theory and Therapy is a comprehensive model of human behavior that emphasizes the importance of cognition or thought in the cause and maintenance of maladaptive emotions and behavior (Ellis, 1962). While typically employed within the context of a psychotherapeutic relationship, the principles of rational–emotive behavior therapy are appropriate tools by which to eliminate belief system incongruity between employer and employee, individual and corporation.

Rational–emotive behavior therapy, as it was originally established, employs a simplistic A-B-C assessment framework to identify and conceptualize a person's psychological problems (Ellis, 1962). In this model A stands for Activating Event, B stands for a person's Belief about that event, and C represents the person's emotional and behavioral response or Consequence to holding or adhering to that particular Belief at B. According to REBT theory, people hold a multitude of beliefs (B's) or cognitions, thoughts, ideas, or values regarding activating events or (A's); and these beliefs exert a strong influence on how one chooses to respond emotionally, behaviorally, and cognitively as a consequence or (C) of the interaction between A and B (Ellis & Dryden, 1987). According to Ellis and Dryden people have many different cognitions or thoughts, both rational and irrational. In REBT, we encourage the maintenance of rational rather than irrational belief states. It is hypothesized that rational belief states lead to goal-directed, self-helping behaviors, while irrational beliefs often, if not always, lead to self-defeating behavior and emotional disturbance.

Ellis and Dryden also point out that at the core of psychological disturbance lies the tendency in humans to entertain absolutist evaluations of the perceived events or happenings in their lives or in the lives of others. These assessments are in the form of dogmatic "musts," "shoulds," "have to's," "got to's," and "ought's." Ellis (1983) believes that this type of cognition or thought is at the root of a philosophy of excessiveness that is central in human emotional and behavioral disturbance.

Within the workplace, Richman (1992) identified three themes which were prevalent in the cognitive structure of both organizations and individuals—commitment, competence, and expectation. Inherent in each theme are the four basic irrational thinking styles: demandingness, "awfulizing," low frustration tolerance, and self-downing. Richman (1992) uses the following examples to illustrate irrational individual and organizational belief states.

> From the employee's viewpoint: I should work for my company permanently; I should only have to do the minimum amount of work for my salary; it would be awful if I made a mistake on my job; my organization should provide me with security and steady promotions. From the organization's viewpoint: employees should work for us through retirement; employees should perform competently at all times; it would be awful if employees were not able to perform their job perfectly; and employees should be grateful to work for us and not complain or expect so much. (p. 239)

Richman (1992) states it is unrealistic to expect individuals and organizations to always agree about work-related events. The A-B-C model of REBT can help both the employee and employer accept their individual differences and work on more realistic ways of interpreting their situation so that long-term goals are mutually achieved.

The writers contend that rational–emotive behavior theory in its applied forms, rational-emotive behavior therapy, rational effectiveness training, rational management training, and emotional management training, is a tool that can be used cooperatively or on an individual basis by either employer or employee. Kirby and DiMattia (1991) believe that corporations need to return to a basic curriculum that teaches how to handle attitudes and beliefs on the job. Rational management training can help managers learn to recognize the causes of their emotional reactions and to change self-defeating emotions. Corporations can begin to reduce attitudinal incongruity between themselves and their employees by first acknowledging incongruity does exist, and that in order to realize their goals it might well be necessary for them to give up authority and control.

Employee assistance programs (EAPs) are a means by which corporations and individuals can work cooperatively to end attitudinal incongruency. Through the development of in-service training programs designed to stress individual ownership of dysfunctional emotions and behavior, and through the use of short-term psychotherapy, goal attainment by both cooperations and individuals can be realized.

Klarreich, DiGiuseppe, and DiMattia (1987) warn us that, since not all EAPs are alike, uniformity should not be considered a priority over the specific intervention strategies to be used by program personnel, i.e., counselors, psychologists, etc. Research has shown that rational–emotive behavior therapy is a cost-effective and helpful tool that warrants special consideration by program personnel and management.

CONCLUSION

It becomes increasingly more apparent when one examines the nature of organizations in the 1990s that belief system incongruity does in fact exist between individuals and employers. While attempts are made to reduce this incongruity by means of job previews, realistic performance measures, and education and counseling programs, attitudinal and performance expectation differences still abound. Many individuals and organizations seem to understand that a cognitive component to goal acquisition does exist. However, an understanding of how attitudes, values, and beliefs affect emotions and behavior is lacking. Rational–emotive behavior theory provides a model for organizations to follow when designing job previews, introducing performance measures, and setting realistic employee and organization goals.

Educational programs such as rational effectiveness training help management deal with the realities of the workplace by teaching an adaptive model of communication and emotion management. The development of a similar program for nonmanagement personnel during their initial orientation would help limit attitudinal incongruity and invariably improve performance by reducing expectations from the onset. In these times of downsizing or rightsizing, it is increasingly more apparent that the corporate culture should be more sensitive to the impact such cost-saving measures have on individuals who are essential to the existence of an organization. Part of changing an organization consists in changing how it perceives and thinks about (1) risk, (2) challenge, (3) success, (4) failure. Rational–emotive behavior theory speaks to all four issues via multiple intervention strategies.

REFERENCES

Bartol, K. M. (1994). Professionalization as a predictor of organizational commitment, role, stress and turnover: A multidimensional approach. *Academy of Management Journal, 22*(4), 815–821.

Bobko, P., & Colella, A. (1994). Employee reactions to performance standards: A review and research propositions. *Personnel Psychology, 47*(1), 1–29.

Cangemi, J. P., & Mitchell, D. W. (1975). A brief psychology of healthy and unhealthy organization. *Psychology, 12*(2), 46–50.

Dawis, R. V., & Lofquist, L. H. (1984). *A psychological theory of work adjustment.* Minneapolis, MN: University of Minnesota Press.

Dugoni, B. L., & Ilgen, D. R. (1981). Realistic job previews and the adjustment of new employees. *Academy of Management Journal, 24*(3), 579–591.

Ellis, A. (1962). *Reason and emotion in psychotherapy.* Secaucus, NJ: Citadel.

Ellis, A. (1971). *Growth through reason.* North Hollywood, CA: Wilshire Books.

Ellis, A. (1983). *The case against religiosity.* New York: Institute for Rational–Emotive Therapy.

Ellis, A. (1985). *Overcoming resistance: Rational–emotive therapy with difficult clients.* New York: Springer.

Ellis, A. (1991). The revised ABC's of rational–emotive therapy (RET). *Journal of Rational–Emotive & Cognitive–Behavior Therapy, 9*(3), 139–172.

Ellis, A., & Dryden, W. (1987). *The practice of rational–emotive therapy (RET).* New York: Springer.

Engel, G. V. (1970). Professional autonomy and bureaucratic organizations. *Administrative Science Quarterly, 15*(1), 12–21.

Kirby, P., & DiMattia, D. (1991). A rational approach to emotional management. *Training and Development Journal, 45*(1), 67–70.

Klarreich, S., DiGiuseppe, R., & DiMattia, D. (1987). EAPs: Mind over myth. *Personnel Administrator, 32*(2), 119–121.

Klimoski, R. J., & Hayes, N. J. (1980). Leader behavior and subordinate motivation. *Personnel Psychology, 33*(3), 543–555.

Kozak, R. E., & Cangemi, J. P. (1977). Individual and corporate objectives: Determinants of human behavior. *Psychology, 14*(3), 33–44.

Lachman, R., & Aranya, N. (1986). Evaluation of alternative models of commitments and job attitudes of professionals. *Journal of Occupational Behavior, 7*(3), 227–243.

Lofquist, L. H., & Dawis, R. V. (1969). *Adjustment to work.* New York: Appleton Century Crofts.

Maccoby, M. (1988). *Why work.* New York: Touchstone.

Maslow, A. (1965). *Eupsychian management.* Homewood, IL: Dorsey Press.

McDermid, C. D. (1960). How money motivates men. *Business Horizons,* Winter, 94–100.

McGregor, D. (1960). *The human side of enterprise.* New York: McGraw-Hill.

Morris, G. B. (1993). A rational–emotive paradigm for organizations. *Journal of Rational–Emotive and Cognitive–Behavior Therapy, 11*(1), 33–49.

Murphy, K., & Cleveland, J. (1991). *Performance appraisal: An organizational perspective.* Boston, MA: Allyn & Bacon.

Porter, L. W., Lawler, E. E. III, & Hackman, J. R. (1975). *Behavior in organizations.* New York: McGraw-Hill.

Porter, L. W., & Steers, R. M. (1973). Organizational, work, and personal factors in employee turnover and absenteeism. *Psychological Bulletin, 80*(2), 151–176.

Richman, D. R. (1992). Working together: Belief systems of individuals and organizations. *Journal of Cognitive Psychotherapy, 4*(6), 231–244.

Sayles, L. R. (1965). *Individualism and big business.* New York: McGraw-Hill.

Schein, E. M. (1978). *Career dynamics: Matching individual and organizational needs.* Reading, MA: Addison-Wesley.

Scott, W. G. (1962). *Human relations in management, a behavioral science approach.* Homewood, IL: Richard D. Irwin.

Senge, P. M. (1990). *The fifth discipline: The art and practice of the learning organization.* New York: Doubleday.

Wanous, J. P. (1973). Effects of previous realistic jobs on job acceptance, job attitude, and job survival. *Journal of Applied Psychology, 80*(2), 151–168.

Wanous, J. P., Poland, T. D., Premack, S. C., & Davis, K. S. (1992). The effects of met expectations on newcomer attitudes and behavior: A review and meta-analysis. *Journal of Applied Psychology, 77*(3), 288–297.

3.

Why Computerized Life-Style Assessment Is Good for Business

STEVEN J. STEIN, Ph.D. and HARVEY A. SKINNER, Ph.D.

Organizational psychologists have discovered that many businesspeople find it hard to justify increased expenditures in health benefits, employee assistance programs, and health promotion. On the other hand, the costs of absenteeism due to preventable illnesses, burnout, poor morale, and stress related causes can be staggering. Because of the difficulties in relating these key but soft measures of human performance to the bottom line, little progress seems to have been made among North American companies in dealing with employee life-style issues.

THE PROBLEM

Over the past 20 years health promotion and disease prevention have become increasingly emphasized. The Institute of Medicine conducted a major study for the U.S. Congress in 1990 arguing that alcohol and drug problems, and community responsibility for early and brief intervention, must be more broadly defined. A number of recent studies have shown how brief interventions by physicians and nurses can motivate patients to reduce excessive drinking or quit smoking (Barbor, 1990; Kottke, Battista, DeFriese, & Brakke, 1988; Wallace, Cutler, & Haines, 1988). Primary care physicians and nurses are often in the best position to recognize health risk behaviors and provide advice or counseling for potential problems, such as risky sexual practices, stress, excessive drinking, smoking, drug misuse, over- or underweight, physical inactivity, or eating problems (Roemer, 1984; Skinner, 1990). These problems often go undetected not only in the workplace, but in schools, health care settings, and in correctional facilities.

In 1974, Canada's National Minister of Health and Welfare, Marc Lalonde, published a report identifying four major determinants: lifestyle, biology, environment, and health care. In the United States, the Surgeon General's 1979 report into the 10 leading causes of death found that "perhaps as much as half of U.S. mortality in 1976 was due to unhealthy behavior or lifestyle: 20% to environmental factors, 20% to human biological factors and 10% to inadequacies in health care."

The importance of life-style issues on physical health has been known for a number of years. For example, Hamburg, Elliot, and Parron (1982) showed that life-style behavior relates to the majority of North American illnesses. Goldman and Cook (1984) estimated that changes in life-styles, such as reducing serum cholesterol levels and smoking, resulted in 54% of the decline in ischemic heart disease between 1968 and 1976, compared to a 39% reduction attributed to coronary care units and other medical advances.

A more recent study by McGinnis and Foege (1993) evaluated the major external (nongenetic) factors that contribute to death in the United States. Of the approximate 2,148,000 total deaths in 1990, almost half could be attributed to: tobacco (19%), diet and activity pattern (14%), alcohol (5%), firearms (2%), sexual behavior (1%), motor vehicles (1%) and illicit use of drugs (1%). These data provide a compelling argument for health policies and practices that would lead to improvements in these life-style factors.

A Canadian study looked at the relationship between premature deaths, medical care, and life-style. It found that over 50% of the 96,100 premature deaths (before age 75) were preventable through life-style change. The life-style influences included cigarette smoking, hypertension (obesity/diet/exercise), serum cholesterol (obesity/diet/exercise), adult onset diabetes (obesity/diet/exercise), and excessive drinking. In contrast, only about 6,000 premature deaths (6%) were estimated to be avoidable through improved medical care (Wigle, Semenciw, McCann, & Davies, 1990).

In another study Berkman and Breslow (1983) studied 6,928 adult residents in Alameda County, California in a 9-year follow-up project. They found that good health, lower disease, and mortality risks were positively and strongly related to no cigarette smoking, moderate or no alcohol use, regular physical exercise, a desirable weight, and sleeping 7 to 8 hours each night. This was found to be cumulative: the more positive personal health habits were practiced, the greater the probability of a longer life. This study also found that the level of social support (family, friends, support groups) was positively associated with good health outcomes over this 9-year period.

THE SOLUTION

While the expectation is that life-style issues will be dealt with in the context of medical examinations, the reality is that they are only dealt with minimally, if at all. Nearly three-quarters of the primary health care practitioners surveyed by Wechsler, Levine, Idelson, Rohman, and Taylor (1983) felt the physician was definitely responsible for educating patients about life-style behaviors such as cigarettes, alcohol, drugs, stress, exercise, and diet. Only about one-quarter (27%) of the practitioners, however, reported routinely gathering information about all of these life-style behaviors.

Organizational health psychologists have assisted and coached employers to take it upon themselves to play a more important role in employee health and life-style issues. One area where this can be seen is through the growth of Employee Assistance Programs. These programs have largely focused on the emotional, interpersonal, and family problems of employees. Increasing awareness of life-style issues have led to effective awareness and educational programs that can be easily implemented in the workplace.

One such program that provides awareness and early intervention is the Computerized Lifestyle Assessment (CLA) by Harvey Skinner (1994). The CLA was designed to provide a simple and comprehensive technique for routine case identification, allowing for early recognition of problems in a variety of settings. Organizational psychologists can use the CLA as a powerful intervention strategy with organizations.

Research has found that people are more likely to give accurate responses to questions about sensitive issues like addictive behaviors if they are part of a broader assessment. The CLA, using a microcomputer, has the advantage of instant feedback by means of computer graphics and detailed printed reports. A life-style "balance sheet" is created and tailored for each individual that highlights her or his strengths as well as areas of concern and health risks.

The CLA has a number of advantages over other methods of life-style programming. The program is comprehensive; it covers life-styles as well as social/family relationships and personal health habits. The CLA is health focused. It emphasizes life-style strengths as well as personal concerns and health risks. The software is ideal for screening purposes as it identifies significant numbers of health concerns or risks among individuals. It can be used in the workplace as well as in educational, correctional, and health care settings.

Unlike most assessment methods, the CLA has been designed to provide immediate feedback through on-screen graphs that include health status for each area. Also included is a life-style summary and detailed printed report. The program is also designed to motivate. It engages the individual to complete a life-style assessment and encourages self-analysis. Another benefit of this approach is that it stimulates change. Built-in features increase readiness for action and change and identify steps the respondent is considering.

In order to be successfully implemented, a program like the CLA must be practical in terms of the individual's time required. The full program can be completed in 20 to 30 minutes. Additionally, the program needs to be flexible and adaptable. It can be customized for specific workplace requirements. For example, certain life-style areas might need to be deleted (e.g., sexual practices). In addition, the option to add a directory of referral sources would be useful, such as the company Employee Assistance Program phone number for further assistance, or the contact for the company sponsored weight-loss program.

Finally, a program such as this should be research based and evaluated. The CLA has had numerous studies published regarding its reliability and validity (Allen & Skinner, 1987; Skinner, 1994; Skinner, Allen, MacIntosh, & Palmer, 1985a, 1985b; Skinner & Allen, 1983; Skinner, Palmer, & MacIntosh, 1988; Skinner, Palmer, Sanchez-Craig, & MacIntosh, 1987; Weekes, Fabiano, Porporino, Robinson, & Millson, 1993).

The content areas that make up the CLA include:

Nutrition
Eating Habits
Caffeine Use
Physical Activity
Weight
Sleep
Social Relationships
Family Interactions

Use of Cigarettes
Alcohol Use
Nonmedical Drug Use
Medical and Dental Care
Motor Vehicle Safety
Sexual Activities
Work and Leisure
Emotional Health

Organizational psychologists can assist organizations to make the CLA available to employees to use when they choose. All that is needed is a computer with privacy around it. All results would be confidential. In some settings, the results are not saved and the individual simply receives feedback upon completion of the program. Thus, no one would have access to the results. In other settings, the results are coded with whatever name the individual chooses (e.g., Mickey Mouse) and the group results are analyzed by department, work group, or company wide. Alternately, an abbreviated scannable paper-and-pencil version can be completed by all employees as a survey. When the scannable paper-and-pencil forms are used, once again code names can be individually created by employees. Each person's results are in a sealed, windowed envelope with the code name visible. The company gets only group reports with the groups being predefined. The results can be scanned in and company or department profiles can be developed. These profiles help point the way toward company interventions that are likely to be utilized and can be set up department or company wide. These can include smoking programs, weight loss programs, exercise programs, nutrition education, safe drinking interventions, insomnia interventions, and others. A special program evaluating Emotional Intelligence (Emotional Quotient Inventory) allows for targeting areas that have been identified as having significant impact on work and personal life (Bar-On, 1997). These areas include assertiveness, empathy, optimism, interpersonal relations, flexibility, stress tolerance, impulse control, and others.

The identification and assessment of life-style issues in the workplace can also help with employee morale. When companies take the time and effort to be concerned about the well-being of the people who work there, a more positive attitude about the workplace can be created. Assessments should be followed up by organizational psychologists with planned interventions in which employees are involved. Priorities for programs can be set up and each intervention evaluated for participation, quality, and effects.

Organizational psychologists can play a key role, using the CLA, in making the workplace a better place to do business.[1]

REFERENCES

Allen, B. A., & Skinner, H. A. (1987). Lifestyle assessment using microcomputers. In J. N. Butcher (Ed.). *Computerized psychological assessment: A practitioner's guide.* (pp 108–123). New York: Basic.

Barbor, T. F. (1990). Brief intervention strategies for harmful drinkers: New directions for medical intervention. *Canadian Medical Association Journal, 143,* 1070–1074.

Bar-On, R. (1997). Bar-On Emotional Intelligence Inventory (EQ = i). Toronto, Canada: Multi-Health Systems.

Berkman, L. F., & Breslow, L. (1983). *Health and ways of living: The Alameda County Study.* New York: Oxford University Press.

Goldman, L., & Cook, F. (1984). Decline in ischemic heart disease mortality rates. An analysis of the comparative effects of medical interventions and changes in lifestyle. *Annals of Internal Medicine, 101,* 825–836.

Hamburg, D. A., Elliot, G. R., & Parron, D. L. (1982). *Health and behavior frontiers of research in the biobehavioral sciences.* Washington, DC: National Academy Press.

Kottke, T. E., Battista, R. N., DeFriese, G. H., & Brakke, M. L. (1988). Attributes of successful smoking interventions in medical practice: A meta-analysis of 39 controlled trials. *Journal of the American Medical Association, 259,* 1883–2889.

McGinnis, J. M., & Foege, W. H. (1993). Actual causes of death in the United States. *Journal of the American Medical Association, 270,* 2207–2212.

Roemer, M. I. (1984). The value of medical care for health promotion. *American Journal of Public Health, 74*(3), 243–248.

Skinner, H. A. (1990). Spectrum of drinkers and intervention opportunities. *Canadian Medical Association Journal, 143,* 1054–1059.

Skinner, H. A. (1994). *Computerized lifestyle assessment.* Toronto: Multi-Health Systems.

Skinner, H. A., & Allen, B. A. (1983). Does the computer make a difference? Computerized versus self-report assessment of alcohol, drug, and tobacco use. *Journal of Consulting and Clinical Psychology, 51,* 267–275.

Skinner, H. A., Allen, B. A., MacIntosh, M. C., & Palmer, W. H. (1985a). Lifestyle assessment: Applying microcomputers in family practice. *British Medical Journal, 290,* 212–214.

Skinner, H. A., Allen, B. A., MacIntosh, M. C., & Palmer, W. H. (1985b). Lifestyle assessment: Just asking makes a difference. *British Medical Journal, 290,* 214–216.

---

[1] The Computerized Lifestyle Assessment (CLA) is available through Multi-Health Systems Inc., 908 Niagara Falls Blvd., North Tonawanda, NY 14120-2060 (US - 1-800-456-3003, Canada - 1-800-268-6011, International - 416-424-1700).

Skinner, H. A., Palmer, W. H., & MacIntosh, M. C. (1988, May). *Lifestyles. What factors patients think are important and what help they expect from their doctor.* Presented at 16th Annual Meeting of the North American Primary Care Research Group, Ottawa.

Skinner, H. A., Palmer, W. H., Sanchez-Craig, M., & MacIntosh, M. C. (1987). Reliability of a lifestyle assessment using microcomputers. *Canadian Journal of Public Health, 78,* 329–334.

Wallace, P. G., Cutler, S., & Haines, A. P. (1988). Randomized controlled trial of general practitioner intervention in patients with excessive alcohol consumption. *British Medical Journal, 297,* 663–668.

Wechsler, H., Levine, S., Idelson, R. K., Rohman, M., & Taylor, J. O. (1983). The physician's role in health promotion: A survey of primary-care practitioners. *New England Journal of Medicine, 308(2),* 97–100.

Weekes, J. R., Fabiano, E., Porporino, F. J., Robinson, D., & Millson, W. A. (1993). *Assessment of substance abuse in offenders, The Occupational Lifestyles & Assessment Instrument.* Paper presented at a meeting of the Canadian Psychological Association, Montreal, Quebec.

Wigle, D. T., Semenciw, M. R., McCann, C., & Davies, J. W. (1990). Premature deaths in Canada: Impact trends and opportunities for prevention. *Canadian Journal of Public Health, 81,* 376–381.

4.

How to Gain Access to a Company as a Consultant

JOHN GALLUP

As the Chief Executive Officer of the Strathmore Paper Company for 22 years, I felt that my primary function was to build upon the considerable foundation that had been created at Strathmore long before I was hired, and to help retain and attract employees who not only believed in the company's philosophy, but who were willing and capable of carrying it forward consistently in an ever-changing, challenging external environment.

This chapter is directed toward organizational psychologists (and other social services professionals) who practice independently or in small-group practices, and who are motivated to contribute to a company's growth by helping the organization meet some of its people challenges and goals and add to the overall health of the organization.

There are important things for those to know who consult with a medium-sized growth company where people are truly appreciated and properly viewed as an integral part of the success of the organization. There will be a description of what to do before making contact with the organization, the importance of sensitivity skills, and the opportunities available for psychological consultants, in a medium-sized growth company, working closely with its chief executive officer in today's fast-changing economic environment. If you are to help companies become healthier organizations, you must find a way to enter this process.

GETTING THROUGH THE GATE

It has been my experience that some chief executive officers will consider hiring skilled consultant organizational psychologists if they perceive them as providing important services that will truly benefit the organization. However, the first challenge for a psychological consultant is to gain entry into the organization. Entry is accomplished in many different ways. This sometimes comes about as a result of having an established reputation. In this instance, the company may initiate the contact based on your reputation. However, in most instances you will increase your chances of contributing to an organization by making yourself and your services known to as many key people in the organization as possible.

Knowing people within the company, or having contacts with people who know management, will yield an advantage. But what if you are starting without established credentials or contacts? You can obtain and use some of the following information about a company and its people that experienced consultants would instinctively gather and use to their advantage.

It is axiomatic that you should know a good deal about a company before you approach the organization and suggest a consulting relationship. Fortunately much company information is readily available for this purpose. For example, information about listed companies is easily downloaded from computer databases. This information is available on most on-line services such as Hoover Company Profiles on Compuserve, company home pages on the Internet, or you can find an abundance of company information in the business reference section at your local library. The company's annual reports will describe current management themes, and often these themes will be consistent with an organizational psychologist's interests and training: growth, change, expansion, challenges, people, and so forth. However, if you plan to approach a division of a corporation, you will normally do better to gather grassroots information about that particular division.

The person who goes beyond the information given in computer databases and annual reports creates a much better advantage in being considered for a consultancy. The more experienced consultants normally make themselves knowledgeable about the company's softer features, such as "personality," "character," and heritage. Some will go through the past year's local newspapers to study news articles about the company. This screening of information can help you identify problems the company is in the process of solving. If you have a workable solution to the problem, you will be at an advantage when contacting management.

Although I cannot speak for all company presidents, I am likely to be impressed by people who come to me with a professional understanding of my company: its heritage, mission, products, market, philosophies, and people. This knowledge demonstrates the person's willingness to take extra steps, to be really involved. You cannot always get this information from a report or via computer data. However, a person's willingness to take the extra steps to find the information demonstrates interest and motivation and suggests that any projects undertaken will be successful.

The following is a sampling of the type of information you can gather about a company, the sort of information that is not available in financial reports, but will help establish your credentials. I'll use Strathmore as an example to illustrate the possibilities for those willing to seek information that goes beyond the ordinary.

- Although I know there is a divergence of opinion about the importance of a corporate culture, in cases where a company has a distinctive history related to its operating philosophy, the consultant would best be intimately aware of that organization's heritage before approaching its management. For example, Strathmore is a company with a rich heritage. I would personally be impressed if a prospective consultant knew that the company was started in the late nineteenth century. Its progenitor, Horace Moses, was an entrepreneurial visionary with a special insight into marketing. This former farm boy built the company through hard work. He traveled extensively to personally deliver his products and to get to know his merchants. He started the world-renowned Junior Achievement organization to help young people learn about business. He was a philanthropist who emphasized service to the community, a tradition that lived on well beyond his death. Strathmore people continue to involve themselves in service to the community. Information, such as the above, is normally available for any established company if you search for it.
- Just as service was part of the company's heritage, so too was marketing. During my time on watch, I can attest that Strathmore was definitely a market-driven company. We'd find out what our customers wanted and we'd produce the product to their specifications. This effort made it possible for us to continue to give stable employment to our people and to keep our company on a growth path. This type of information is important because it shows the company's areas of emphasis.

- Strathmore is best known for its top-of-the-line printing and artist paper products. It is the market leader in this area. It has high product recognition among artists and other consumer groups who seek value and quality. Its highest volume and highest market penetration is in fine paper sales. The company also is *the* undisputed leader in the specialized end-of-the-text and cover paper market. I would expect a consultant to understand our position and role in those market areas and how we got there.
- Strathmore is a growth company. We grew 125% in production during the last 10 years of my tenure. This growth required that we not only expand our production capacity, but that we also upgrade our advertising and marketing efforts, and assure that the various aspects of our operation were properly supported by people who could perform at above average levels of competency. Although I wouldn't expect an outside consultant to have access to the numbers, I would want to feel confident that the person understood whether our company was growing, stable, or declining. Each phase in a company's normal growth cycle will partially determine the types of personnel hired or retained, and suggest the types of challenges the company faces.
- The company's mission can either say a lot or a little about the internal workings of the organization. The Strathmore mission happened to fairly reflect how we conduct our business: Everyone in the company will be involved in supporting and advancing the mission of providing customer satisfaction in speciality niche markets by, (1) understanding and meeting customer needs; (2) fostering sound supplier relationships; (3) focusing on the quality of product and services; (4) striving to broaden market penetration, both nationally and internationally; (5) achieving strong profit performances by utilizing sound financial controls and by improving the costs; (6) operating a safe and secure workplace; (7) treating all employees with respect, and fostering a climate that involves and develops the full potential of its members; and by (8) being ethical in all activities, being a good neighbor in our communities, and having a responsible concern for the environment. The format for a mission statement will vary from organization to organization but should be readily attainable and may provide valuable insights.

Your knowledge of a company's heritage, service orientation, products, marketing approach, and mission is also going to be important to your decision about whether or not to approach the organization. For example, if you are likely to be empathic toward a company's position, company management is likely to be sympathetic toward your approach. Thus, any consulting arrangement between you and company management has a better chance of working to your mutual benefit.

Armed with the above background information, you are now in a position to contact management and ask for an opportunity to survey the organization's present and future human services consultation plans and to describe what you are prepared to contribute.

Personal meetings arranged by a mutual contact are normally more productive, but you can also accomplish a positive result through a letter in which you state who you are, highlight your knowledge about the organization, and ask for a meeting. Of course, such "cold calling" has limitations. Although I answer my relevant correspondence, you may not get a response from the majority of companies you contact. In a certain percentages of cases, you'll get a form letter thanking you for your inquiry. You may, however, hear from a contact person who will talk with you over the phone or arrange to meet with you. That's an encouraging start.

Doing in-depth homework on a company takes time. You may gather extraordinary information about a company with no guarantee that this effort will result in a consulting arrangement. However, the more prepared you are, the more chance you will have to succeed. So if you make a few contacts and do not receive a favorable response, don't let these results discourage you. Your success will partially be a numbers game. The more contacts you make, including repeat contacts, the more likely you are to succeed. Developing a consultation practice with a CEO is like climbing an experience curve. At a certain point you will have your presentation refined and the program refined to such an extent that you are in a better position to succeed.

THE BASICS OF A GOOD CONSULTING RELATIONSHIP

Assuming you have passed through the gate, the next step involves establishing a relationship. The kind of information exchanged by a consultant and a CEO defines the consulting relationship. Some managements prefer to focus consultation efforts into a defined area and to explain as little as possible about the company beyond what the consultant needs to know. At Strathmore, our psychological consultant had free reign to come and go within the company and to examine all aspects of the operation. He became personally familiar with all of our key people and many of our key customers. These experiences gave him the opportunity to both learn and contribute in a broad range of areas. Further, when there was an assignment that required an objective overview, confidentiality, and familiarity with our operation, I knew from experience that I could call upon him to get the job done right.

This "open door" approach was valuable and supportive of Strathmore's growth objectives and helped to maintain the interest and commitment of the consultant. Thus, the free flow of information between our people and our psychological consultant was actively encouraged. However, a consultant in this more "open" environment must be able to separate important from nonessential information and demonstrate ability to create consulting structures that have positive payback to the organization. The person must have excellent communications skills, understand his or her role, and be perceived as effective.

Relationships are important in most business environments. Most of us prefer to get along with the people we transact our business with. Few of us would want to work with people we disliked or did not respect. Thus, a good consulting relationship will normally include mutual respect on the part of both parties exemplified by the following: (1) a workable rapport; (2) compatible problem-solving styles; (3) integrity; (4) open communications; (5) clear goals; and (6) reasonable outcome measures. These six consultant-relationship attributes should be important for both company management and the consulting psychologist. Good consulting relationships then are built on both the six-step process by which we obtain results for the organization and personal satisfaction for ourselves.

CONSULTING OPPORTUNITIES IN A GROWTH COMPANY

Once a psychological consultant to a CEO has proven his or her effectiveness, the individual will often have as many opportunities to contribute to the organization as his or her interests, training, and abilities allow. I will describe some that I found of special value. You may consider this as a partial list of possibilities. Nevertheless, they illustrate a range of opportunities within a rapidly growing organization.

The Assessment Center

Recruiting, hiring, and retaining highly qualified key people is of significant importance to any growing organization. At Strathmore we sought people who could perform at above average levels, had the competencies to serve as backups at least at the next level of authority. It was also realized that if you hire high-competency people, they will start making a contribution sooner and with less training.

I was frustrated by traditional selection methods that primarily relied on personal interviews. Although the interview is still the most prevalent selection method, it is subject to the vicissitudes and whims of the interviewer, and is likely to reflect the result of biased judgments. Moreover, how well a person presents him- or herself may bear little relationship to the job functions the person will eventually perform. Accordingly, the interview method was rejected in favor of a selection procedure where properly screened candidates went through multiple measures, with multiple observers, using multiple criteria. Some of the assessment center strategies involved resumé reviews and interviews, but the most significant part of the process relied on simulations where the candidates demonstrated their ability to perform real job functions under mildly stressful conditions. Clearly, it is better to see what people actually can do in preference to what they say they can do.

Our psychological consultant devised a selection method that built upon assessment center technology that could be rapidly employed on an as needed basis. The method afforded Strathmore the opportunity to screen single individuals as opposed to the traditional assessment center model that involved multiple candidates. I found this individualized procedure to be quite valuable for our organization because of its flexibility, efficiency, and cost effectiveness. Over time, I observed that the method was unwaveringly accurate and that the selected individuals proved most valuable in their support of Strathmore's growth. Because of the high degree of its objectivity, the method was especially valuable in evaluating both external and internal candidates for a position. As Dr. Knaus notes in Chapter 1, Strathmore's assessment center had an impressive 91.8% accuracy rating and this translated into less turnover and greater organizational consistency and stability.

Despite its impressive supportive research, utility, predictive validity, and reliability, few medium-sized companies use this assessment center selection method. However, there is no question that medium-sized companies that use this technology in a careful and objective manner should gain a competitive edge, as happened at Strathmore. I would think that by virtue of their training in test construction, in using scientific methods, and in people assessment, that psychologists would be uniquely qualified to devise and implement assessment centers. Their professional background also gives the psychologist a credibility that can yield a marketing edge over nonprofessionally trained competition in this area.

Cross-Transfer Program

Bright and talented people often flourish under conditions where they can challenge themselves, learn new things, and grow. As a by-product, their contributions to the company broaden, and both the individual and the organization normally prosper as a result. In medium-sized organizations, some talented persons may feel limited in their advancement opportunities if the managerial position to which they aspire is blocked by an individual who, for one reason or another, does not advance. To meet this challenge, it was routine to create opportunities for talented individuals to assume responsibilities outside of their training and discipline, providing they showed the necessary attributes to succeed and their qualities matched up to the job. Thus, throughout the organization, talented people knew they were not locked into a particular job or department.

Cross-transfer strategies opened up promotional opportunities that benefited both the individual and the organization. It increased Strathmore's retention of people we wanted to keep. This cross-transfer promotional system also strongly signaled the company's intent to promote from within.

Our psychological consultant provided valuable insights into the match-up between person and position. He had access to test data and to reports of his assessment center findings. He directly observed all key staff and management personnel. He was intimately familiar with the job requirements for each position. Because of this background, our joint efforts in placing people greatly strengthened our management team and supported our efforts to retain key people.

I found our problem-solving dialog beneficial to both myself and our organization. I know there are important opportunities for psychologists to contribute in this area. However, this contribution is again predicated on the psychologist having detailed information about the organization, its people, and its challenges. In my view, it is well worth the effort for a psychological consultant to develop the knowledge about an organization in sufficient depth to be able to make this valuable contribution.

Staff Development

In all organizations, some talented people inhibit themselves and do not approach their potential. Our psychological consultant was used to individualize training programs to create opportunities for company people to better use their talents. This involved a hands-on individualized training approach where Strathmore people would improve their delegation skills, assert their organizational roles effectively and constructively, recognize and deal effectively with drug and alcohol problems in the workplace, improve their people assessment and management skills, overcome procrastination, improve their problem-solving skills, run brief but effective staff meetings, and so forth.

Psychologists seem particularly well suited to the task of providing individual training to key personnel in areas that relate to psychology and that provide personal as well as professional benefits. I see substantial opportunities for psychological consultants working in these key areas. However, the reader is likely to improve his or her ability to contribute through developing working relationships with the key people in the organization, maintaining confidentiality, and genuinely supporting the growth and development of organizations that have finite human resources capabilities.

Mental Health Interventions

Unfortunately, alcoholism and mental illness can strike anyone, and we had our fair share of such challenges. Over time, I learned to deal with these matters with sensitivity and compassion. Our psychological consultant made a significant contribution in this area. He intervened in a wide range of mental health matters including monitoring the rehabilitation of persons with drug and alcohol related problems as well as severe mental disorders, such as a bipolar disorder. When appropriate, he gave direction to mental health professionals about the employees' job demands and he made sure that the treatment was appropriate. He also advised the employees on how to get the most from their treating professional. This form of oversight proved valuable. People who might have been lost to the company were able to return to their jobs and continue to contribute and prosper.

In this age of managed care, where cost savings too often rank above the quality of care for a temporarily handicapped employee, our psychological consultant was able to find a balance between cost and care and to assure that a Strathmore employee with emotional or substance related problems was ready to return to work.

Based on our experience, there appear to be important opportunities for clinically qualified, licensed psychologists to provide an oversight to managed care organizations in order to assure that the mental health care dollars are used wisely and well. We have observed that it is short-sighted to "short-change" individuals on their mental health treatment in order to save dollars. Such savings may prove transitory and ultimately drive up costs through increased primary care physician visits.

We need to take a long-term view on the benefits of mental health care in relationship to job performance, recruitment costs for those who do not receive adequate treatment, and insurance costs. That aside, we need to consider the individual and his or her sense of well-being. Appropriately trained psychologists will attempt to initiate such oversight efforts at a company level. Many CEOs may not have access to the empirical research on the relationship between good mental and physical health and costs of care factors and performance factors. A skilled psychologist can provide this information to the benefit of the company personnel and certainly to the overall health of the organization.

Employee Conferences

It was found to be of special value to discuss Strathmore's key people with a knowledgeable outside consultant who was intimately familiar with our people and operations. As a result, and with professional insight, I was better able to do the right thing both for our people and the company. Although it is difficult to put a dollar amount on the value of this service, I can say that we were a far stronger company for anticipating and dealing with challenging problems before they rose to a level of critical concern. This level of involvement with a company CEO only comes about over time and with the consultant's proven ability to show an objective perspective and insight into the organization's people and their relationship to various aspects of the company.

Outplacement Services

As is commonly known, outplacement is a costly but important service for employees who, for whatever reason, were eventually unable to meet the standards for their positions. Fortunately, the implementation of the assessment center reduced the need for these services at Strathmore, as did our cross-transfer model. However, in a few select cases, our psychological consultant was able to coordinate the company's outplacement services, provide information, and give direction to a severed employee. In all cases, the individuals were reemployed within 6 months.

Psychologists with experience in outplacement services can provide valuable assistance, and presumably at a cost less than the normal outplacement firm costs. Further, clinically trained psychologists are prepared to help the individual deal more effectively with the "shock" that sometimes accompanies a dismissal. As a company president, I found it beneficial to have former employees receive high quality services from a person trained in this area than to entrust this responsibility to someone whose training and ability is equivocal in dealing with persons with job loss stress.

Career Counseling for People in the Community

Bearing in mind Strathmore's belief in service to the community, we found it occasionally important to provide career counseling and direction for people referred to us from the community or who independently inquired about general opportunities within the company. In selected cases, our psychological consultant provided this career counseling service. As a result, we were able to hire several excellent managers and staff. We also found that some individuals could profit from a career direction unrelated to any of our company functions. We gave them the necessary information and direction to find their career path. I am gratified that many took this advice and appreciated our effort.

Although other chief executive officers may hesitate to engage a psychologist for this purpose, I found external career counseling to be a humanitarian endeavor. For those who are more closely keyed to economic issues, I offer this observation: There is a compelling economic argument for this service. Hiring one person out of ten for whom this service is provided, is likely to be less costly than paying a search firm fee for one position.

Market Research

Because psychologists are trained behavioral scientists, they may have many skills that can benefit medium-sized growth organizations. For example, our consultant conducted national marketing surveys to define both our market and market share. He also surveyed artist preferences for artist paper products to help us decide what to produce and sell. The costs of these services were considerably less than if we had contracted with a large consulting firm that must pay salaries, overhead costs, and, of course, make a profit. Moreover, many consulting firms hire people who are not as well credentialed as a licensed psychologist.

Market research is a specialized area. Organizational psychologists with training, talent, and experience in this area will surely find these skills welcomed by organizations that seek quality information at an affordable cost. In our information age, with rapid market changes taking place, this role is likely to gain in value with time. Based on our experience, I encourage the reader to prepare to meet this challenge.

CONCLUSION

I'm told that psychologists face many challenges in a managed care environment and opportunities in academe have become more limited. On the other hand, consultation work with a growth company—or direct employment—can provide many challenges and rewards, as we have outlined in this chapter. For those organizational psychologists who wish to avail themselves of the opportunity of working with a chief executive officer, I offer this advice: Do plenty of advanced planning; get to know as much about the company as possible; determine where your skills can make a real contribution to the prospective organization; and then plan to have persistence, persistence, and persistence. If you succeed, it will be an extraordinarily rewarding experience to serve a medium-sized growth company that emphasizes the people side of the equation.

5.

Reducing Procrastination in the Workplace

HANK ROBB, Ph.D.

Prioritizing means putting off until tomorrow what would be wiser to do tomorrow. Procrastination means putting off until tomorrow what would be wiser to do today. For dedicated procrastinators, tomorrow rarely comes soon enough and prioritizing can become just another rationalization for further procrastination. Procrastination can be a serious problem in many life areas including the workplace.

Procrastination has been studied most widely and thoroughly among college students. An early study of 500 college students attending five different colleges found that as many as 50% of them reported procrastinating with regard to their studies *at least* half the time. This finding was consistent across types of educational institution, which ranged from a community college to an Ivy League school (Hill, Hill, Chabot, & Baral, 1978). Other studies have found that between 20 and 30% of college students have significant procrastination problems which lower their grades and disrupt other areas of their lives (Aitken, 1982; Briordy, 1980; McCown, 1986; McCown, Johnson, & Petzel, 1989; Solomon & Rothblum, 1984). More intelligent people, as measured by the Shipley (1940) Intelligence Test, are as likely to procrastinate as less intelligent people (Ferrari, 1991). There is also evidence that while students who fail to act until the last minute may not make lower grades than their counterparts who start earlier, they retain much less of the material they studied (McCown & Ferrari, 1995).

Only a little work has been done with nonstudent populations and published in peer reviewed outlets (Ferrari, 1992b; Ferrari, 1993; McCown & Johnson, 1989). Even less appears to have been done within a business setting (Ferrari, 1992a). However, what has been done again suggests procrastination is a significant problem for 20 to 30% of the general population. Though most businesses cannot track procrastination and its effects, records of disciplinary action for attorneys are kept and offer a potential index to the frequency of the problem. In the state of Oregon, for example, it is estimated that as many as one-third of complaints against licensed attorneys involve failing to act in a timely fashion (Sapiro, 1995, personal communication). The law is a profession that requires 3 years postgraduate education for entry-level workers and meeting deadlines as an essential aspect of the profession for which they trained.

Intelligence and education may not greatly reduce procrastination but age, to a point, has a salutary effect. McCown and Roberts (1994) randomly conducted a telephone survey of 360 individuals from 18 through 77. Women were found to procrastinate less than men, and both groups tended to decline in self-reported procrastination until approximately age 60 at which time both groups began a sustained increase in self-reported procrastination, with women now reporting higher levels of procrastination than men. Since this was cross-sectional rather than longitudinal data, it is impossible to know what role environmental (e.g., living through the Great Depression and World War II) or health factors (e.g., increased chronic illness) may have played in determining this result.

There is strong evidence for five "big" factors which make up human personality (Costa & McCrae, 1989; Eysenck, 1970). These factors include a greater or lesser tendency toward: (1) anxiety, worry, and depression; (2) outgoingness, sociability, and impulsiveness; (3) openness to experience; (4) agreeableness; and (5) conscientiousness. There is agreement that at least one and possibly two other of these well-documented human tendencies play a role in procrastination (Ferrari, Johnson, & McCown, 1995). First, some humans simply seem more diligent than others about attending to what is to be done. If one is less focused, it is easier to procrastinate. Second, some humans are more impulsive than others. If one is more likely to impulsively dive into and dive out of things, one is more likely to procrastinate. Finally, some humans are more prone to anxiety, worry, and depression. When the very act of doing something leads a person to become more worried, anxious, or depressed about the outcome and what it means for them, procrastination becomes more probable. These factors are orthogonal (i.e., having one tendency says nothing about the probability of having another). Those with the most difficulty have problems in all three areas, others have problems in only one or two. It is the, potentially, multiply determined aspect of procrastination that requires it to be addressed in several ways for some individuals but not for others. *Procrastination and Task Avoidance* (Ferrari, Johnson, & McCown, 1995) also provides evidence that, for many, procrastination is a chronic condition, much like near sightedness. If, like many, an individual chronically procrastinates, then the best thing that individual can do, analogically speaking, is learn to wear his or her glasses. For others, procrastination only occurs at certain life transitions, with certain people, or certain tasks. Whether one has a chronic or only occasional problem with procrastination, the approaches to reducing it are largely the same.

COMPASS SETTING

Setting priorities and acting on them is the opposite of, and the antidote to, procrastination. People will not act effectively if they are spending their time on those activities with the most payoff, and neglecting those with the least. With regard to prioritizing, Steven Covey (1989) has noted four categories of potential activities involving urgency (events or activities calling for immediate attention) and importance (events or activities relevant to your most central goals or desires): (1) urgent and unimportant; (2) urgent and important; (3) not urgent and unimportant; and (4) not urgent and important. Urgent events can vary from a ringing telephone, to a greeting from a colleague, to a summons from either one's manager-supervisor or the majority stockholder. Urgent is not necessarily important. The importance of an activity is determined by it relevance to the individual's overall life goals.

Helping Individuals Set Their Goals

If people are to reduce their own tendency to procrastinate or help someone else reduce *their* tendency, then, at some point, they will have to decide, "I had better get this done." Why? If the answer is only to avoid short-term pain, discomfort, or difficulty, people will not have nearly as effective a motivation to reduce procrastination as if the answer is to acquire, achieve, or experience something they find deeply moving and central to their lives.

Many people have difficulty getting things done because those things are not themselves experienced as deeply moving or central to their lives nor are those things connected to anything deeply moving or central to their lives. Confronting and tolerating, rather than avoiding, short-term pain, discomfort, or difficulty, is usually the thing required to overcome procrastination. If avoiding certain instances of these types of experiences (e.g., "the boss will yell at me and, perhaps, not give me a raise or fire me if I don't get this done") are the only reasons individuals have for confronting and tolerating other instances of them (e.g., confronting and tolerating boring, tedious, or lengthy tasks), they will not have much motivation to reduce procrastination relative to the motivation they will have to keep it up. Essentially, individuals are telling themselves, or encouraging others, to confront and tolerate one instance of relatively short-term discomfort in order to avoid some other instance of relatively short-term discomfort. It is far easier to confront and tolerate discomfort in the service of acquiring, achieving, or experiencing something people deeply desire as compared to confronting and tolerating discomfort in the service of merely avoiding something they do not care deeply about.

Determining what one really wants to be doing with one's life is not usually done easily or quickly, but once an individual has set their compass they will have a distinct advantage in prioritizing activities because they can more readily decide which activities are more important and which are less so. In fact, figuring out what one really cares about in life is one of those activities that falls in the category of important but not urgent, because there will almost always be other events pressing for a response. However, until individuals set their respective compasses, they will not know which events are actually important and which are not. Thus, there will be an increased probability for individuals to engage in tasks based on whether they are immediately pleasant or unpleasant. That is because Covey's category "important" means, "important to the individual" and not merely important to the individual's manager, company, or stockholders. The first step in assisting individuals to reduce their procrastination is to set up time to assist them in evaluating what they really want to acquire, achieve, or experience in life.

Fiore has suggested the "unschedule" as the first place to start (Burka & Yuen, 1983). The idea of the unschedule is to find the places in an individual's life where they actually have time to get things done. The individual lists the days of the week across the top of a sheet of paper and the hours of the day they are likely to be awake down the side. Next, the individual fills in all the activities that are regularly going to occur during the week (e.g., wake up and prepare for activities, commute to work, eat, read the newspaper, watch TV, attend regularly scheduled staff meetings, etc.). What is left are the time periods available to work on figuring out what the individual really cares about in life. Encourage individuals to schedule at least an hour, and preferably two or three, a week to deal with this issue. Encourage them to recall that this is the most important thing they have to do all week because the results of this activity are meant to structure the rest of their lives.

We learn what is important to us by having different kinds of experiences and reflecting on them. If one has had enough experiences to get a clue about what one finds deeply moving in life, then one's job is to reflect on them and sense which are most important. If individuals find, on reflection, that they actually do not know what they deeply care about, then encourage them to write down some experiences that might help them to find out. Of course, these experiences can include asking others about what they have found important in life or reading about what people have written about this issue. However, what others have found deeply moving may not be what an individual finds deeply moving and the point of this activity is to help determine what someone finds deeply moving.

The organizational practitioner must be careful when encouraging this activity not to position him- or herself in the middle of a conflict between the interests of the employer and those of the individual. For example, an individual may determine that maximum productivity for their employer is incompatible with their child rearing goals and that the latter is more important to the individual. This potential conflict of interest can best be addressed by encouraging and structuring the process but not requiring individuals to detail the outcome to the practitioner. In this way, confidentiality about employees' long-term goals can be maintained, but the mechanism for establishing priorities essential for the reduction of procrastination can be instituted.

Individuals may change as they grow older regarding what they deeply care about. Thus, each person had better be encouraged to set time aside on a regular basis to check, and possibly reset, his or her compass. A midlife crisis has been defined as, "Getting to the top of the ladder and discovering it's against the wrong wall." It results from not systematically attending to the fact that what one really cares about may change over time, thus requiring regular re-charting of one's life course.

If individuals procrastinate planning or following through on activities to establish their life priorities, the remainder of the material in this chapter can be used to help them address this most important issue. It has become common for decision makers at or near the top of organizational charts to recognize that if the company does not know where it is going, it has much less chance of getting there. The same maxim applies to individuals.

The Problem of Should

In the previous discussion, individuals were encouraged to reflect on their experience and sense what is important to them as opposed to sense what should be important to them. *Should* is a word with several different meanings and is, therefore, potentially a source of problems when providing assistance to those with procrastination problems. In the following discussion it will become obvious that some meanings of should can be categorized as "good sense" while others can be categorized as "nonsense." Individuals often can see this distinction readily. They often mistakenly believe that because they "know the right answer," the "knowledge" will control their behavior without much further effort on their part. However, "knowing the right answer" does not ensure people will stick with it. A thought experiment often helps get this point across.

Suppose you are in England. Imagine you are at a street corner and then imagine crossing the street. Which way did you look just before you stepped into the street? Chances are it was to the left when it should have been to the right. Visitors to England have this problem quite frequently. They "know" people drive on the left in England, but they don't stick with it. In order to get themselves to act appropriately, visitors often have to frequently, forcefully, and repeatedly remind themselves of something they already "know." Thus, when it comes to working against procrastination, individuals may often have to frequently, forcefully, and repeatedly go over things they already "know" in order to get themselves to stick with that "knowledge" at the appropriate times. "Knowing the right answer" does not equal "sticking with the right answer." The latter may take considerable work and effort.

The "Should of Prediction"

Take the phrase, "I *should* get this work done by the close of business today." One meaning of should might be called the "Should of Prediction" as in, "I *predict* I will get this work done by the close of business today." We use the same meaning when we say, "It should rain tomorrow."

A potential area of procrastination problems lies with the should of prediction. Individuals with these problems may find they do not accurately predict how long a task will take and so do not get it done in a timely fashion. This is not procrastination in the sense of setting a plan and then failing to follow it. However, it is procrastination in the sense that the individual has put off until tomorrow what would have been wiser to do today. The individuals may have followed their work plans, but failed to complete their work in a timely fashion because when the work plans were made the amount of time necessary to complete them was underestimated.

Lay and Schouwenburg (1993) failed to verify poor prediction of the time necessary to complete a task as a problem for procrastinators, but clinical reports (Burka & Yuen, 1983; Ellis & Knaus, 1979) suggest this problem does occur. Ferrari, Johnson, and McCown (1995) report students in their structured treatment for procrastinators underestimate the time necessary to complete tasks by approximately one-half, and must, therefore, double the amount of time they predict the task will take if they are to succeed.

Often, the problem of misprediction can be overcome only by experience. You can ask others with experience you do not have how long it takes them to get a similar project done, but that may not accurately translate to how long it will take you. Learning from experience may also require being open to certain unpleasant realities because refusing to accept them may play a role in procrastination, especially the feeling of being "under the gun" as deadlines draw closer. For example, individuals may realize that considering: (1) the amount of effort typically required to complete work projects; (2) the pace at which they typically work; and (3) the amount of time available during a typical project means that during at least one week of the project period, they will be working more hours than in their normal work week. Perhaps such individuals can lobby for more time to complete projects. However, if that is not possible, they can at least choose which week they will "burn the midnight oil." If they hate the feeling of "being behind," they can choose the first, rather than the last, week to put in the "extra" time.

The "Should of Approval"

"I *should* get this work done by the close of business today" can also mean it is wiser, preferable, or more approvable to get this work done by the close of business today. This meaning might be called the

"Should of Approval." But, whose approval is being considered: one's manager-supervisor's, coworker's, subordinate's, your mate's, or society's? If we want to maximize individual motivation, whatever is asserted as being "more approvable" had better be more approvable to the individual. Chronic procrastination can, of course, lead to an individual's being dismissed and, in this era of downsizing or rightsizing, some may find it tempting to adopt the "lump it or leave it" point of view toward such individuals. However, if one wants to focus on maximizing an individual's motivation rather than dismissing that individual, then it is best to recognize that whether the chain of events associated with "Why should I get this work done by the close of business today" is short or long, the individual had better be able to end the chain with, "Because that is what *I* truly and deeply care about," rather than, "Because that is what other individuals or groups want me to care about."

Admittedly, getting what the individual wants may mean doing what other people tell him or her to do. However, individual motivation is maximized not by allowing individuals to stay focused on the fact that other people are telling them what to do but by getting them focused on the fact that compliance will get them what *they* want. As stated above, what one really and deeply desires is to be discovered by taking the life experiences one has had by accident or design and reflecting on them. No person can answer this question for another, but people can be encouraged to find out for themselves. Practitioners wishing to aid individuals with procrastination problems will be wise to provide such encouragement.

Must's and the "Should of Demandingness"

"I *should* get this work done by the close of business today" can also mean, "I must get this work done by the close of business today," which contains yet another linguistic ambiguity. One meaning of "must" shows a necessarily contingent connection between events (e.g., "If I am to have a chance of getting the contract, I must submit a proposal by the close of business today"). However, a second meaning is a demand issued as if one were the ruler of the universe, a universe which *must* conform to its ruler's commands. Thus, "I should get this work done by the close of business today," becomes "I *must* get this work done by the close of business today," and even "I *must* get the contract." Such demandingness toward oneself, others, or the world in general has been cited as a root cause of emotional disturbance and is almost always counterproductive (Ellis, 1962, 1972, 1994). It is hypothesized to generate emotional disturbances such as anger, anxiety, and depression which do not help to reduce tendencies toward procrastination and often increase them.

If a practitioner asks others, or even him- or herself, why such and such must occur, the typical ruler of the universe answer, "Because that's the way I want it!" will rarely be given in response. People typically realize, "I am running the universe," is not the right answer. Instead, individuals usually cite the reasons why it would be *approvable* for such and such to happen. Unfortunately, just because an individual or group of individuals designate some acquisition, achievement, or experience approvable hardly means it *must* happen as if ordained by some absolute ruler of the universe. If such were the case, we would live in a very different world; a world in which by simply designating some acquisition, achievement, or experience approvable we would automatically bring it about. In such a world there would be no need for effort and little opportunity for procrastination.

Acceptance: The Antidote to Demandingness

When shown the reasons something is approvable do not prove it *must* happen, many people often respond with something like, "Well what am I supposed to do, just accept the situation?" In a word, *yes*. They can work to accept things of which they do not approve, and encourage others to do likewise, because accepting can be differentiated from either approval or acquiescence. Individuals can be shown that acceptance means making the best out of things whether they approve of those things or not. A useful analogy is suggesting that acceptance means playing the hand one is dealt the best one can regardless of whether or not one approves of the way the hand was dealt or the cards one received. Demanding one *must* not have the cards one is dealt, or even demanding one *must* play them well, does not help one get new and different cards nor does it help one play one's cards better. One does not have to approve of the task itself, or the circumstances by which it came one's way, in order to accept that, indeed, this is the task before one and, if the outcome associated with completing this task is to be obtained, then, I, contingently speaking, must do the work. In short, individuals can be both trained and encouraged to accept, even gracefully accept, things they do not rate as approvable.

Conversely, acceptance need not mean acquiescence. A very popular prayer reads, "Lord, give me to ability to accept the things I cannot change, to change the things I can, and the wisdom to know the difference." This prayer leaves one with the notion that acceptance means acquiescence to things as they are, the opposite of doing something about them. On the contrary, acceptance that things are as they are, whether or not one approves of them, is not an alternative to change, it is a virtual prerequisite to change. Individuals can often grasp the importance of this point with the following example. Suppose your work situation includes a poor office procedure, poor training procedure, or poor procurement procedure. If one does not first accept the unsatisfactory procedure as an unpleasant fact in one's life, there is, literally, nothing for one to consider changing. Logically speaking, before one can decide whether or not to attempt a change, one must accept that there is something there to change. Such acceptance, by itself, does not determine whether one will choose to leave things as they are or work to change them. In short, acceptance that something is as it is need not mean acquiescence to its continuing to be as it is.

Busyness and Bingeing

Boice (1989) has shown that new university professors suffer from "busyness and bingeing," and it is reasonable to believe they are not the only group of workers to have these problems. If new faculty members are to retain their positions, they, contingently, must write, submit, and obtain publication for their articles. Boice found new faculty tended to view this task as requiring large blocks of time which they could not arrange in their schedules. This inability to "control time" led to a high sense of stress and anxiety. It also led to high levels of "busyness." These new faculty members did not sit around twiddling their collective thumbs or playing computer games. They became immersed in other tasks which had more immediate deadlines, such as preparing lectures.

Similarly, while studying procrastination by college students taking a summer class, Lay and Schouwenburg (1993) found there was little difference, during the last week of the marking period, in time-on-task between those with high and low levels of "trait procrastination." The nearness, or temporal proximity, of the events of concern, namely a final paper and exam, seemed to allow both groups to focus on the relevant task.

Ainslie (1992) has suggested that people naturally tend to devalue future rewards but do not devalue more immediate rewards, resulting in a phenomenon labeled *temporal myopia* (Ainslie, 1975; Hernstein & Mazur, 1987). With temporal myopia the further out in time an individual projects a reward, the less valuable the reward tends to be rated by that individual. Thus, temporally proximate rewards are viewed as relatively more valuable. Skinner (1953) and Ellis (1962) have also made the point that temporally distant consequences tend to control behavior less effectively than more immediate consequences. These all too human tendencies mean that it is essential that individuals be encouraged to continually evaluate what it is they really care about so as to be gaining the refreshment of those experiences as often as possible and not simply anticipating them "sometime" in the far distant future.

The new faculty Boice studied not only focused on preparing their lectures, they "binged" in their preparation, and generated considerably more material than they could use. For them, only *too much* was enough. This view further created a sense of pressure. It was as if the faculty were operating with the following maximum, "Well, at least this is something I *can* get done." The more they *could do* the more they did.

In summary, they suffered from both busyness, a sense of too much to get done, and bingeing, over doing the things they did get done. They seemed to be insisting to themselves, and did assert to the researcher, that contingently, they must have large chunks of time to do their scholarly writing. Since they could not find the big chunks of time they insisted they needed, they focused on other tasks with deadlines closer at hand. However, they not only focused on these activities, they overfocused on them. They not only worked on them, they overworked on them. It was a cycle that left the faculty feeling exhausted, frazzled, and more convinced than ever they had an inadequate amount of time available to do their work, especially their scholarly writing.

Boice not only documented the "busyness and bingeing" phenomenon, but also provided a way to overcome it. The heart of that program was getting participants to accept, at least tentatively, the possibility of doing their scholarly writing for only short periods of time. Even those who agreed to participate in the program began skeptically.

The faculty had been correct in asserting they did not have large blocks of time available to do their scholarly writing. The problem was not their assessment of the situation but their conclusion, "therefore such work cannot get done." Using something like the "unschedule" described above, participants were helped to identify smaller blocks of time which could be devoted to scholarly writing instead of other tasks (e.g., preparing lectures). Program participants agreed to try doing this kind of work during these time periods. They also agreed to variable and unannounced visits from the researcher to "see how things were going." Somewhat to their surprise, program participants found they were making headway with their articles. Since they very much wanted to write and submit articles, there was little trouble getting their vigorous continuation of these procedures once they saw the procedures did, in fact, work.

Analogically individuals can be encouraged to "walk and chew gum at the same time." One bite at a time doesn't necessarily mean one thing at a time. Using an unschedule may help individuals realize that doing one thing at a particular time doesn't mean they cannot do something else as well. Those who commute to work by means other than a car may be able to work on projects while commuting. Those who commute by bicycle can get their daily exercise while providing their own transportation. If work involves telephone contacts which frequently put individuals on "hold," a speaker phone or a headset can free them to work on other tasks while waiting. If individuals move from place to place during the work day (e.g., making calls on prospective clients) and/or regularly spend time waiting to be seen, that time also could be used to accomplish other tasks. Hand-held recorders allow dictation while doing other tasks. Even if the individual is the one who has to transcribe the tape at a later time, at least they are making headway with the task. Once individuals begin applying this principle, they often generate highly creative and personally relevant means to increase their effective use of time.

PLANNING

Planning is essential to reducing procrastination. If work provides individuals with an opportunity to procrastinate, it also provides them at least some control over their time. Planning provides the best opportunity to exert that control effectively. Individuals do not need an elaborate daily planner but they almost certainly need a simple one along with a pocket notebook. The pocket notebook is used to write down things that call on a person to be done. Their life priorities allow individuals to decide which of these things get a high priority and which get no priority at all. Their own experience and input from others allow them to predict, with greater or lesser accuracy, how long it will take to get things done. Recognizing they can walk and chew gum at he same time, along with the pocket notebook of "things to do" and their daily planner, allow them to schedule time to do them.

Should's that Block Planning and How to Deal with Them

The first should that causes planning problems is the should of prediction. People with procrastination problems typically underestimate the amount of time necessary to complete a task, and by as much as 50%. They also overestimate the time left to perform a task. If it takes 30 minutes to get from one's home to one's workplace when there is no traffic, how reasonable is it to predict it will take a 30-minute commute during the rush hour? If a task can be finished in 30 minutes providing there are no interruptions, how reasonable is it to predict it will take 30 minutes to complete the task when there are several interruptions an hour? People "know" the right answers to these questions but they do not stick with them. Given Murphy's Law: Anything that can go wrong will and at the worst possible time, no one will predict the amount of time it takes to get something done with perfection which probably accounts for nonprocrastinators typically overpredicting how long it will take to complete a task.

Individuals regularly mispredicting how long it will take to get something done are often helped by this four-step process. First, list each activity associated with an overall task. Second, make an estimate of how much time that activity will take. Third, compare the estimated time to the actual time spent. Fourth, continually perform this routine until the individual becomes fairly accurate at predicting all the activities necessary to complete a task, and the estimated and actual time for a task are close.

This brings up a typical next problematic should, demanding that the world operate differently from the way it does because one wishes, desires, or approves of it operating differently. Because the individual wants it to take less time, they stick with and act as if it *should/must*. Unfortunately, however long something takes, that's how long it takes. There is no reason it should/must take less time simply because individuals, their organizational subordinates, and superiors, customers or corporate stockholders want it to take less time. This is not a rationalization for refusing to search for and use time-saving mechanisms. But if they don't exist or can't be found, then, that is the way it is. The fact of one's wanting them to exist or be available does not prove they should/must exist or be available to the individual. People with procrastination problems often "know" these right answers, but, again, knowing the right answer does not necessarily mean sticking with the right answer. The question for them is, "Are you sticking with the right answer when you are procrastinating?"

"But I *should/must* not have to put up with such a hassle to get what I want" is another common response which contributes to procrastination. The illogic underlying the response is something like, "Because planning is a hassle or reveals other hassles I will have to put up with and because I strongly dislike hassles, they *should/must* not exist." Individuals can be helped to work against this illogic by challenging it. Here is an example.

"Why shouldn't you have to put up this hassle? Suppose I or you or the entire human race deem it wrong, unfortunate, undesirable, or bad that in order to get what you want you, contingently, must deal with hassles. Does that prove a hassle should/must not exist for you or anybody else? No! Much as any individual might like to have a 'Get Out of Hassles Free' card, no one does. It's nice when we get a choice about which hassles we have, but living and working involve hassles."

Ferrari, Johnson, and McCown (1995, p. 197) note that in addition to poorly estimating the time required to complete a task, and the time available to devote to it, individuals who procrastinate have other motivational problems. First, they overestimate future motivational states (e.g., "I'll feel more like doing it later"). Second, they wrongly believe the only right time to work is when you feel like working ("People should only tackle a task when they feel ready for it"). Third, they wrongly believe that nothing useful can be accomplished if you attempt to work when you don't feel like it (e.g., "It doesn't do any good to work when you're not motivated"). The last is a particular problem for bright people who may believe that because they are bright, hard work is unnecessary, at least for them. Each of these is a variation on the theme, "I should/must be able to get what I want without hassle."

Individuals can be taught to stop sticking with these variations with tactics similar to the example given above. Namely, they can frequently and forcefully and repeatedly show themselves they are sticking with nonsense when they procrastinate despite the fact that they "know" better.

"Awfulizing": How It Blocks Planning and How to Overcome It

"It's awful," as in, "It's awful that I have to do all this planning to get what I want," is a response to the discomfort of planning that makes planning even harder to accomplish. When individuals awfulize about planning, it can quickly come to a halt.

Awfulizing comes in two different forms. The first is, "This planning stuff is worse than 100% bad." Here is an example of how individuals can challenge their tendency to stick with this type of awfulizing. Despite football commentator assertions that, "He gave 110%," 100% is all there is—the totality. However bad something is, it will never be worse than 100% bad (i.e., totally and completely bad). Consider something truly bad, such as a loved one being in an automobile accident and living on for many years with constant and painful suffering. Thinking about how bad things really could be shows one that, regardless of how uncomfortable planning activities are, the discomfort does not come close to 100% bad and is certainly not more uncomfortable than it possibly can be.

A second form of awfulizing is overestimating how bad things actually are. Individuals act as if things that are less then 1% bad are 50, 75, or even 99% bad. To combat this tendency, individuals can be taught to build a "Badness Scale." The central attribute of the scale is suffering over time. Thus, 100% bad, the top of the scale, might be having had a car wreck which left one paralyzed from the neck down and in constant pain for the next 20 years. Because it makes it worse when a person's loved ones suffer as well, one can add that the individual's mate, children, or other important people were in the accident resulting in their having been disfiguringly burned and maimed. Clearly, this would make the situation worse. Importantly, these are not fanciful events. They actually have happened and will continue happening to some people. With such events projected over 20 years at 100% bad, one can easily see that 50% bad would be such events projected over 10 years; 25% over 5 years, and 1% bad over approximately 72 days of being paralyzed from the neck down and in constant pain with my loved ones also suffering with maiming and burning from an auto accident? Almost certainly they will see they are overestimating how bad their work related suffering actually is.

When working to help individuals give up or at least reduce their awfulizing, practitioners often hear, "Well, it feels awful." This is sometimes called "emotional reasoning." Here is an example of how individuals can learn to recognize their emotional reasoning and begin to stop sticking with it.

Many things feel or seem a certain way but are not, in fact, as they seem or feel. Consider rising before daylight and looking to the east. It may feel or seem as if the sun is rising, but it is not. The earth is turning. The sun may feel or seem to grow smaller as it "rises" in the sky, but the size of the sun is not shrinking any more than its size is increasing as the sun "sets." If you put your arm in clear water, the portion in the water seems or feels suddenly to have adopted a new angle relative to the portion of your arm out of the water. In fact, it has not. Many things seem or feel to be different than they are and this distinction is also true for many uncomfortable things. Yes, they are uncomfortable and no, they are not so uncomfortable as to be awful even though they seem to be. Specifically, events outside your body or sensations inside your body are (1) not worse than they can possibly be and (2) not likely to be nearly as bad as they actually could be.

Person Rating: How It Blocks Planning and What to Do About It

Many people experience anxiety when they begin planning for work activities. This anxiety may not be caused by their contemplating how "awful" it will be to plan for or do the work. Instead, it is anxiety about their personhood, more commonly known as their self-esteem. Rational–emotive behavior therapy (REBT), originated by Ellis (1962, 1972, 1994), is one of the few approaches to handling life problems which advocates giving up your self-esteeming rather than trying to build more of it. Self-esteeming encourages the view: "If I do good, I am good. If I do dirt, I am dirt," while REBT encourages people to "Rate what I do, not who I am." With this approach individuals can be confident that their selfhood or personhood is never on the line. A person always remains a person—a person who may do well or poorly, but a person nonetheless.

An approach to life which encourages individuals to rate their "selves" or their personhood based on how well they perform will work well as long as the person performs well. Unfortunately, none of us performs well all the time. The knowledge that one sometimes performs poorly, and may do so quite often, combined with a self-esteeming approach to life, tends to lead to anxiety when contemplating action. To avoid this anxiety, many people avoid performance. Even when they force themselves to act despite their anxiety, their performance often is reduced by it. Fortunately, a person's worth as a worker does not equal their worth as a human. One can work against the tendency to rate one's personhood based on performance and get off the self-esteem yo-yo.

Suppose we took a DNA sample from a person who had excellent work performance and another sample from a person who had poor work performance to a laboratory with equipment capable of performing multiple DNA analysis. Suppose we then asked the laboratory workers to tell us which sample is from the "excellent human" and which is from the "poor human." Could we get an answer to this question? Of course not. Either you are a human or you are not. While there are good or poor performances, there are no good or poor people.

Plan Worst Things First

"Eat a live toad first thing each morning, and nothing worse will happen the rest of the day." This aphorism has an implication for planning. Plan to do unpleasant things first. Ross Van Ness (1988) cleverly refers to tasks which are Difficult, Uninteresting, and Distasteful as DUDs. Remind individuals there is no reason one should/must not be stuck with one or more DUD tasks nor is being stuck with one or more DUDs awful. It is best to plan to get DUDs out of the way as early as possible, whether that be early in the day, early in the week, early in the quarter, or early in the year.

Plan to Make Work Easier When Possible

Delegation can often help procrastination. In preparing this chapter, I was able to get a research librarian to complete computer searches of popular and technical literature on procrastination rather than having to do it myself. I was also able to pay my daughter to make copies of articles so I could work on other matters and still review the articles without having to leave my office. Many individuals profit from including more delegation as part of their planning.

While individuals may not be able to delegate, they may be able to trade. They may have a workmate, or even someone outside their work setting, who would be willing to do something for them if they provide an alternative service for him or her. They may be able to arrange to work on tasks "side by side" with someone. In some companies work pods are replacing work cubicles. Such an arrangement may help assuage feelings of loneliness and isolation in an individual's work. It may not be awful that one is alone and isolated in one's work but, if one finds it undesirable, why not try to modify the work situation, at least for certain tasks? Individuals have the additional benefit of having agreed to work on a certain task at a certain time and such "public declarations" may make it easier to stick with business (Burka & Yuen, 1983).

Rewards

Scheduling rewards for partially or fully completing a task may also help get it done. The biggest reward is recognizing that the task is in some way linked to that which moves one in life and that by accomplishing this task, having this experience, or achieving this outcome, one is gaining, or making it more probable that one will gain, that fulfillment.

Even so, short-term immediate enjoyments can provide encouragements to keep going. When planning rewards for partially or fully completing tasks, small but frequent enjoyments are more effective than large but infrequent ones. Most importantly, the reward is not to be obtained without the performance on which it was made contingent. This can be a problem when an individual's plan calls for self-provided or self-withheld rewards. Not completing a task and still providing a reward constitutes active self-training in procrastination.

Planning for the Unplanned

Work often involves many immediate tasks of short duration. Some of them can be predicted (e.g., daily mail), others cannot (e.g., unanticipated telephone calls). One can prioritize some of these events as unimportant and wisely refuse to respond. However, many will be important regardless of how mundane. "Do it now" is the planful motto for these events. Something as mundane as the daily mail can provide a good example. (1) Open the mail and act on what you open. (2) If there are things to be filed, file them yourself or delegate the task. (3) If there are immediate actions to be taken, take them. (4) If mail brings requests for action that require relatively longer periods of time to generate a response, schedule time to produce that response.

ACTION

The demandingness, awfulizing, and person rating that worked against making effective and realistic plans can also work against carrying out those plans. Responses to these blocks in action are the same as when they are blocks in planning. With regard to demanding that things should/must: (1) not take so long, (2) be easier, or (3) generally be other than they are, individuals can be taught and encouraged to forcefully, frequently, and repeatedly show themselves that their approving of the world and the actions of the people in it is not the basis on which the world works or others act. One can expect hassles when one attempts to implement one's plans. Considering the issue from the perspective of the should of prediction, these problems definitely should exist because hassles and problems are, predictably, a part of life. Hassles may be bad but they are hardly awful.

It may help to teach individuals and encourage them to remind themselves that the amount of energy it takes to get started is not the amount of energy it takes to keep going. By forcing one's self to do a task for at least 15 minutes, one proves to one's self that, indeed, one *can* stand the task even though it is unpleasant. Individuals can use the momentum of having gotten themselves going to help keep themselves going. As the aphorism says, "You eat elephants one bite at a time." One is not required to eat every bite at one sitting.

High Work Standards

Self-generated high performance standards are the "enemy" of procrastination and will actually help individuals work against their tendency to procrastinate (Flett, Hewitt, & Thomas, 1995). The "friend" of procrastination is the fear generated by the conviction that if others judge one's work harshly, then one's worth as a human being decreases (Ellis, 1962, 1972, 1994; Flett, Hewitt, & Thomas, 1995). Below is a additional example of what individuals can be taught and encouraged to review for themselves.

> If your work is severely criticized and your worker worth is rated low, that does not mean your human worth is low. You can show yourself that those who think so are simply wrong by reminding yourself of the DNA thought experiment. Your worth as a human being does not go up or down as your worth as a worker goes up and down, any more than the sun "rises and sets" over a flat earth. It may feel bad to be harshly criticized but it does not, and cannot, make you bad. No matter how poor or perfect your performance, that is all it will be—a poor or perfect performance, not a poor or perfect you.

If individuals find themselves getting so anxious that it is hard to remind themselves of the facts as outlined above, they might find a relaxation technique helpful as a prelude to more actively working against their tendency toward self-downing. There are many different techniques to achieve relaxation. Here is one which focuses on breathing.

> In this technique, you want to do abdominal or "belly" breathing. Find a comfortable place to sit or lie. Put one hand on your chest and the other on your abdomen. Notice that you can breath so the hand on your chest barely moves but the hand on your belly rises and falls rhythmically. Imagining you are blowing up a balloon in your belly often helps achieve this breathing pattern. (Pause.)
>
> Next, focus your attention on your breathing. Closing your eyes may help you do this. Notice that you can control your breathing, but you need not. Your body breathes all on its own. Allow yourself to focus on your body performing rhythmic abdominal breathing, all on its own. (Pause.)
>
> No turn your attention to various parts of your body, beginning with the top of your head and proceeding down to the tips of your toes. With each part, allow yourself to focus on any tension. Then focus on "exhaling" that tension with each exhalation of breath. Continue until you feel more calm, peaceful and relaxed in that part of your body. (Pause.)
>
> It may help to "hear" yourself saying words like, *calm*, or *peaceful*, or *relaxed* with each exhalation. Then go to the next part (e.g., from the top of your head to your face and neck). First "notice" and then "breathe away" tension in that part of your body. Continue in this fashion until you have "breathed away" tension from each part of your body.

Relaxation should be used as an aid to help individuals reduce the power of beliefs that buttress procrastination by showing themselves these beliefs are false. It is not a substitute for this activity.

Excuses

Many people who regularly procrastinate also regularly make excuses for their procrastination. Blame and condemnation are common responses to shortcomings in Euro-American society. However, blaming and condemning self or others does not help. It is more useful to adopt an attitude of compassionate understanding plus firmness. Life is difficult. It may prove difficult to acquire, achieve, or experience the things that each of us finds moving and central to our lives. Procrastination is an added difficulty. About these aspects of the human condition we can show compassionate understanding both to ourselves and to others. However, we can also be firm. If individuals failed to make plans to get the work done, then it is *they* who failed to make them. If individuals made inadequate plans which did not leave time to get the work done or did not follow through on the plans they made, then it is *they* who made inadequate plans or did not follow through. An individual does not become a bad person for acting badly, but she or he is the one who acted badly. No excuses.

SUMMARY

Procrastination at work is quite often a chronic condition. Whether chronic or transitory, the treatment involves first recognizing what is deeply important in an individual's life so as to then effectively prioritize, plan, and follow through. Planning will be difficult because people with procrastination problems tend to both underpredict the amount of time necessary to complete a task and overpredict the time available. They can work to increase their predictive abilities by estimating all the activities associated with completing a task as well as the time it will take to complete each of those activities, and then comparing their estimates with actuality. Individuals can also anticipate and overcome problems tolerating the necessity to work even when they do not feel like working. Both planning and follow through can be enhanced, and anxiety and depression reduced, by systematically countering tendencies to (1) demand that self, others, and the world be different than they are because it would be preferable if they were different, (2) awfulize by acting as if unpleasant realities are either worse than they can possibly be or at least worse than they actually are, and (3) rate one's personhood based on one's performance or agree with anyone else's rating of one's personhood based on performance.

REFERENCES

Ainslie, G. (1975). Specious reward: A behavioral theory of impulsiveness and impulse control. *Psychological Bulletin, 82*(4), 463–496.

Ainslie, G. (1992). *Picoeconomics.* Cambridge, U.K.: Cambridge University Press.
Aitken, M. (1982). *A personality profile of the college student procrastinator.* Unpublished doctoral dissertation, University of Pittsburgh.
Boice, R. (1989). Procrastination, busyness, and bingeing. *Behavioral Research & Therapy, 27*(6), 605–611.
Briordy, R. (1980). An exploratory study of procrastination. *Dissertation Abstracts International, 41*(2a), 590.
Burka, J. B., & Yuen, L. M. (1983). *Procrastination.* Reading, MA: Addison-Wesley.
Costa, O. T., & McCrae, R. R. (1989). *The NEO-PI/NEO-FFI manual supplement.* Odessa, FL: Psychological Assessment Resources.
Covey, S. (1989). *The 7 habits of highly effective people.* New York: Simon & Schuster.
Ellis, A. (1962). *Reason and emotion in psychotherapy.* Secaucus, NJ: Citadel Press.
Ellis, A. (1972). *Executive leadership.* New York: Institute for Rational–Emotive Therapy.
Ellis, A. (1994). *Reason and emotion in psychotherapy: Revised and updated.* Secaucus, NJ: Carol.
Ellis, A., & Knaus, W. J. (1979). *Overcoming procrastination.* New York: Penguin.
Eysenck, H. J. (1970). *The structure of human personality* (2nd ed.). London: Methuen.
Ferrari, J. R. (1991). Compulsive procrastination: Some self-reported personality characteristics. *Psychological Reports, 68*(2), 455–458.
Ferrari, J. R. (1992a). Procrastination in the workplace. Attributions for failure among individuals with similar behavioral tendencies. *Personality & Individual Differences, 13*(3), 315–319.
Ferrari, J. R. (1992b). Psychometric validation of two adult measures of procrastination: Arousal and avoidance measures. *Journal of Psychopathology & Behavioral Assessment, 14,* 97–100.
Ferrari, J. R. (1993). Christmas and procrastination: Explaining lack of diligence at a "real-world" task deadline. *Personality & Individual Differences, 14*(1), 25–33.
Ferrari, J. R., Johnson, J. L., & McCown, W. G. (Eds.), (1995). *Procrastination and task avoidance: Theory, research and treatment.* New York: Plenum.
Flett, G. L., Hewitt, P. L., & Thomas, R. M. (1995). Dimensions of perfectionism and procrastination. In J. R. Ferrari, J. L. Johnson, & W. G. McCown (Eds.). *Procrastination and task avoidance: Theory, research and treatment* (pp. 113–136). New York: Plenum.
Hernstein, R. J., & Mazur, J. E. (1987). Making up our minds. *The Sciences, Nov.–Dec.,* 40–47.
Hill, M., Hill, D., Chabot, A., & Baral, J. (1978). A survey of college faculty and student procrastination. *College Student Personnel Journal, 12*(3), 256–265.
Lay, C. H., & Schouwenburg, H. C. (1993). Trait procrastination, time management, and academic behavior. *Journal of Social and Personality, 8*(4), 647–662.
McCown, W. (1986). Behavior of chronic college-student procrastinators: An experimental study. *Social Science & Behavioral Documents, 6*(1) (man. 2745)8.
McCown, W., & Ferrari, J. R. (1995). *A meta-analysis of treatments for procrastination in high school and college students.* Unpublished manuscript, Northeast Louisiana University.
McCown, W., & Johnson, J. (1989, April). *Validation of an adult inventory of procrastination.* Paper presented at the Society for Personality Assessment, New York.

McCown, W., Johnson, J., & Petzel, T. (1989). Procrastination, a principal components analysis. *Personality & Individual Differences, 10*(2), 197–202.

McCown, W., & Roberts, R. (1994). *A study of academic and work-related dysfunctioning relevant to the college version of an indirect measure of impulsive behavior* (Integra Technical Paper 94–28). Radnor, PA: Integra.

Shipley, W. C. (1940). A self-administering scale for measuring intellectual impairment and deterioration. *Journal of Psychology, 9*(1), 371–377.

Skinner, B. F. (1953). *Science and human behavior.* New York: Free Press.

Solomon, L. J., & Rothblum, E. D. (1984). Academic procrastination: Frequency and cognitive-behavioral correlates. *Journal of Counseling Psychology, 31*(4), 503–509.

Van Ness, R. (1988). *Eliminating procrastination without putting it off.* Bloomington, IN: Phi Delta Kappa Educational Foundation.

6.

Creating the Family Friendly Workplace: Barriers and Solutions

MARK FRANKEL, Ph.D.

> Family issues will redefine our political, economic and social agenda over the next decade . . . forcing both the public and private sectors to restructure their focus. (Naisbitt & Aburdene, 1990, p. 137)

This is how John Naisbitt, popular business futurist, and other observers heralded the rapidly expanding emphasis on reconciling the demands of work and family at the beginning of the 1990s. Employers, both private and public, would finally come to grips with the dramatic demographic shifts that have seen vastly increased numbers of women in the workplace, a shrinking pool of highly skilled labor, a rapidly aging population, and an increase in both men and women's desire to balance work with family commitments.

Work–family programs would be fueled by the outpouring in the 1980s of work–family articles in the popular media and business press, as well as by a myriad of professional symposia, conferences, scholarly articles, workshops and research institutes. A majority of employers were supposedly on the verge of initiating programs to rationally integrate work and family life. Such family-responsive programs would relieve employees of crushing work–family overload and stress while simultaneously improving productivity, work attendance, morale, recruitment, retention, employee health, and work involvement (Friedman & Galinsky, 1992).

And why not? By 1990, many of the brightest and most progressive corporations in America, including IBM, AT&T, Merck, Aetna, Dupont, NationsBank, Johnson & Johnson, Prudential Insurance, and American Express had already implemented impressive, exemplary programs offering employees family friendly job conditions. Employees in these corporations enjoyed such benefits as flexible work arrangements, information and referral services, family-responsive training for supervisors, financial aid, family friendly leave policies, and funding to expand the pool of child and elder care services in the community. To add further momentum to the effort, the popular magazine, *Working Mother,* began producing an annual list of the 100 most family friendly companies for working parents.

Now, more than halfway through the 1990s, how family friendly is the typical North American workplace? The answer, unfortunately, is "Not!" Although Naisbitt's forecast is not entirely unfulfilled, the vast majority of employers have so far chosen to do little or nothing about making their workplaces more responsive to employees' family needs or concerns (Crain, 1994; Saltzman & Wiener, 1993; Seyler, Monroe, & Garand, 1995). In 1994, after a decade of concerted effort, it was estimated that a total of approximately 6,000 American employers offered employees some form of child care support (e.g., flextime, information and referral services, financial aid) (Crain, 1994). In a country with 8 million employers, that represents a penetration rate of less than one-tenth of 1%! Elder care programs are found in even fewer workplaces. The picture was equally gloomy when *Personnel Journal* (Solomon, 1994) had a panel of 13 distinguished work–family experts grade corporate America (from "A" to "F") on its use of a comprehensive list of possible work–family programs or policies. The grades for use—18 D's or F's, 7 C's, no B's, no A's.

What is more, work–family surveys often credit image-conscious employers with family friendly practices based on the flimsiest of evidence (Saltzman & Wiener, 1993). Detailed operational definitions of family friendly terms such as *flextime, flexplace,* or *information and referral* are rare in workplace surveys. As a result, companies counted as providing work–family benefits sometimes include those which allow a handful of employees among thousands to telecommute, or which provide a "token" information and referral service consisting of little more than a list of child care names and telephone numbers drawn from an outdated directory.

Of equal concern, many of the programs actually implemented are barely used by employees, begging the question of whether they represent real solutions to real problems in the first place. While it is claimed that the vast majority of employees in North American workplaces face serious, stressful work–family conflicts in some form (e.g., Galinsky & Hughes, 1987), most family-responsive programs report single digit usage rates. For example, Genasci (1995) reports that only 6% of employees offered work-at-home options in 129 companies surveyed by The Conference Board had ever used that option, and that the average usage of programs such as child care information and referral, job share or part-time work is usually seen by observers to be between 3 and 5% of a company's workforce. At AT&T, less than 1% of employees take family leaves each year and at American Express, only 4% of eligible employees took advantage of a tax-free dependent care spending account over a period of $6^1/_2$ years (Saltzman & Wiener, 1993). Some company-financed on-site child care centers have been opened with great fanfare and then quietly closed later on, due to high expenses and low enrollment (e.g., Global TV, Toronto; ISI, Philadelphia) and a similar fate has befallen several programs providing sick-child care and respite care benefits to employees.

If the promise of work–family initiatives is going to be realized for most working North Americans, then it is time that the methods for promoting, designing, and implementing family friendly programs be rethought. This chapter discusses the rationale for and the barriers to implementing family responsive programs in the workplace, and suggests some possible ways to achieve better results. It is proposed that in order to persuade employers to adopt and then maintain truly family friendly workplaces, organizational developers, psychologists, and human resources practitioners need to conceptualize both work–family problems and their solutions in more complex, three-dimensional terms, relying less on ideology and more on available research and professional experience.

WORK AND FAMILY CONNECTIONS

It is still possible to find individuals at all organizational levels in the workplace who believe that work and family are entirely separate worlds (Piotrkowski, 1978) and can be kept that way. But those who hold that the two domains can be completely compartmentalized are a shrinking minority. As noted above, the previous decade marked a rapid expansion of articles and books addressing work and family connections (see reviews by Barling, 1990; Friedman & Galinsky, 1992; Voydanoff, 1988; Zedeck, 1992). Indeed, as early as 1977,

Kanter explored the linkages between work and family life and persuasively showed that the notion of work and family life as isolated and separate from each other no longer accurately described postindustrial society. The following years saw a large volume of research papers examining various aspects of the work–family relationship.

This research repeatedly demonstrated how closely the domains of work and family are connected, although there has been little agreement about a comprehensive model which describes and explains that relationship (Zedeck, 1992). Different theoretical models have conceptualized the essential work–family relationship in terms of:

1. *Spillover,* i.e., feelings, experiences, and behaviors in one sphere are carried over to the other.
2. *Compensation,* i.e., needs and deficiencies experienced in one sphere are fulfilled and counterbalanced in the other.
3. *Conflict,* i.e., the two life spheres are in inevitable competition and conflict for the individual's time and involvement.
4. *Integration,* i.e., the two spheres are actually part and parcel of the same phenomenon and should not be studied separately.
5. *Instrumental Linkage,* i.e., activity in one sphere is directed at gaining resources and rewards needed in the other sphere.

Barling (1990) summarized this body of research by noting that much of it assumes that it is work which impacts on family life, not vice versa, and that the impact is generally negative. He reviews evidence calling both of these assumptions into question and suggests that (1) there is a reciprocal, bidirectional relationship between work and family; and (2) that impacts may be either positive or negative. He further suggests that it is most useful to look at work and family domains as open systems which exhibit typical open system dynamics and properties such as ripple effects, subsystem interactions, mediation effects, and boundaries (see Minuchin, 1974, for an overview of system dynamics in families).

Despite the primacy of research concentrating on the effects of work on the family, other research began emerging in the mid-1980s asserting that family life impacts negatively on work, often mediated by the strains or conflicts of meeting responsibilities in both domains (e.g., Crouter, 1984; Emlen & Koren, 1984; Fernandez, 1986; Friedman & Galinsky, 1992; Galinsky & Hughes, 1987; Goff, Mount, & Jamison, 1990). As two paycheck and single-parent families juggle responsibilities at work with the demands of child or elder care, negative workplace impacts which have been highlighted included absenteeism, tardiness, increased sick leave, low morale, reduced job satisfaction, lessened work involvement, and resistance to proposed relocations and promotions.

It should be noted that this research had underlying it the assumption that people have limited time and energy to give to the work and family domains and that both are in competition with each other for that finite time and energy (the "conflict" model of work-family described above). Furthermore, "family" demands were almost exclusively considered to be those related to child care, with little attention paid to responsibilities involved in marriage or adult partnerships or in the care for elderly or disabled family members.

In any case, the main thrust of this body of research is that (1) the work performance and family lives of employees are impaired by work–family conflict, and (2) there is need to find ways to reconcile, harmonize, or balance the demands of work and family. It is also often predicted that this reconciliation will result in a workplace which attracts and retains more highly qualified employees and which maximizes their health and productivity (Galinsky & Stein, 1990).

A number of workplace initiatives have appeared to support these contentions. For example:

1. NationsBank reported its part-time work option for employees improved retention rates and lowered employee stress (Solomon, 1994).
2. American Bankers Insurance Group opened a "corporate kindergarten" and reported a 30% reduction in absenteeism and a 10% reduction in turnover (Ward, 1991).
3. Hewlett-Packard opened an on-site public school for employees' children and reported absenteeism reduced (*HRMagazine* 1994).
4. WMX Technologies estimates that it saves $1,600 a year in absenteeism and turnover costs for every employee who participates in its parent support groups (Fierman, 1994).
5. Steelcase reports that offering flexible work schedules to employees has dramatically reduced recruitment and retention costs (Luciano, 1992).
6. Aetna Life & Casualty Group introduced a family leave program for employees and reduced by half the number of employees who leave the company permanently after a maternity leave (Nelson, 1995).
7. Fel-Pro Inc. provided a package of family-responsive benefits, including on-site child care, summer day camps, and college scholarships. A research study found that employees who used the

programs had the best job performance evaluations (Solomon, 1994).
8. A study of 2,000 pregnant employees in companies which offered parental leave, flexible scheduling, supportive supervision, and health insurance found that these employees took fewer sick days, worked later into their pregnancies, were more satisfied with their jobs, and were more likely to return after maternity leave than employees in workplaces where these benefits were absent (National Council for Jewish Women, 1988).
9. Executives surveyed in companies where flextime, family leave, and information and referral services were offered to employees strongly believed that these benefits improved productivity and morale and reduced absenteeism and lateness (Seyler et al., 1993).
10. A meta-analysis of flextime studies in 92 different workplaces found reduced absenteeism and some limited reductions in turnover (Pierce, Newstrom, Dunham, & Barker, 1989).

In summary then, much research in the 1980s and early 1990s confirmed that: (1) The workplace and the home are the two most salient and central settings or domains in most people's lives. (2) Events in each of these settings have powerful effects on the other. (3) The interdependence of work and family offers opportunities for lowering employee stress, absenteeism, and tardiness and improving morale, job involvement, retention rates and recruitment results.

On a practical basis, the research and published anecdotal evidence of this period has offered employers and organizational developers their choice of a wide and varied array of benefits believed to help reduce work–family strain, i.e., a program suited for every human resources budget. The "family friendly" label has been assigned to everything from on-site day care centers for children and/or seniors to dependent care savings accounts, and from liberal maternity and family leave policies to employee assistance programs.

Hall and Richter (1988) and Kirchmeyer (1995) have suggested that it is useful to group these family responsive interventions according to the degree which they either (1) blur the work–family boundary, casting the work organization as provider of needed family services ("integration" strategies) or (2) help employees to keep that boundary distinct but flexible by enabling or empowering employees to meet their own nonwork responsibilities ("respect" or "mutuality" strategies). Table 6.1 summarizes work–family interventions according to whether they reflect an integration or mutuality strategy. There is some controversy over whether one or the other strategy is more effective in both helping employees achieve work–family balance and benefiting the organization. Richter (1992) stresses that mutuality strategies, but not integration strategies, assist employees in limiting the penetration of work into family life and vice versa. On the other hand, integration strategies appear to directly reduce some work–family conflicts. It is suggested that choice of strategies should be based on careful consideration of both the organizational culture and the workforce in question.

Those planning work–family interventions would also be wise to consider initiatives which are aimed not just at the employee and family, but at the organization itself (Friedman & Galinsky, 1992). Accordingly, Table 6.1 offers a comprehensive listing of organizational activities designed to improve family-responsiveness, also sorted according to whether they reflect an integration or a mutuality approach.

It should be noted that the "integration" versus "mutuality" distinction represents more of a continuum than a dichotomy, and that placement of a particular activity on the continuum may depend on the content or delivery style of that activity. For example, an information and referral service may simply supply the data employees need in order to make informed decisions themselves (mutuality) or might become heavily involved in problem solving and counseling with employees (integration). Nevertheless, the distinction between the two general approaches is a salient one which can help to identify which work–family programs might fit best in different organizational and family cultures.

BARRIERS TO WORK–FAMILY INITIATIVES

The majority of the measures described in the last section are modest in cost and require little or no administration time (Jenner, 1994a; Van Alphen, 1995). With the exception of day care center construction, many family friendly program costs are nil or trivial compared to "big-ticket" benefits such as medical, drug, disability, and pension benefits or even compared to smaller budget items like company picnics, golf tournaments, or executive retreats.

Furthermore, the costs of "untreated" work–family problems appear to be substantial. It has been estimated that the annual cost to American businesses of absenteeism due to the breakdown of child care arrangements is about $3 billion (Hand & Zawacki, 1994). The

TABLE 6.1
Family-Responsive Interventions: Employee Focus

Integration	Mutuality
On-site or near-site day care center	Flexible work hours, flextime
Reserved spaces—local day care center	Supportive maternity, parental, adoptive & family leave policies
After school child care service	Option to "buy" time off via salary or benefits trade-offs
Sick child care services	
Respite care services for the elderly	Part-time and job share options
Geriatric case management service	Condensed work week
Elementary public school on-site	Pretax dependent care savings accounts
Warm-line for latchkey children	
Company sponsored summer camp	Child & elder care information & referral service
On-site holiday child care	
Child care subsidy or voucher	Child or elder care seminars
Long-term care insurance	Child & elder care resource library
Adoption benefits	Family care newsletter
Convenience or concierge services	Caregiver fair
Employee Assistance (EAP)—counseling	
Family, legal, or financial counseling	
Relocation counseling	
Parent or elder care support groups	
Children visiting the workplace	
Work at home/telecommuting	

TABLE 6.2
Family-Responsive Interventions: Organizational Focus

Integration	Mutuality
Corporate funding for community child care and elder care programs	Regular consideration given to impact of company travel, work time, benefits and personnel policies on family life
Corporate strategic plan links work–family issues to corporate objectives	Supervisors trained in resolution of employee work–family conflicts
Family life workshops conducted with senior executives	Written policy on work–family benefits developed
Work–family coordinator appointed	Work–family needs assessments conducted

Conference Board of Canada (Van Alphen, 1995) reported that absenteeism due to family commitments is costing medium and large Canadian corporations between $1 million and $1.5 million each annually. It has also been estimated, in a recent, careful, and conservative cost analysis, that the elder care provided to family members by the employees of a single large (87,000 employees) U.S. manufacturing firm is costing that company more than $5 million annually (Coberly & Hunt, 1995). Beyond direct costs in absenteeism, work–family conflicts may cost both corporations and families in indirect ways, via employee, marital, and family stress, with attendant costs in stress-related disorders (Cooper & Cartwright, 1994; Ironson, 1992).

With respect to benefits from family-responsive policies, it has been shown that employees generally attach great importance to their family life (Galinsky & Hughes, 1987), consider the family friendliness of a company to be of value to them, and respond to work–family initiatives with improved attendance, performance, and loyalty. Given this compelling pattern of both costs and benefits, it might be expected that every workplace would be family friendly by now. The actual situation is quite different.

Following more than a decade of effort by articulate and determined proponents, sustained positive media attention, and a substantial body of encouraging research and practical experience in high-profile corporations, only small numbers of North Americans work in organizations which have seriously incorporated *any* family friendly measures. In fact, there now exists an organization, *ChildFree Network,* with 2,000 members across the United States, whose mission is to oppose work–family benefits (Jenner, 1994b, 1994c)!

Obviously, there must be powerful barriers to family friendly efforts. It is tempting to lay the entire blame for these barriers with traditional corporate culture and its "henchman," the middle-aged male executive. It is unlikely this simple explanation will bring about effective efforts to overcome barriers to the family-responsive workplace. In fact, some important barriers to work–family efforts are hardly ever acknowledged in the literature or in practice. But the multiple sources of resistance to family friendly change need to be confronted honestly and thoroughly in order to overcome and remove them (Friedman & Galinsky, 1992). It is most useful to review barriers separately as (1) obstacles to adoption and (2) obstacles to usage.

OBSTACLES TO ADOPTION

Low Employee Need

In some organizations, work–family problems are simply not seen as primary by employees. Employees voice other priorities such as salary, job security, training, workplace conditions, or health benefits, even when given completely free choice via anonymous surveys. While large numbers of employees may report experiencing significant work–family strain at some times, many of these employees feel that, overall, they have achieved a reasonable work–family "fit" (Frankel, 1988). In such organizations, managers can conclude that work–family initiatives are only responsive to a small special interest group.

Low Business Need

There are companies in which recruitment, retention, and absenteeism are not considered serious problems. As one manager remarked, "Our main problem is getting our employees to go home!" The popular appeals of family friendly programs appear irrelevant and unrelated to any strategic business need in these companies. Without a clear business rationale, appeals to a corporate social conscience often don't sell well and "family friendly" can be equated with "fluff."

Negative Effects

Although contrary to actual research, many employers still see work–family initiatives as unnecessarily complicating business operations and customer service delivery (Kush & Stroh, 1994) and/or encouraging abuse by some employees (e.g., Peak, 1994). In these workplaces, work–family programs or policies are seen as antagonistic to "getting the job done." They are also seen as generating workforce resentment because they will not be used by all employees and may result in extra workload for nonparticipating employees (Jenner, 1994b).

Perceived Cost

Without proper education, corporate decision makers sometimes see work–family programs as costly and likely to create expectations of still costlier programs in the future. Employers fear encouraging employee demands for building expensive day care facilities and/or providing open-ended flextime policies.

Inappropriate Corporate Role

Many organizations believe that it is inappropriate for them to become involved in the nonwork lives of their employees (Covin & Brush, 1993; also see Guzzo, Nelson, & Noonan, 1992, for an historical review of corporate attitudes about involvement in nonwork). Employers and senior managers who hold this attitude are not alone. In more than one organization known to this writer, small numbers of employees have complained strenuously about intrusion and invasion of privacy when their employer merely sought to directly inform employees' families about benefits for which they were eligible.

Antagonistic Culture

Some organizations oppose the adoption of family friendly measures because those with influence and power in the organization see work-family as a "women's issue" and a sign that proponents are not "serious" about their careers or their commitment to the job. This culture is nurtured by the opposition and resentment of supervisors, managers, and senior executives who have either never experienced work–family strains and crises themselves or have silently suffered through such problems without any acknowledgment or assistance from their employer.

OBSTACLES TO USAGE

Poor Quality Control

Some so-called family responsive programs are simply not effective. Family friendly programs are sometimes poorly conceived, poorly designed, or poorly executed. For example, several investigators have concluded that telecommuting, although frequently labeled "family friendly," is a questionable strategy for employees with young children at home (Shamir, 1992). Other examples include slow, superficial information and referral services, low quality parent seminars, complicated dependent care savings plans, flextime programs with hardly any flex, job share programs which do not effectively match prospective partners, expensive on-site day care centers for employees who want family day care near their homes, and respite care or sick child care programs for employees who would never leave an ill family member in the care of a stranger.

It is hardly surprising that programs which do not meet needs are not used. Nevertheless, poor program quality is usually the last thing considered when low program usage occurs. Instead, "friends" of the program cite negative corporate culture and "enemies" cite lack of need. As a result, opportunities are lost to refine needs assessment measures, improve delivery methods, more clearly target user groups, and define outcome goals.

Poor Marketing

Many work–family benefits are unused because nobody knows about them. It seems paradoxical at first that corporations would spend money on family-responsive programs and then keep them virtually secret from employees. But that is precisely the case in many instances. Initiation of work–family programs is often accompanied by management fears that they will actually be used!

One company known to this writer designated a visiting day for employee's children but insisted on barely visible announcements about the event. The low profile approach was dictated by the vice president of human resources, who feared a flood of children in the workplace. Other organizations worry about high usage of family leave or flextime. As a result, family friendly programs are kept low profile. In addition, when actual internal marketing is done, it is often primitive or inept, bearing no resemblance to that organization's skillful marketing efforts with its own customers. Other organizations appear to feel that if they announce the launch of a family friendly benefit with great fanfare, followed by complete and prolonged silence, then an employee needing that benefit 2 or 3 years later will remember it and use it!

Outmoded Concept of Work

Another primary obstacle to use of family friendly benefits is the widely held notion of work as "face time." Many supervisors do not trust that work is being done unless they can see it being done. Furthermore, these supervisors see flexible work arrangements as a threat to the control they feel that they must have over workers in order to reach corporate objectives. Such attitudes equate productivity with time expended, reward the inefficient and punish the efficient employee (Perlow, 1995).

Antagonistic Culture

As noted above, some corporate cultures support the notion that work always comes first and total devotion to work is necessary for success. In such cultures, employees may well be intimidated into avoiding use of family friendly benefits, even when they are made available. Making use of technically available benefits such as flextime or part-time job opportunities in these organizations can be a "career killer" in the eyes of management (Kush & Stroh, 1994; Perlow, 1995; Saltzman & Wiener, 1993).

FAMILY FRIENDLY CHANGE

Successful family friendly change needs to start with awareness of the potential obstacles and an assessment of which of these barriers are operative in the work setting. The limited progress to date in making North American workplaces more family responsive also suggests that change agents need to systematically and strategically plan new efforts to overcome these barriers. It is proposed that such new efforts can rest on three supportive "pillars":

1. A more sophisticated, research-based understanding of the relationships and *interactions between work and family* systems.
2. A more complete vision of the *organizational benefits* of a healthy work–family interface.
3. A more *effective* approach to *marketing* family-responsive policies and programs.

These requirements are, of course, interrelated. They are equally necessary in order to effectively deliver the fundamental changes required in the many workplaces currently unresponsive to the family needs of employees.

Interactions between Work and Family

A full examination of recent work–family research yields a picture of work and family as dynamic, interdependent settings. Systems-based conceptualizations of the work and family spheres offer a conceptual foundation for more sophisticated and effective work–family programming (Barling, 1990; Hall & Richter, 1988; Richter, 1992; Zedeck, 1992). Rather than viewing work and family in simplistic terms which assume unidirectional effects, a growing number of researchers see both domains as multidimensional systems, with potential to affect each other in both positive and negative ways. Rethinking work and family in these ways can lead to new and interesting ways of examining the work–family relationship and seeing how attributes and perceptions of each system might positively impact on the other.

Much of the popular rhetoric about work-family assumes that "conflict" is the central dynamic in the relationship. However, some work–family research demonstrates that the relationship between the two domains is neither simple nor predominantly negative (Barling, 1990). There is now convincing documentation to show that family life can have powerful, positive impacts on the workplace (Kanter, 1977; Kirchmeyer, 1992a, 1992b) and that multiple work–family responsibilities can coexist together with high levels of job involvement and satisfaction (Burden, 1986; Frankel, 1988).

Kirchmeyer (1992a, 1992b), in fact, describes substantial evidence which challenges the whole basis of much popular thought about work–family relations, namely, the notion that individuals have only limited resources to give to work and family, leading inevitably to conflicts ("the scarcity model"). Alternatively, she proposes that people function more frequently on the basis of "the expansion model" which holds that personal resources are increased and enriched by multiple involvements in certain nonwork domains (family, community, and recreational settings). She found that her subjects, a group of business school alumni, reported greater job satisfaction and organizational commitment at work when their family and community time commitments and involvements were greater.

Such "positive spillover" from nonwork to work has been virtually ignored by change agents anxious to portray overwhelmed employees struggling with work–family conflicts. Yet, if employers were convinced of the workplace benefits of employees' nonwork involvements, including the acquisition of problem solving, time management, delegating, interpersonal and teamwork skills, as well as increased job satisfaction and commitment (Kirchmeyer, 1992a), would they not have a powerful reason for supporting and facilitating those nonwork involvements? Clearer recognition of the workplace benefits of nonwork involvements may lead to the creation and legitimization of completely new initiatives to support these activities.

In addition, research has also demonstrated that it is often not so much the fact of family-responsive programs in an organization which has a positive impact on employees' work involvement, job satisfaction, and performance, but rather employees' perception that the organization is supportive of family life (Goff et al., 1990; Orthner and Pittman, 1986). Also highlighting the importance of perceptions as mediators in the work–family relationship, Barling (1994) concluded that more evidence exists for the influence of "subjective employment experiences" on family functioning than for the direct impact of "objective" work circumstances on families.

These studies collectively suggest that organizations interested in positive benefits from family friendly initiatives need to pay more attention to how these initiatives as a whole are perceived. Nevertheless, many discrete family friendly programs are currently launched, administered, and evaluated with little formal attention paid to whether these programs have improved either employees' perception of the organization's support for families or employees' perceptions about their own level of coping with work–family strains. It seems evident that organizations which keep their family friendly efforts "low-profile" may virtually guarantee that no organizational benefits result. Family friendly proponents need to expend more effort teaching organizations about the crucial importance of employee and family perceptions, notwithstanding the adoption of exemplary programs.

Finally, just as most proponents of family friendly programs tend to ignore the positive contributions of the family to the workplace, they also often ignore the positive impacts which the workplace has on family life. In fact, researchers have documented many positive effects of work on family life (Barling, 1990; Crouter, 1984; Hoffman, 1986). Specifically, Crouter (1984) graphically described how participatory work experiences increased parents' confidence and ability to negotiate differences at home. Barling (1994) has also reviewed research in support of the notion that satisfying job experiences, even when they involve increased work time and decreased access to family members, lead to positive family interactions. These studies suggest that it is the quality of work, rather than the amount of family time available, which has major effects on family interactions. It is hypothesized by Barling that these positive job effects on family functioning are mediated by employee mood and personal satisfaction.

If valid, these findings indicate that proponents of family-responsive efforts might usefully refocus some of their efforts on helping organizations design better jobs. It is well established that jobs maximize employees' psychological well-being when they provide increased autonomy, decision making, variety, and task significance (Hackman & Oldham, 1980). Quality of work life could prove to be more important to family well-being than increased family access via on-site child care or work at home!

Organizational Benefits

Before they will enthusiastically participate in change efforts, work organizations need to understand how they can benefit from improved work–family relations. As documented above, there is already a good deal of research linking work–family initiatives to reduced absenteeism and improved recruitment and retention. These findings can be powerful in the workplace because discrete business costs can be calculated for these variables. Unfortunately, when family care costs and family-responsive cost savings have been discussed in print, the cost calculation methods and assumptions have usually been either unstated, vague, or questionable and therefore easily dismissed. *The Metlife Study of Employer Costs for Working Caregivers* (Coberly & Hunt, 1995) is a rare and welcome exception. This study of workplace costs stemming from personal caregiving for elderly relatives clearly details the cost factors considered, the rationale for their use, and the calculation methods used to compute the costs. In each case where arbitrary judgments about cost had to made, the authors chose conservative (and therefore more credible) assumptions. The work–family field would benefit greatly from more studies done in this manner and from some concerted effort to reach a consensus about proper cost accounting methods which could be replicated from study to study.

It has been observed, on the other hand, that many organizations find cost savings related to absenteeism, recruitment, and retention of limited practical appeal or remain convinced that workplace features other than family friendliness (e.g., salary, prestige, career opportunities) will more powerfully impact on these variables. It is therefore necessary to formulate a broader rationale for family-responsive efforts in order to appeal to these organizations.

The research on positive spillover from family to work outlined above (Crouter, 1984; Kanter, 1977; Kirchmeyer, 1992a) provides a initial basis for such an enriched portrait of how an organization may profit from a healthy work–family interface. The most important implication of this work is that the workplace and the family are "systems in partnership." This partnership can be negative, competitive, and costly or it can be mutually supportive and enriching. Kirchmeyer's formulations identify some of the potential workplace benefits of a positive partnership that includes the family:

1. It acts as a buffer for employees' work-related stresses, failures, and disappointments.
2. It enhances employees' sense of personal competence and self-esteem.
3. It increases employees' motivation to work.
4. It improves employees' self-management skills including time management, patience, and flexibility.
5. It strengthens employees' organizational commitment and job satisfaction.

Such a list of benefits looks like the sort of "payoff" for which most organizations would (and do) devote substantial supervisory and training dollars. Families do not charge for these services! Despite this potential, almost no effort has been expended to further explore and document these particular benefits or to communicate them in compelling fashion to corporate decision makers. Framed as a strategic resource, the workplace relationship with employees' families could take on new salience and potential for business organzations. However, few senior executives have been encouraged to see the families of employees as a valuable corporate asset, to be supported and encouraged. As a result, an opportunity is being lost.

Effective Marketing

The final requirement for a strengthened and renewed work–family effort is a better developed marketing effort. Work–family programs are in direct competition with a host of other programs and products for the time, money, and attention of organizations. Promoters of training programs, computers, motivational products, information systems, software, office furniture, and wellness programs all promise improvements in recruitment, retention, and absenteeism. Family friendly programs need to "position" themselves effectively in relation to these competing initiatives. Even when in place, work–family programs must compete with other programs for the attention of employees not only concerned about family care but also about job security, career development, training, and economic survival. An effective work–family marketing effort must include:

Influencing key decision makers—The chances of success with key corporate decision makers can be greatly enhanced by a more informed grasp of how decisions are actually made. Kossek, Dass, and DeMarr (1994) have argued persuasively that work–family initiatives are mostly adopted in response to "institutional" forces, quite apart from whether key decision makers are exposed to evidence that these initiatives will directly benefit their organization's bottom-line. They cite three key institutional forces (mimetic, normative, and coercive) which shape management's "dominant logic," i.e., the beliefs and values used to make a decision. Mimetic pressures are determined by the desire to "keep up with" and imitate competitors. Normative pressures result from the perception that respected experts and professionals endorse a particular course of action. Coercive pressures are caused by public opinion and/or government regulations about a specific course of action. The research links managers' perceptions of these forces with decisions about whether or not to adopt family friendly programs.

These results suggest that family friendly proponents would be well advised to find ways to reinforce such institutional pressures in the minds of decision makers; for example, highlighting competitors' family-responsive programs, marshalling family friendly recommendations from respected business experts, and demonstrating the strength of public opinion favoring family responsive initiatives. Another concrete way to implement this strategy might be for family friendly proponents to agree upon and disseminate an objective, attainable national standard for family friendly organizational performance and to arrange for public recognition of all (not just the best 100) qualifying organizations.

Finally, for real change to occur, it is essential that middle managers and supervisors "buy in" to family friendly efforts (Friedman & Galinsky, 1992; Michaels & McCarthy, 1993). Supervisory training in work–family conflict resolution, setting of work–family performance measures for managers, and communication of strong support for work–family goals from senior management, are all useful methods for influencing this key organizational group (Regan, 1994).

Broadening the base of support—It has been noted earlier that family-responsive proposals can be regarded as discriminatory and as favoring one special interest group. Domination of work–family initiatives by child care programs often aggravates this problem (Jenner,

1994c). Family friendly efforts can pick up additional support by emphasizing benefits for employee groups concerned with elder care and care for the disabled. And beyond this approach, a growing number of companies (e.g., AT&T, Johnson & Johnson) are reframing work–family programs as work–life programs (Cronin, 1993; Sladek, 1995). Consistent with Kirchmeyer's (1992b) positive findings with regard to nonwork involvements, these companies have come to believe that fostering employees' nonwork responsibilities (e.g., community volunteer work, parenting, adult education) strengthens the workplace. Such programs have the potential to put work–family benefits in a context which is appealing for a broader base of employees.

Promoting smarter—Although some family friendly programs have foundered because of low usage, a search of the literature revealed virtually nothing published to guide the promotion of program usage (see Sladek, 1995, for a welcome exception). If work–family programs are not highlighted and carefully explained to employees at least every 6 to 12 months, they are soon forgotten in the continuous flow of information in the workplace. It also seems useful, in the light of previously cited research about the importance and value of employees' perceptions (Orthner & Pittman, 1986), to "bundle" together all family-responsive programs and policies active in the workplace when communicating about them, while keeping the work–family "bundle" separate and distinct from other human resource programs.

Proponents of family friendly programs need to be energetic and creative in assisting busy administrators to use all corporate communications channels possible for promotion, including e-mail, newsletters, video, and CD-ROM. Finally, it is critical to emphasize the word *family* in work–family promotions. If the beneficiaries of family-responsive programming are supposed to be families, why not communicate with them? Promotions aimed solely at or only distributed to individual employees often miss the mark because usage of flextime, information, and referral or a work–family seminar is heavily influenced by family members.

While considering these and other marketing measures, companies which have become convinced of the "partnership" quality of their relationship with the families of employees might also consider formulating a written communications plan aimed at keeping employees' families well informed about and involved in all corporate developments of potential interest to them.

CONCLUSION

Despite some notable successes, the work–family "movement" is underachieving. Efforts to institute family friendly measures in North American workplaces have gone slowly. However, substantial work has been done which points to ways of overcoming obstacles to adoption and usage. Because of major changes in the demographic composition of the workforce and because of our strong cultural values about the family, the need for a more family responsive workplace will not go away. It is anticipated that the empirical and conceptual work recently done in this area will serve as the foundation for family friendly proponents to mount a renewed and reenergized work–family effort in the future.

REFERENCES

Barling, J. (1990). *Employment, stress and family functioning.* Chichester, U.K.: Wiley.
Barling, J. (1994). Work and family: In search of more effective workplace interventions. In C. L. Cooper & D. M. Rousseau (Eds.), *Trends in organizational behavior,* Vol. 1 (pp. 63–73). Chichester, U.K.: Wiley.
Burden, D. S. (1986, January). Single parents and the work setting: The impact of multiple job and homelife responsibilities. *Family Relations, 35,* 37–43.
Coberly, S., & Hunt, G. G. (1995). *The Metlife study of employer costs for working caregivers.* Washington, DC: Washington Business Group on Health.
Conference Board (1995). Manager and employee perceptions. *Work-Family Roundtable, 5*(1), 1–14.
Cooper, C. L., & Cartwright, S. (1994). Healthy mind: Healthy organization—a proactive approach to occupational stress. *Human Relations, 47*(4), 455–471.
Covin, T. J., & Brush, C. C. (1993). Attitudes toward work–family issues: The human resource professional perspective. *Review of Business, 15*(2), 25–27.
Crain, J. (1994). Who's raising America? *Colorado Business Magazine, 21*(10), 72–77.
Cronin, M. P. (1993). One life to live. *Inc., 15*(7), 56–57.
Crouter, A. C. (1984). Spillover from family to work: The neglected side of the work–family interface. *Human Relations, 37*(6), 425–442.
Emlen, A. C., & Koren, P. (1984). *Hard to find and difficult to manage: The effects of child care on the workplace.* Portland, OR: Portland State University, Regional Research Institute for Human Services.
Fernandez, J. P. (1986). *Child care and corporate productivity: Resolving family/work conflicts.* Lexington, MA: Heath.
Fierman, J. (1994). Are companies less family-friendly? *Fortune, 129*(6), 64–67.
Frankel, M. L. (1988). *Families at work research project.* Unpublished manuscript.

Friedman, D. E., & Galinsky, E. (1992). Work and family issues: A legitimate business concern. In S. Zedeck (Ed.), *Work, families, and organizations* (pp. 168–207). San Francisco: Jossey-Bass.

Galinsky, E., & Hughes, D. (1987). *The Fortune magazine study.* New York: Families and Work Institute.

Galinsky, E., & Stein, P. J. (1990). The impact of human resource policies on employees. *Journal of Family Issues, 11*(4), 368–383.

Genasci, L. (1995, June 27). On the job: Work-family. *Associated Press.*

Goff, S. J., Mount, M. K., & Jamison, R. L. (1990). Employer supported child care, work-family conflict, and absenteeism: A field study. *Personnel Psychology, 43*(4), 793–809.

Guzzo, R. A., Nelson, G. L., & Noonan, K. A. (1992). Commitment and employer involvement in employees' nonwork lives. In S. Zedeck (Ed.), *Work, families, and organizations* (pp. 236–271). San Francisco: Jossey-Bass.

Hackman, R. J., & Oldham, G. R. (1980). *Work redesign.* Reading, MA: Addison-Wesley.

Hall, D. T., & Richter, J. (1988). Balancing work life and home life: What can organizations do to help? *Academy of Management Executive, 2*(3), 213–223.

Hand, S., & Zawacki, R. A. (1994). Family-friendly benefits: More than a frill. *HRMagazine, 39,* 79–84.

Hoffman, L. W. (1986). Work, family and the child. In M. S. Pollock and R. O. Perloff (Eds.), *Psychology and work: Productivity, change and employment* (pp. 173–220). Washington, DC: American Psychological Association.

HRMagazine (1994, October). Editorial. Five companies offer benchmarks. *HRMagazine, 39*(10), 82–83.

Ironson, G. (1992). Work, job stress and health. In S. Zedeck (Ed.), *Work, families, and organizations* (pp. 33–69). San Francisco: Jossey-Bass.

Jenner, L. (1994a). Work-family programs: Looking beyond written policies. *HR Focus, 71,* 19–20.

Jenner, L. (1994b). Family-friendly backlash. *Management Review, 83*(5), 7.

Jenner, L. (1994c). Issues and options for childless employees. *HRFocus, 71*(3), 22–23.

Kanter, R. M. (1977). *Work and family in the United States: A critical review and agenda for research and policy.* New York: Russell Sage Foundation.

Kirchmeyer, C. (1992a). Perceptions of nonwork-to-work spillover: Challenging the common view of conflict-ridden domain relationships. *Basic and Applied Social Psychology, 13*(2), 231–249.

Kirchmeyer, C. (1992b). Nonwork participation and work attitudes: A test of scarcity vs. expansion models of personal resources. *Human Relations, 45*(8), 775–795.

Kirchmeyer, C. (1995). Managing the work-nonwork boundary: An assessment of organizational responses. *Human Relations, 48*(5), 515–535.

Kossek, E. E., Dass, P., & DeMarr, B. (1994). The dominant logic of employer-sponsored work and family initiatives: Human resource managers' institutional role. *Human Relations, 47*(9), 1121–1149.

Kush, K. S., & Stroh, L. K. (1994). Flextime: Myth or reality? *Business Horizons, 37*(5), 51–55.

Luciano, L. (1992). The good news about employee benefits. *Money, 21*(6), 90–94.

Michaels, B., & McCarthy, E. (1993). Family ties and bottom lines. *Training & Development, 47*(3), 70–72.

Minuchin, S. (1974). *Families and family therapy.* Cambridge, MA: Harvard University Press.

Naisbitt, J., & Aburdene, P. (1990). *Megatrends 2000: Ten new directions for the 1990's.* New York: William Morrow.

National Council for Jewish Women (1988, August). *Employer support for child care.* (NCJW Center for the Child Report). New York: Author.

Nelson, K. L. (1995). Insurers get rewards out of helping parents. *Best's Review—Property-Casualty Insurance Edition, 95*(9), 16.

Orthner, D. K., & Pittman, J. F. (1986, August). Family contributions to work commitment. *Journal of Marriage and the Family, 48,* 573–581.

Peak, M. H. (1994). Why I hate flextime. *Management Review, 83*(2), 1.

Perlow, L. A. (1995). Putting the work back into work-family. *Group & Organization Management, 20*(2), 227–239.

Pierce, J. L., Newstrom, J. W., Dunham, R. B., & Barber, A. E. (1989). *Alternative work schedules.* Needham Heights, MA: Allyn & Bacon.

Piotrkowski, C. S. (1978). *Work and the family system: A naturalistic study of working-class and lower-middle-class families.* New York: Free Press.

Regan, M. (1994). Beware the work-family culture shock. *Personnel Journal, 73*(1), 35–36.

Richter, J. (1992). Balancing work and family in Israel. In S. Zedeck (Ed.), *Work, families, and organizations* (pp. 362–394). San Francisco: Jossey-Bass.

Saltzman, A., & Weiner, L. (1993). Family friendliness: What workplace revolution? *U.S. News & World Report, 114*(7), 59–63.

Seyler, D. L., Monroe, P. A., & Garand, J. C. (1995). Balancing work and family: The role of employer-supported child care benefits. *Journal of Family Issues, 16*(2), 170–193.

Shamir, B. (1992). Home: The perfect workplace? In S. Zedeck (Ed.), *Work, families, and organizations* (pp. 272–311). San Francisco: Jossey-Bass.

Sladek, C. (1995). A guide to offering work/life benefits. *Compensation and Benefits Review, 27*(1), 41–46.

Solomon, C. M. (1994). Work–family's failing grade: Why today's initiatives aren't enough. *Personnel Journal, 73*(5), 72–81.

Van Alphen, T. (1995, March 31). Family duty cited for rising absences. *The Toronto Star,* p. B1.

Voydanoff, P. (1988). Work role characteristics, family structure demands, and work-family conflict. *Journal of Marriage and the Family, 50,* 749–761.

Ward, B. (1991, April). Corporations and kindergartens. *Sky,* pp. 28–39.

Zedeck, S. (1992). Introduction: Exploring the domain of work and family concerns. In S. Zedeck (Ed.), *Work, families, and organizations* (pp. 1–32). San Francisco: Jossey-Bass.

7.

How to Prevent Job Burnout in the Workplace

DIANA R. RICHMAN, Ph.D.

Given the current economy, focusing on job burnout may seem an indulgence. Dealing with job loss and learning job finding strategies in a tight labor market have been discussed more recently in the professional and self-help literature (Jud, 1993; Kuhnert & Vance, 1992; Leana & Feldman, 1992). Individuals feel relieved about not yet having been laid off from jobs that they once perceived as dead-end drudgery, while organizations believe that employees should feel grateful to have their jobs, and as a result symptoms of burnout tend to be minimized or negated.

Job burnout is a complex phenomenon (Lowman, 1993; Schonfeld, Rhee, & Xia, 1995) that individuals may experience at various stages of their careers, throughout the cyclical fluctuations of the economy. Whether at the exploration stage of career development, fearing to leave an unfulfilling job during an economic downturn, or at the career maintenance stage, observing coworkers receiving termination notices, burnout may occur. Job burnout creates serious problems for employees and their organizations (Roach, 1994) in all professions and at all levels of the organization hierarchy (Stallworth, 1990). Costly employee turnover and poor work performance reflect just some of the behavioral manifestations of burnout among individuals in the workplace (Weisberg, 1994). Particularly during the current period of unstable conditions in the workplace and economy, identifying causes and early signs of job burnout, and learning preventive techniques, can help employees and their organizations to avoid the debilitating effects of the phenomenon.

BURNOUT BACKGROUND

The Job Market

During the 1980s, an increase of professional and public interest in job burnout was evidenced in research on the burnout syndrome among professionals in human service occupations (Cherniss, 1980; Maslach, 1976), and in the popularity of self-help books on burnout (Freudenberger, 1980; Maslach, 1982; Pines & Aronson, 1988). Through the late 1960s and through the 1970s many young adults obtained their graduate degrees and entered their chosen careers in human services with idealistic views of helping others. The early 1980s was a time when it became clear that a fast track business mindset was necessary to achieve a more affluent life-style. Graduate students, including some burned-out human service professionals, sought MBA degrees to acquire state-of-the-art business skills in their pursuit of the American dream. Older workers remained on their jobs, looking forward to a secure benefits package that would be theirs upon a planned retirement date. For a period of time, the career expectations of many employees seemed to be consistent with the external conditions of what professions and organizations had to offer.

Through the mid-1980s real estate prices soared as higher incomes enabled some individuals to purchase second homes. On the surface the economy seemed stable and strong. Expectations reflected a quick fix societal mentality. Immediate and greater rewards, already acquired by some colleagues in the early 1980s, were driving forces for the frenzied, stress-evoking work behaviors that followed. Although experiencing signs of stress, depression, and beginning stages of burnout, employees were willing to expend more energy, and work longer hours, motivated by underlying beliefs that they would be guaranteed permanent, worthwhile rewards for their efforts. Believing that they were in control of their future, the reality of the economic cycle was denied. Working longer hours, and harder, would result in a life of security and comfort. The race to move up the organization hierarchy rapidly shifted the balanced life-style of many individuals. Whether the ideal was to help others, gain wealth, or maintain the status quo, employees were reporting a variety of debilitating attitudinal, emotional, and physical symptoms, and exhibiting an array of nonproductive work behaviors (Stewart, 1990).

The Workplace

Around the same period, health practitioners were responding to the need for stress reduction, and organizations were reacting to complaints of stress and related symptoms among their staff. The evident deterioration in work habits among some upper echelon employees seemed to serve as a red flag. Organizations could no longer deny the debilitating symptoms exhibited by their top level staff.

Organizations made attempts to address worker wellness and to recognize that workplace conditions have been associated with symptoms of burnout (Carayon, 1992; Corey & Wolf, 1992). Programs were developed to improve worker performance instead of hiring new staff. Employee assistance programs (EAPS) were introduced, and consultants were hired to train employees in relaxation, stress management, and wellness techniques.

However, state-of-the-art programs do not necessarily result in the acceptance and application of the newly learned knowledge. As Fassel (1980) points out, treating symptoms of burnout and stress without treating the cause will exacerbate the problem. The reality of unstable, unfair workplace conditions, and individuals' unrealistic cognitions about workplace realities, continue to influence the occurrence of job burnout. The nonproductive work behaviors, attitudes, and emotions experienced by burned-out employees may be masked during the current economy, but continue to pervade the workplace.

Considering the dynamic changes in the workplace and job market, it is not surprising that burnout and stress have been top research priorities through the past decade (Schaufeli, Keijsers, & Miranda, 1995). The concern about the effect of burnout and stress on both the labor force and the bottom line, and on the well-being of organizations, has been reflected in studies by psychologists specializing in work-related issues. Recent publications by the American Psychological Association indicate that health issues of employees have reached crisis proportions (Gebhardt & Crump, 1990). There is a serious need to address workplace wellness and fitness (Keita & Hurrell, Jr., 1994; Keita & Sauter, 1992; Quick, Murphy, & Hurrell, Jr., 1992; Sauter & Murphy, 1995).

The Individual

In an effort to prevent the causes and symptoms experienced by individuals, as well as to understand the construct of burnout, psychologists continue to study factors related to stress, including job satisfaction, motivation, and work performance (Katzell and Thompson, 1990). While research has found that individuals most highly motivated by a task are less likely to respond to negative external changes (Mawhinney, 1990), worksite conditions can directly result in debilitating psychological, physiological, and behavioral symptoms (Elder, 1987; Ivancevich, Matteson, Freedman, & Phillips, 1990; Vallen, 1993). Cordes, Dougherty, and Blum (1995) emphasize the importance of correctly identifying job and organizational variables that contribute to burnout if individual and workplace factors are to be successful. Their research substantiates the need to study components of burnout among individuals within the corporate work environment. Workplace strains of work overload, noncontingent punishment, and uncontrollable changes are pervasive realities confronted by individuals in the public and private sector.

Through the late 1980s and the 1990s, the trend toward lean and mean, forced early retirement, layoffs, and cutbacks in benefits have intensified many of the conditions associated with burnout. Burned-out individuals seeking new options are now concerned about getting laid off. Perceived security is no longer a reality for those experiencing job burnout but expecting the long-term rewards for remaining committed to an unfulfilling job. Burnout is not alleviated when forced unemployment occurs. The process of accepting the job loss and seeking new employment adds to the burnout syndrome for many individuals. Employed individuals often experience symptoms of burnout when they are assigned workloads from recently laid off coworkers. The decrease in opportunities for promotions and alternative sources of employment can only serve to intensify the burnout syndrome among individuals in the labor force.

Individual differences should be considered when examining the burnout phenomenon. Polance (1988) explains that each employee has a unique job burnout threshold with a varied pattern of symptoms. Individuals have different attitudes and responses to stress. Nowack (1986) refers to hardy employees as those who are less likely to experience burnout. As Senge (1990) points out, those employees who maintain a realistic perspective about themselves and their organizations will not be let down.

DEFINITION OF JOB BURNOUT

Although individuals may experience burnout in relation to a variety of situations in their lives, throughout this chapter, the word *burnout* will refer to work unless otherwise specified.

Maslach's (1982) definition of job burnout is the one most often used as a basis for research to understand and clarify the construct. Maslach describes burnout as "a syndrome of emotional exhaustion, depersonalization, and reduced personal accomplishment that can occur among individuals who do 'people work' of some kind" (p. 3). As a response to the emotional strain of dealing with people, it can be considered one type of job stress arising from the social interaction between helper and recipient. This three-factor model has been substantiated, modified, and challenged (Jackson, 1986; Lee, 1993; Leiter, 1988), and more recently has been applied to organizations and professions other than direct human services (Cordes, Dougherty, & Blum, 1995). Cordes (1993) explains that a developing literature on burnout has begun to clarify the position of burnout in a network of variables included in the study of organizational behavior. Cordes' research substantiates that burnout is based on an overriding common construct.

Some definitions of burnout acknowledge a cognitive component in addition to the external workplace factors related to the syndrome. Cherniss (1980) describes burnout as involving professionals' attitudinal and behavioral changes in response to demanding, frustrating, unrewarding work experiences. Freudenberger (1980) reports that burnout occurs when the job fails to produce the expected reward. When individuals perceive that they are giving more to their job than they receive in return, burnout may result (Stallworth, 1990).

Burnout and/or Stress

Burnout has been frequently defined as an outcome of stress (Nowack, 1986). Towery (1992) suggests that unrelenting stress is a major factor in burnout. Filipczak (1993) states that some people do not notice stress until they burn out. Umiker (1989) views burnout as an advanced stage of overstress characterized by physical, emotional, and attitudinal exhaustion. Byrne (1993) described burnout as the inability to function effectively in one's job as a consequence of prolonged extensive job-related stress. Firth (1989) agrees that job burnout is characterized by psychological strain resulting from occupational stress. Grensing (1991) defines burnout as a debilitating psychological condition that is brought about by unrelieved work stress. It has been agreed that stress is a component of this multidimensional phenomenon.

Katzell (1994) differentiates between stress, strain, and burnout. Stress refers to environmental forces impinging on employees to create strain, and may also be viewed as a cause of burnout. Strain refers to feelings of emotional exhaustion associated with prolonged strain. Stress has consistently been associated with the burnout syndrome as both an external workplace condition, and as a symptom experienced by individuals. Definitions of job burnout have emphasized the negative effects of external workplace stressors. However, job demands alone do not automatically lead to stress (Stellman, 1987). Identifying employees' attitudes about stressful work-related situations, and examining their responses to external conditions, may contribute to the understanding, treatment, and prevention of the burnout phenomenon.

Burnout and/or Depression

Schonfeld (1992) has found that two of the components of burnout, emotional exhaustion and a reduced sense of personal accomplishment, constitute symptoms of depression. He suggests that the way to distinguish between stress and burnout factors and depressive symptoms is to measure aversive environmental conditions defined as stressors and depressive symptoms as the distress independently. Although depression and burnout have been found to overlap, Meier and Davis (1982) report that burnout has good construct validity. Pines and Aronson (1988) distinguish between burnout and clinical depression, explaining that depression is pervasive. In the early stages of burnout on the job, workers are often productive in other areas of their life. Job burnout is usually viewed from a social rather than from an individual perspective. As with stress, identifying employees' attitudes about workplace conditions often associated with depression, and examining the different symptoms of depression among those individuals, may contribute to research on the treatment and prevention of job burnout.

COGNITIVE COMPONENTS OF JOB BURNOUT

While it has been substantiated that external stressful workplace conditions, and external factors in individuals' personal and family lives are associated with burnout symptoms, it is essential to acknowledge the internal cognitions maintained by individuals about the external events in their lives. Especially during the present period when uncontrollable events at work are pervasive, by addressing the cognitive components, individuals can learn to control their own self-defeating, unrealistic attitudes about these work-related realities. Since there is an indication that depression and stress overlap with burnout, and cognitive behavioral techniques have been found to reduce or eliminate nonproductive symptoms of depression and stress (Beck, 1976; Ellis, 1994), it seems logical to apply a cognitive–behavioral approach to the treatment and prevention of burnout. Examining the attitudinal factors of both individuals and their organizations may most effectively contribute to understanding the syndrome (Richman, 1988b, 1992; Roach, 1994).

Cognition has been suggested but rarely examined as a factor in the prevention and treatment of burnout. Several self-report measures of burnout reflect an attitudinal component. Freudenberger (1980) reported that using his checklist of 10 attributions may indicate if an individual's thought patterns are producing burnout symptoms. Maslach's (1976) three-factor theory alludes to workers' direction of attribution in the description of the mea culpa reaction as a tendency to blame oneself. However, the attitudinal component needs to be delineated. Schaufeli (1993) emphasizes that burnout in the Maslach burnout inventory can be employed as a reliable and valid multidimensional construct consisting of an affective and an attitudinal component. A study of burnout and locus of control found that respondents expressing feelings of burnout tended to have an external locus of control orientation, while those not experiencing burnout exhibited an internal locus of control (Glogow, 1986).

While cognitive themes suggest that core belief systems about oneself and work-related events may increase the probability of experiencing burnout and its related symptoms (Richman & Nardi, 1985), the application of cognitive–behavioral techniques by practitioners specializing in work problems is lacking. Emphasis on a quick fix approach to effect behavioral change in the workplace, and the belief systems of professionals specializing in work issues, may have sabotaged efforts to apply the combination of cognitive–behavioral techniques to the prevention and treatment of job burnout.

UNREALISTIC EXPECTATIONS AND BURNOUT

Maintaining unrealistic expectations about oneself and the workplace is a recurrent underlying theme in the burnout literature. The term *expectations* may be used interchangeably with aspirations, goals, and ideals. While unmet expectations occur daily in the workplace, not everyone will experience burnout symptoms. Those who maintain unrealistic expectations about the fact that the workplace will not meet their perceived needs will be more likely to develop the symptoms. Montaque (1994) states that burnout happens incrementally as unrealized expectations conflict with reality, thwarting a quest for growth. Cherniss (1980) believes that human service professionals' unmet goals and aspirations are related to job burnout. Individuals entering the beginning stages of their careers, or moving to new positions, often hold idealistic views about their jobs (Richman, 1988a, 1993). Pines and Aronson (1988) point out that burnout tends to afflict individuals who enter their professions highly motivated and idealistic, expecting their work to give their lives a sense of meaning. Senge (1990) explains that those with idealistic expectations will tend to end up as cynics. Often the brightest are most susceptible to burnout, putting unrealistic pressures on themselves to achieve (Filipczak, 1993).

Discrepancies between employees' and organizations' expectations and values can result in the burnout phenomenon (Richman, 1992). Unrealized expectations and lack of opportunities for self-actualization are two causes of burnout. Hunt (1986) describes a relationship between a person's adjustment to demands of the organization and burnout, and the importance of gaining a realistic perspective and objectivity about work. In a study of the effect of perceived achievement of expectations on an individual's job satisfaction and on the perceived level of occupational stress, Savery (1988) suggests that failure to achieve expectations causes occupational stress and low job satisfaction which may be related to the job burnout syndrome.

BURNOUT BELIEFS

Many definitions of burnout describe an accumulation of external stressors as a major causal factor, and approaches to treatment emphasize situational change. Since reality reflects the unlikelihood that work situations will be modified to fulfill the perceived needs of individual employees, identifying and modifying workers' unrealistic attitudes may serve as a strong mediator in helping individuals to deal with workplace events.

The definitions, symptoms, and recurrent themes in the burnout literature substantiate the premise of rational–emotive behavior therapy (REBT), based on a cognitive–behavioral approach, that our beliefs about situations, and in particular our unrealistic demands about ourselves, others, and the world, result in our nonproductive behaviors and emotions (Ellis, 1994). Rational–emotive behavior therapy provides a framework within which to identify and modify unrealistic expectations about work-related events in order to prevent and treat job burnout (Richman and Nardi, 1985).

Burnout beliefs consist of an accumulation of perceived and real discrepancies between individuals' idealistic expectations and their work experiences. When taken to an extreme, their views of unmet expectations over time may escalate to intense demands resulting in debilitating burnout symptoms. Demandingness about self, others, and the world represents the core style of irrational thinking that Ellis (1982) describes as causing emotional disturbance: (1) "I *must* do well at the tasks I perform and be approved by others for doing well"; (2) "You *must* treat me fairly, kindly, and justly"; (3) "The conditions under which I live *must* be easy, unfrustrating, and enjoyable." It is evident that these absolutist views can easily apply to how individuals view their jobs. By identifying and modifying their unrealistic beliefs about themselves and work-related events, in relation to cognitive themes suggested in the job burnout literature, individuals may be able to prevent or reduce their burnout symptoms.

In their description of a cognitive–behavioral approach for treating burnout, Richman and Nardi (1985) show how the burnout themes of commitment, competence, and overall unrealistic expectations about oneself, others, and the work world can be extinguished and rekindled to a renewal spark of light on more productive views for dealing with work realities. This chapter presents five basic cognitive themes within which individuals maintain burnout beliefs about themselves, others, and the work world. The absolutist degree of each term is defined by the individual and the organization maintaining the belief:

1. Commitment—Attachment, bonding, loyalty to and from oneself and the workplace.
2. Competence—Adequate performance by and for oneself and the workplace.
3. Control—Domination over others maintained by and experienced from oneself and the workplace.
4. Challenge—Growth, development, use of full potential experienced by and presented from oneself and the workplace.

5. Comfort—Convenience, security, ease, experienced by and offered from oneself and the workplace.

These five themes can guide practitioners in helping individuals to recognize their unrealistic demands directed toward themselves, others, and events in the work world. Their organizations and coworkers, as well as themselves, may maintain unrealistic expectations about these five burnout themes.

Within each theme employees can learn to identify their burnout beliefs (BB) about themselves and work-related events. By extinguishing (EXT) their BB through active, logical, pragmatic questions and statements, they can develop a renewal spark (RS) of nonburnout beliefs about themselves and the work world.

Commitment

Commitment as cognitive theme serves as a focal point for a variety of burnout beliefs about oneself and work-related events. Overcommitment is described as one of three factors found in patterns of job burnout, and may involve characteristics of individuals or their jobs (Lowman, 1993). Employees who are excessively committed to their jobs or careers tend to experience burnout (Sperling, 1988). When employees and their organizations maintain realistic expectations of commitment to themselves and each other, commitment to the larger whole might be the best outcome for all. Senge (1990) emphasizes the need not only for individuals, but for organizations as well to tap a level of commitment beyond self-interest. However, the need for a balance between work and personal life is essential for an individual's well-being (Killinger, 1991) before an employee can effectively commit to an organization without experiencing the debilitating symptoms of job burnout.

Perceptions of commitment often differ between organizations and their employees (Richman, 1992). Organizations may expect more than they are willing to give (Landy, 1992). Since today's organizational behaviors reflect a move away from considering worker needs, it becomes more crucial for individuals to develop a realistic perspective on this harsh reality and to seek balance in their lives. Individuals who work hard, expecting immediate, or any, rewards for their dedicated behaviors, tend to burn out sooner than employees who accept the reality of lack of recognition for work well done (Pines and Aronson, 1988). Cherniss (1980) found that helping professionals in the public sector started out their careers with a strong commitment to work and willingness to make self-sacrifices for others. Over time their commitment often resulted in alienation and withdrawal from clients. The balance between commitment to oneself and the organization can assist workers in preventing burnout.

Commitment may be described in terms of attitudinal and behavioral commitment. Katzell (1994) states that attitudinal commitment reflects a potentially intense moral involvement, attachment, and identity with an organization. Behavioral commitment represents the costs that tie an employee to an organization. Attitudinal and behavioral commitment maintain a reciprocal relationship. Cognitive–behavioral practitioners can assist individuals in achieving a realistic attitude to achieve a balance of commitment between their personal and work lives. The following represents burnout beliefs directed toward oneself and the workplace within the commitment theme:

BB: I *must* remain dedicated to my job even though I may get laid off. (self)
EXT: What rule exists that I have to maintain my feelings of loyalty and dedicated behaviors to a firm that may lay me off?
RS: While I do not have to remain dedicated to my job, it would be preferable for me to continue to perform adequately.
BB: My company *should never* lay me off. (workplace)
EXT: What is the reality that companies never lay off good workers?
RS: I may not like it, but my company has the right to lay me off.

Competence

It would appear, based on ideal conditions, that employees are suitably selected for their positions, and that they will perform to their highest level of competence, receiving recognition for work well done. While ongoing poor performance, or a deterioration in worker job competence may reflect a direct response to external workplace stressors, patterns of incompetent worker behaviors may also be symptomatic of job burnout.

In order to assess the causes of incompetent job behaviors, a differentiation must be made between external workplace conditions, and individual factors of job skills and attitudes. The underlying reasons for competent and incompetent performance may be internally based, particularly in the undercommitted worker (Lowman, 1993). By identifying the cognitions of competent workers who exhibit poor work performance, the individual factors causing burnout can be examined and addressed.

Competence is so often measured and evaluated in the workplace by individuals who are not well versed in cognitive–behavioral techniques and interpersonal communication skills. Beliefs about the whole individual may contaminate the evaluation of specific work behaviors. Employees may rate themselves based on the specific behaviors being evaluated. The reality of politics in the workplace rewards aligning oneself with people in power and looking good on paper, even when the work behaviors are incompetent. Workers often say, "I am" rather than "I do," when asked what they do for a living. They equate their personage and worth with whom they work for, their job title, and how much they earn, thus modifying the definition of competence in the workplace.

Some employees find themselves in work situations in which their boss gives them negative feedback no matter how well or hard they work, while others are given rewards although their work performance is incompetent. To avoid conflict with the more aggressive workers, some supervisors may fulfill the needs of these workers while neglecting to reward and support their competent staff. Burnout may result among the most competent employees. By understanding the congitions of competent, hard-working employees, and those who tend to overwork or exhibit poor performance, organizations can more readily differentiate between skill deficits and attitudinal issues among staff, as well as identify external workplace barriers related to job burnout. However, only employees themselves can decide to apply their best abilities within the realistic framework of the unfairness and routine tasks characteristic of the workplace. The following represents burnout beliefs directed toward oneself and the workplace within the competence theme:

BB: I *must always* perform more competently than others in my department. (self)

EXT: Where is the evidence that I can or must always outperform others or that my performance must be rated higher than others?

RS: I may like to perform the best in my department, but I can stand it if others perform more competently or disagree with my view.

BB: My boss *should* give me positive feedback for my competent work. (workplace)

EXT: The reality in the workplace is that my boss tends to give only negative feedback.

RS: While I would like recognition for work well done, I can accept the reality that my boss will probably continue to give only negative feedback.

Control

Control over others, as represented by job titles, financial compensation, and the overall organization hierarchy and structure as it relates to the delegation of power, is an integral part of the workplace. When workers have minimal personal control over how their job is done, stress will result (Shalowitz, 1991). Lack of control at work can even disrupt family life (Lang, 1991). Finneran (1991) explains that people feel the greatest pressure when they have responsibility but no control. So often those demanding to control others at work achieve the more powerful positions in the organization hierarchy. As dedicated competent staff lower in the hierarchy begin to complain, they are often ignored or punished. Over time many staff will quit, act out, or withdraw; burnout occurs when they see no way out and experience a total lack of power and control to make constructive changes.

Low decision latitude among employees in organizations, and perceived control held by organizations are factors related to job burnout (Glogow, 1986; Hunt, 1986; Landsbergis, 1988). The combination of a demanding job and little or no control over how tasks are carried out may cause burnout (Stellman, 1987). In Montaque's (1994) study of health care providers in a hospital setting, it was recommended that physician leaders must include many more of their organization's members in the decision-making process to avoid burnout. When work does not allow for or encourage growth, burnout can occur (Pines & Aronson, 1988). Hogan (1992) believes it is essential to give employees as much authority as possible and to empower employees. Learned helplessness can explain burnout in terms of workers' lack of control in their work environment. Repeated exposure to uncontrollable events reinforces beliefs of helplessness, hopelessness, and self-downing, which are cognitive themes in depression and burnout.

When organizations provide rewards for those manifesting a need to control others, those valuing competence, hard work, and equality may begin to believe that they do not count, something must be wrong with them, and that they had better stay out of the way. They may begin to withdraw and exhibit behavioral, emotional, attitudinal, and physiological symptoms of burnout. It is common to find some of the brightest and most competent workers exhibiting burnout symptoms as the less competent gain control and rise to the top. Since the workplace is not necessarily fair, unrealistic expectations about gaining control in the organization need to be addressed and workers' goals need to be reexamined. The following represents burnout beliefs directed toward oneself and the workplace within the control theme:

BB: I *should* have more staff working for me by now. (self)
EXT: Where is it written that I need to have more staff under me now?
RS: While I like to be in charge of others, I can stand it, and it does not mean anything negative about me if I do not have more subordinates.
BB: My organization *should* give me more say in making the important decisions. (workplace)
EXT: The reality is that my organization has control over how much power it decides to give to me.
RS: I can continue to share my ideas while accepting that my organization has the final word.

Challenge

Individuals maintain different views about the meaning of work (Maccoby, 1988). Some consider work an expenditure of energy that they must endure in order to survive financially. Others view work as their sole identity, equating their position in the workforce as a determinant of their worth as a person. Those who seek constant challenge, growth, and development through their career life may experience difficulty accepting the reality that routine tasks exist in all positions, and that organizations tend to pigeonhole workers into positions based on their initial skills and the needs of the organization when they entered the firm. However, even during the current tight labor market, some individuals will pursue careers that coincide with their intrinsic values, interests, and potential.

Those who seek growth, development, and personal challenge are often assigned to status quo positions. For all the career counseling concepts of matching individual abilities and aptitudes to a career path, reality usually reflects that most jobs do not require the intellect, education, or skills of their workers. In fact, most jobs label and compartmentalize employees into routine tasks with minimal room for growth. It is up to the individual to maintain realistic expectations about themselves and their work as they strategize to develop their potential.

Burnout often occurs when individuals unrealistically demand that their organization should provide them with a daily challenge. Burnout may also result when employees are placed in positions beyond their competency. They tend to experience a great deal of stress and pressure in these positions. Challenge may be viewed as an opportunity to deal with the uncontrollable, unfair decisions and changes so frequent in the workplace. Seeking challenge in a variety of areas in one's life instead of expecting work to provide the daily stimulation and challenge may prevent burnout. The following represent burnout beliefs directed toward oneself and the workplace within the challenge theme:

BB: I *must* use my full potential daily at work. (self)
EXT: Given the reality that many daily job tasks do not require the use of my full potential, I would be placing stress on myself to demand a higher level of functioning at work.
RS: I will seek challenge in varied areas of my life while accepting that I do not have to use my full potential at all times in every situation.
BB: My job *should* provide me with challenging work daily. (workplace)
EXT: Where is it written that my organization has to provide me with daily stimulation and challenge to fulfill my potential?
RB: While I would prefer daily challenge at work, my organization has a right to assign tasks based on organizational needs.

Comfort

Human beings tend to seek comfort, which is reflected in their behaviors at work. Beliefs about what is comfortable depend on an individual's cognitive appraisal about what is necessary for his or her survival. Individuals with low frustration tolerance (LFT) demand convenience in the short term and often exhibit inappropriate work behaviors which result in self-defeating consequences over the long term.

Avoidance of change and discomfort are reflected in a variety of nonproductive work behaviors of both individuals and their organizations. When employees find a comfortable niche, and comfort is their goal, they will experience a great deal of stress when change occurs. Especially during the current organizational restructuring, beliefs that change should not occur, and attempts to maintain sameness are in vain. Over time, these individuals may develop burnout symptoms.

Individuals demanding absolute comfort and security are unwilling to risk the discomfort of taking the actions necessary to achieve their career goals. Employed by large bureaucracies, these individuals, often labeled as paper pushers or dead wood, usually remain in the same position, experiencing burnout as they wait to receive their pensions. The need for comfort is so strong that burnout is viewed as a normal ritual to be endured in order to achieve future security. With the present changes, including a reduction in retirement benefits, stress increases. Comfort seekers may also include those in comfortable, challenging positions who demand that they permanently remain there. While definitions of comfort vary, loss or the threat of loss of perceived comfort is often related to burnout symptoms in the workplace. The following represents burnout beliefs directed toward oneself and the workplace within the comfort theme:

BB: I *should* feel secure and comfortable in my present job without having to worry that I might lose it one day. (self)

EXT: Since change in workplace conditions will inevitably change, where will it get me to constantly worry about what might happen?

RS: Instead of worrying about the future and demanding that I have to feel comfortable, I will prepare myself for dealing with change when and if it occurs while continuing to make the most of my present situation.

BB: My company *should* give me time off when I need it. (workplace)

EXT: What is the logical basis for me to expect my company to place my needs before its business oriented goals?

RS: I may not like it, but my company, which conducts a successful business, has the right to decide when and why to allow employees to take leave.

PREVENTION

Over the years a variety of recommendations for preventing job burnout have been introduced. Since job burnout is multidimensional, a holistic approach is advocated to focus on affective, cognitive, physical, and spiritual aspects (Romano, 1984) and to be flexible and adaptable to different workplace settings and professions. In addition to identifying nonproductive cognitions early on, and practicing realistic thinking about burnout themes, many behaviorally oriented recommendations have been made to prevent the symptoms of job burnout.

Social Support

Social support has been frequently suggested to help prevent job burnout. Teachers who communicated extensively about work but had relatively few informal supportive relationships experienced higher levels of burnout than those who reported having supportive supervisors (Russell, 1987). Andersen (1990) emphasizes the important role health care supervisors can play in helping their employees learn to deal with occupational stress. When head nurses were viewed as considerate, staff nurses were more likely to be satisfied with their jobs and less subject to burnout (Skinner, 1993). Shalowitz (1991) reports that stress-related illnesses are less likely among workers at companies with supportive work and family policies.

Proper training, positive feedback for work well done, employee empowerment through participation in decision making, and acknowledgment of family pressures are just some of the social supports that the workplace can provide to prevent job burnout among staff. Interpersonal factors are often ignored when addressing work performance. However, social support, or lack of it, at all levels of the organization hierarchy plays an important role in the occurrence of job burnout.

Career Development

Job burnout occurs when employees remain in positions that are a mismatch, that they have outgrown, or that have not met their expectations. To prevent job burnout, it would be preferable if individuals could make smooth transitions through the career cycle to achieve their goals. However, the work world rarely provides the perfect niche to meet the career development needs of individuals. Since so many employees reach a position in their organization from which they are not likely to receive a promotion, it is imperative that managers communicate that career plateauing need not interfere with individual effectiveness (Appelbaum, 1994). In fact, Schiska (1991) suggests that supervisors can help to prevent burnout by informing employees that plateauing is a normal phase of career development.

Employees may recognize that they must take steps to explore other alternatives to develop their careers, but their work schedule makes their desired transition impossible to complete. Sabbaticals provide employees with time to examine and experience new options and return to their job renewed. Toomey (1988) believes that sabbaticals are good for both the company and employees.

Human resource professionals, trained in cognitive career counseling (CCC) (Richman, 1993), can assist individuals in reducing the cognitive barriers to pursuing their career goals, even if leaving the company is the most appropriate plan. It is preferable for employees and their organizations to terminate their relationship when employees are dissatisfied with their position in remaining with their organization. Counselors may help employees to recognize when their expectations are unrealistic, particularly during a tight economy, and learn how to strategize career moves for the future while maintaining a productive attitude about their present position, and a balanced life-style to prevent job burnout.

Balanced Life-Style

Whether or not organizations provide services to help prevent job burnout among employees, individuals can take responsibility for their own life-style. Achieving a balance between work and personal areas of life is essential for preventing job burnout. Cook (1988) recommends maintaining a balanced life-style by avoiding overdiversification and information overload within the work arena. Johnson (1988) found that being physically active, focusing on nonbusiness relationships, stimulating the intellect, and working for enjoyment are important components of job burnout prevention. Developing outside interests and balancing work and home responsibilities can help to prevent job burnout (Hunsaker, 1986; Pines & Aronson, 1988; Potter, 1993).

Employees who spend most of their lives on work-related activities would do well to examine what they are avoiding in other areas of their lives. Especially during a period when organizations have shifted the balance far away from individuals' needs, employees should take control of how they spend their time within the realistic parameters of the work arena. Even with the restricted time constraints of so many employees, incorporating into one's life such habits as meditation, exercise, new hobbies, and social interactions can result in a balanced life-style and prevent the occurrence of job burnout.

Cognitive Control

The purpose of this chapter has been to apply a combination of cognitive–behavioral techniques to the treatment and prevention of job burnout. Since job burnout can be influenced by beliefs about oneself and work-related events, individuals may prevent symptoms from occurring by developing and maintaining realistic, moderate habits of thinking as they pursue their career goals within the external realities of an extremely stressful work world.

Both positive attitudes and powerful thinking to eliminate thoughts of helplessness and unrealistic expectations can help individuals to let go of what they cannot control (Goodwin, 1988; Potter, 1993). A positive self-image and developing realistic outlook skills can help to prevent job burnout (Polance, 1988: Raudsepp, 1988). Maintaining cognitive clarity as to what can be changed and not changed instead of giving up and just doing one's job can also prevent burnout (Pines & Aronson, 1988).

It is important to recognize the early warning signs of job burnout and to actively identify and modify burnout beliefs about oneself and workplace events in relation to the five cognitive themes of job burnout. If burnout symptoms have already occurred, it is essential to challenge any self-downing beliefs about having the symptoms, and to replace the dysfunctional thinking with more productive beliefs.

To prevent further symptoms, burnout may be understood and viewed as purposeful in warning individuals that they have continually neglected to provide self-care for themselves, unrealistically expecting external factors to meet their perceived needs within a stressful work environment. It is time to evaluate their situation, modify their unrealistic expectations, accept work realities, and strategize to take productive actions toward their career goals.

While there is no guarantee that job burnout can be entirely prevented by modifying burnout beliefs, changing cognitions that are incompatible with workplace realities is a good place to begin. As employees take responsibility for defining and acting toward their goals instead of unrealistically expecting the work arena to consistently fulfill their perceived needs, they will no longer alienate themselves from their chosen career, diminish their sense of personal accomplishment, and emotionally exhaust themselves to the point of burnout as they experience the uncontrollable, unstable, unfair realities of the world of work.

REFERENCES

Andersen, C. M. (1990, July). A departmental stress management plan. *Health Care Supervisor, 8*(4), 1–8.

Appelbaum, S. H. (1994). Revisiting career plateauing: Same old problems—avant-garde solutions. *Journal of Managerial Psychology, 9*(5), 12–21.

Beck, A. T. (1976). *Cognitive therapy and the emotional disorders.* New York: Meridian.

Byrne, B. M. (1993, September). The Maslach burnout inventory: Testing for factorial validity and invariance across elementary, intermediate and secondary teachers. *Journal of Occupational and Organizational Psychology, 66*(3), 197–212.

Carayon, P. (1992). A longitudinal study of job design and worker strain: Preliminary results. In J. C. Quick, L. R. Murphy, & J. J. Hurrell, Jr. (Eds.), *Stress & well-being at work* (pp. 19–32). Washington, DC: American Psychological Association.

Cherniss, C. (1980). *Professional burnout in human service organizations.* New York: Praeger.

Cook, M. (1988, November). Stress management. *Management Success, 32*(11), 18–21.

Cordes, C. L. (1993, October). A review and an integration of research on job burnout. *Academy of Management Review, 18*(4), 621–656.

Cordes, C. L., Dougherty, T. W., & Blum, M. (1995). *A test of competing models of burnout for managers and professionals.* Paper presented at the annual meeting of the Society for Industrial/Organizational Psychology, Orlando, FL.

Corey, D. M., & Wolf, G. D. (1992). An integrated approach to reducing stress injuries. In J. C. Quick, L. R. Murphy, & J. J. Hurrell, Jr. (Eds.), *Stress and well-being at work* (pp. 64–78). Washington, DC: American Psychological Association.

Elder, V. T. (1987, December). Gender and age technostress: Effects on white collar productivity. *Government Finance Review, 3*(6), 17–21.

Ellis, A. (1982). The treatment of alcohol and drug abuse: A rational–emotive approach. *Rational Living, 7,* 15–24.

Ellis, A. (1994). *Reason and emotion in psychotherapy.* New York: Birch Lane Press.

Fassel, D. (1989, January). The high cost of workaholism. *Business and Health, 7*(1), 38–42.

Filipczak, B. (1993, February). How to avoid burnout. *Training, 30*(2), 15–25.

Finneran, M. (1991, January). People issues: They are business issues. *Business and Communications Review, 21*(1), 80–82.

Firth, H. (1989). "Burnout," absence and turnover amongst British nursing staff. *Journal of Occupational Psychology, 62*(1), 55–59.

Freudenberger, H. (1980). *Burn-out: The high cost of high achievement.* Garden City, NY: Doubleday.

Gebhardt, D. L., & Crump, C. E. (1990). Employee fitness and wellness programs in the workplace. *American Psychologist, 45*(2), 262–272.

Glogow, E. (1986). Burnout and locus of control. *Public Personnel Management,* Spring, *15*(1), 79–83.

Goodwin, W. R. (1988, June). Avoiding burnout in development work. *Fund Raising Management, 19*(4), 38–43, 99.

Grensing, L. (1991, September). Seven causes of job burnout. *Office Systems, 8*(9), 50–54.

Hogan, J. J. (1992, February). Turnover and what to do about it. *Cornell Hotel and Restaurant Administration Quarterly, 33*(1), 40–45.

Hunsaker, J. S. (1986, November/December). Burnout: The culmination of long-term stress. *Industrial Management, 28*(6), 24–28.

Hunt, J. W. (1986). Alienation among managers: The new epidemic or the social scientists' invention? *Personnel Review, 15*(1), 21–26.

Ivancevich, J. M., Matteson, M. T., Freedman, S. M., & Phillips, J. S. (1990). Worksite stress management interventions. *American Psychologist, 45*(2), 252–261.

Jackson, S. E. (1986, November). Toward an understanding of the burnout phenomenon. *Journal of Applied Psychology, 71*(4), 630–640.

Johnson, K. L. (1988, December). Coping with burnout. *Broker World, 8*(2), 88–96.

Jud, B. (1993). *Coping with unemployment.* Avon, CT: Marketing Directions.

Katzell, R. A. (1994). Contemporary meta-trends in industrial and organizational psychology. In H. C. Triandis, M. D. Dunnette, & L. M. Hough (Eds.), *Handbook of industrial & organizational psychology:* 2nd ed. (Vol. 4, pp. 1–94). Palo Alto, CA: Consulting Psychologists Press.

Katzell, R. A., & Thompson, D. E. (1990, February). Work motivation: Theory and practice. *American Psychologist, 45*(2), 144–153.

Keita, G. P., & Hurrell, Jr., J. J. (Eds.). (1994). *Job stress in a changing workforce.* Washington, DC: American Psychological Association.

Keita, G. P., & Sauter, S. L. (Eds.). (1992). *Work and well-being: An agenda for the 1990s.* Washington, DC: American Psychological Association.

Killinger, B. (1991). *Workaholics the respectable addicts.* New York: Simon & Schuster.

Kuhnert, K. W., & Vance, R. J. (1992). Job insecurity and moderators of the relation between job insecurity and employee adjustment. In J. C. Quick, L. R. Murphy & J. J. Hurrell, Jr. (Eds.), *Stress & well-being at work* (pp. 48–63). Washington, DC: American Psychological Association.

Landsbergis, P. A. (1988, July). Occupational stress among health care workers: A test of the job demands-control model. *Journal of Organizational Behavior, 9*(3), 217–239.

Landy, F. J. (1992). Work design and stress. In G. P. Keita & S. L. Sauter (Eds.), *Work and well-being: An agenda for the 1990s* (pp. 119–158). Washington, DC: American Psychological Association.

Lang, J. M. (1991, January). Foodservice industry: Career burnout. *Restaurant Business, 90*(4), 131–148.

Leana, C. R., & Feldman, C. D. (1992). *Coping with job loss.* New York: Lexington.

Lee, R. T. (1993). A further examination of managerial burnout: Toward an integrated model. *Journal of Organizational Behavior, 14*(1), 3–20.

Leiter, M. P. (1988, March). Burnout as a function of communication patterns: A study of a multidisciplinary mental health team. *Group and Organization Studies, 13*(1), 111–128.

Lowman, R. L. (1993). *Counseling and psychotherapy of work dysfunctions.* Washington, DC: American Psychological Association.

Maccoby, M. (1988). *Why work.* New York: Simon & Schuster.

Maslach, C. (1976). Burned-out. *Human Behavior, 5*(9), 16–22.

Maslach, C. (1982). *Burnout—the cost of caring.* NJ: Prentice-Hall.

Mawhinney, T. C. (1990). Decreasing intrinsic motivation with extrinsic rewards: Easier said than done. *Journal of Organizational Behavior Management, 11*(1), 175–191.

Meier, S., & Davis, S. (1982). *Burnout: A term in search of a theory.* Carbondale, IL: Southern Illinois University.

Montaque, J. (1994, December). Burning out: Handling stress crucial to health of caregiver and hospital. *Trustee, 47*(12), 23.

Nowack, K. M. (1986, May). Who are the hardy? *Training and Development Journal, 40*(5), 116–118.

Pines, A., & Aronson, E. (1988). *Career burnout causes and cures.* New York: Free Press.

Polance, C. (1988). Avoiding burnout. *American Salesman, 33*(5), 9–11.

Potter, B. (1993). *Beating job burnout.* CA: Ronin.

Quick, J. C., Murphy, L. R., & Hurrell, Jr., J. J. (Eds.). (1992). *Stress & well-being at work.* Washington, DC: American Psychological Association.

Raudsepp, E. (1988). Are you obsessed with your work? *Chemical Engineering,* Mar. 28, *95*(4), 65–66.

Richman, D. R. (1988a). Cognitive career counseling for women. *Journal of Rational-Emotive and Cognitive-Behavior Therapy, 6,* 50–65.

Richman, D. R. (1988b). Cognitive psychotherapy through the career cycle. In W. Dryden & P. Trower (Eds.), *Developments in cognitive psychotherapy* (pp. 190–217). London, U.K.: Sage.

Richman, D. R. (1988c). Cognitive career counseling for women. *Journal of Rational–Emotive and Cognitive–Behavior Therapy, 6*(1), 50–65.

Richman, D. R. (Guest Ed.). (1992). Working together: Belief systems of individuals and organizations. (Special Issue). *Journal of Cognitive Psychotherapy, 6*(4), 231–244.

Richman, D. R. (1993). Cognitive career counseling: A rational–emotive approach to career development. *Journal of Rational–Emotive and Cognitive–Behavior Therapy, 11*(2), 91–108.

Richman, D. R., & Nardi, T. J. (1985). A rational–emotive approach to understanding and treating burnout. *Journal of Rational–Emotive Therapy, 3*(1), 55–64.

Roach, B. L. (1994). Burnout and the nursing profession. *Health Care Supervisor,* June, *12*(4), 41–47.

Romano, J. L. (1984, May). Stress management and wellness: Reaching beyond the counselor's office. *Personnel & Guidance Journal, 62*(9), 533–537.

Russell, D. W. (1987, May). Job related stress, social support, and burnout among classroom teachers. *Journal of Applied Psychology, 72*(2), 269–274.

Sauter, S. L., & Murphy, L. R. (Eds.). (1995). *Organizational risk factors for job stress.* Washington, DC: American Psychological Association.

Savery, L. K. (1988). Reacting to incongruencies: Job expectations and reality. *Journal of Managerial Psychology, 3*(4), 8–12.

Schaufeli, W. B. (1993, December). The construct validity of two burnout measures. *Journal of Organizational Behavior, 14*(7), 631–647.

Schaufeli, W. B., Keijsers, G. J., & Miranda, D. R. (1995). Burnout, technology use, and ICU performance. In S. L. Sauter & L. R. Murphy (Eds.), *Organizational risk factors for job stress* (pp. 259–272). Washington, DC: American Psychological Association.

Schiska, A. (1991, September). Revitalizing the plateaued employees on your staff. *Supervisory Management, 36*(9), 1–2.

Schonfeld, I. S. (1992). Assessing stress in teachers: Depressive symptoms scales and neutral self-reports of the work environment. In J. C. Quick, L. R. Murphy, & J. J. Hurrell, Jr. (Eds.), *Stress and well-being at work* (pp. 270–285). Washington, DC: American Psychological Association.

Schonfeld, I. S., Rhee, J., & Xia, F. (1995). Methodological issues in occupational-stress research: Research in one occupational group and wider applications. In S. L. Sauter & L. R. Murphy (Eds.), *Organizational risk factors for job stress* (pp. 323–340). Washington, DC: American Psychological Association.

Senge, P. (1990). *The fifth discipline: The art and practice of the learning organization.* New York: Doubleday.

Shalowitz, D. (1991, May). Another health care headache—job stress could strain corporate budgets: Study. *Business Insurance, 25*(20), 3, 21–22.

Skinner, K. (1993, August). Depression among female registered nurses. *Nursing Management, 24*(8), 42–45.

Sperling, J. (1988, May 23). Burnout causes and cures. *Chemical Engineering, 95*(8), 152–153.

Stallworth, H. F. (1990). Realistic goals help avoid burnout. *HR Magazine, 35*(6), 169–171.

Stellman, J. M. (1987, October). Environmental factors affecting job stress. *Business and Health, 4*(12), 16–19.

Stewart, T. A. (1990). Do you push your people too hard? *Fortune, 122*(10), 121–128.

Toomey, E. L. (1988, April). Employee sabbaticals: Who benefits and why. *Personnel, 65*(4), 81–84.

Towery, T. L. (1992). Extinguishing healthcare burnout. *Healthcare Executive, 7*(2), 34–35.

Umiker, W. (1989, October). Dealing with people who fail to produce. *Health Care Supervisor, 8*(1), 68–74.

Vallen, G. K. (1993, February). Organizational climate and burnout. *Cornell Hotel and Restaurant Administration Quarterly, 34*(1), 54–59.

Weisberg, J. (1994). Measuring workers' burnout and intention to leave. *International Journal of Manpower, 15*(1), 4–14.

8.

A Cognitive Perspective on Absenteeism

NANCY HABERSTROH KNAUS, Ph.D., M.B.A.

Unnecessary voluntary absenteeism can prove costly in numerous ways, including its potential negative impact on the morale of some workers who responsibly and consistently have good work attendances. Staff who must routinely cover for a colleague who takes excessive time off, may eventually sour on the system. Although the effects of such patterns are known to managers, the dollar costs and moral costs are often obscured by the numerous other demands required to keep an operation productive. Absenteeism comes into focus, however, when it is clear that the time and dollar losses resulting from absenteeism in the workplace are excessive and where such patterns impact the health of the organization.

From a health perspective, it makes sense to view absenteeism from a multiple perspective in terms of costs, motivations, advantages, and disadvantages. To begin, let's look at the scope and costs of absenteeism.

ABSENTEEISM COSTS

A summary of the U.S. Department of Labor, Bureau of Labor Statistics (1981) surveys, identifies the prevalence of absenteeism:

- 3.2% of all scheduled working hours
- 90 million lost work hours per week

- 416 million lost work days per year
- Nine days per employee per year
- One employee in every 15 is absent at least once a week

These time losses translate into these direct dollar costs:

- $26.4 billion per year in the United States
- $66 per day for each day lost to absenteeism
- $150 for each 1% of absenteeism per worker
- a 1% increase in employee absence can cut profits by 4%.

ABSENTEEISM PATTERNS

Actuarial factors contributing to these labor losses, and associated dollar costs of absenteeism, show several clear patterns. Gender presents a significant difference for total number of days absent. Women average an absence rate of 6.3% compared to 3.7% for men. Women are more likely to be absent during the child rearing years; after that the rate declines. For men and women, the highest absence rates occur during the 16- to 19-year teenage period. For men, rates decline until age 55, then again increase.

Other factors associated with absence behavior include union membership and unemployment rate. Union members are 29% more likely to be absent than nonunion members. Economic conditions also influence absenteeism rates. During the 1982 recession, average absence rates dropped from 6.1 to 4.7% (Rhodes & Steers, 1990).

Differences across occupations show technicians (3.0%) with the lowest absence rates, executive and managerial positions take low rates of absence leave (4.2%), compared to unskilled laborers with the highest (6.7%) rate of absence. Comparisons of the public and private sector show that education (6.2%), health services (5.9%), and public agencies (5.9%) have the highest average absence rates compared to finance, insurance, and real estate (4.1%) and goods producing industries (4.4%) (Klein, 1985).

ABSENTEEISM MODELS

Despite agreement that the explicit costs of absenteeism are excessive, one must caution against the conclusion that absence behavior represents costly or unnecessary excess in corporate America. Absence is a real and necessary feature of life and human existence. People get ill, become injured, and productively use "mental health" days as a release from stress. Effective and otherwise healthy employees need to maintain their health via routine preventive dental and medical visits. These legitimate, and sometimes, *cost saving*, reasons for absenteeism need acknowledgment. The employee who takes an occasional mental health day, but averts a bleeding ulcer or chronic depression, may experience less stress and have lower medical costs. Employees who use sick leave to seek preventive medical care will likely have fewer total days of sick leave than those who neglect routine medical care. Thus, when looking at absenteeism we need to define clearly the terms and perceptions we use. The above measures of absenteeism costs often do not calibrate for cost savings attributed to preventive care.

In defining these terms and perceptions of absenteeism, efforts have focused on identifying causative and predictive variables, but mostly without regard to legitimate, *positive* uses of sick leave. Absenteeism models from the 1960s to the present seek to explain the absenteeism phenomenon to make it more understandable.

Steers and Rhodes (1978) developed a model of absenteeism that has interested investigators. They focus on two major causes of absence behavior: attendance motivation and ability to attend work. Looking at 104 absenteeism research studies, Steers and Rhodes argued that we can identify two distinct types of absence: voluntary and involuntary absence. The authors theorize that since involuntary absence relates to true illness, which we can do little to relieve, organizations need to concentrate on voluntary absences, which depend on employees' motivation to attend work. Attendance motivation includes job satisfaction (job scope, job level, role stress, work group size, leader style, coworker relations, and opportunity for advancement) and pressures to attend work (economic/market, incentive reward systems, work group norms, personal work ethic, and organizational commitment). The predictive validity of this model consistently shows zero to weak correlations between attendance and attendance motivation variables (job satisfaction/job involvement) and lacks power.

Nicholson and Johns (1985) developed a social view of absenteeism using the psychological contract between the employer and employee and cultural salience among employees to identify four distinct types of absence cultures. They argue that the amount of allowed independence/creativity (trust) and cultural salience (horizontal likeness of the work peer group) distinguish among causes of absenteeism such that four cultures emerge: type I, dependent (high trust, low salience) characterized by deviant absence; type II, moral (low trust, high salience) characterized by constructive absence; type III, fragmented (low trust, low salience) characterized by calculative absence; and type IV, conflictual (low trust, high salience) characterized by defiant absence. Although these prototypes take important environmental influences on absenteeism into account whereas Steers and Rhodes did not, this model does not lend itself to rigorous research.

Brooke (1986) extends the Steers and Rhodes 1978 process model of absenteeism in his causal model of employee absenteeism, and he draws upon the health and alcoholism literature to hypothesize that high levels of role ambiguity, conflict, and overload exert positive indirect effects on absenteeism, through the intervening variables of lower satisfaction, poorer employee health, and increased alcohol involvement. This model lacks supporting research.

Other models (Lawler & Porter, 1967; Newman, 1974; Porter & Steers, 1973; Vroom, 1964) have borrowed from expectancy and equity theory to find causes of absenteeism. Newman (1974) found Fishbein's model of expectancy theory to predict employee turnover, but not absenteeism. Vroom (1964) and Lawler and Porter (1967) view individuals as making choices to absent themselves based upon the probability that they will receive valued results. These theoretical underpinnings have added to the development of the research in this field, but have not achieved validity via supportive empirical evidence.

Dittrich and Carrell (1979) and Patchen (1960) have looked at equity theory to explain causes of absence (that absence is a means of restoring equity to an inequitable employee/employer relationship).

Geurts, Buunk, and Schaufeli (1994) investigated correlations between health problems and objectively recorded absence frequency with 245 blue-collar workers and 199 other workers. The more these workers experienced health problems (attributed to the work environment), the less well off they felt compared to workers outside the company, which results in absence as a means of reducing an inequitable relationship with the company. Results also found that workers adjusted their personal absence norm to that of the work group. Although many veins of research in absenteeism draw upon the idea of employee withdrawal behavior due to dissatisfaction with their job as a cause of absenteeism, equity theory has not adequately explained the research findings.

Although the above models have helped focus the empirical research in this area, none adequately accounts for the broad and varied findings in this literature.

ATTITUDES AND ABSENTEEISM

While some investigators seek explanations for absenteeism behavior, others have identified flaws in the research to explain the broad and often contradictory empirical results of attitudinal research in absenteeism.

Empirical studies of the causes of absenteeism, absence behavior, and attendance have yielded little corroboration or replication during the past 25 years. The authors of a plethora of empirical studies have looked at alterations and variations of employee attitudes hypothesized to predict or correlate with absenteeism, or its inverse, attendance. Latham and Pursell (1975, 1977) argue that recording error contaminates measurements of absence. Recorders may incorrectly categorize days away from work as absence, when such days may represent other processes, such as turnover. These authors suggest counting "number of people who come to work" since this is the variable of interest. Ilgen (1977) and others find that measuring absence has the same inherent potential error as measuring presence and provides little advancement to the field.

Varying criteria for absenteeism represent one area of difference in the empirical investigation of attitudes associated with the phenomenon. When researchers disagree on the basic construct to measure, synthesizing research findings often results in comparing apples and oranges. Fortunately over the years two common measures of absenteeism have evolved: frequency of absence (number of absence periods independent of duration of each absence period) and total time lost (duration of absence independent of the periodicity). Unfortunately, both measures are subject to recording error and differences between studies regarding what gets included or excluded as a "period of absence" or "total days lost." Some studies have excluded vacation time, bereavement leave, excused absence, etc., while others have included all absence taking for any reason as measures of absenteeism.

In most absenteeism research, frequency of absence has predicted absenteeism and absenteeism attitudes more powerfully than total time lost. Steers and Rhodes (1978) among others have suggested that frequency data reflect a category of "voluntary absence" and time lost absence involves "involuntary absence." These authors suggest research efforts concentrate on voluntary absence, under the employee's control, whereas involuntary absence (absence due to illness) is not under the employee's control and thus can show little change. Hammer and Landau (1981) fault this view because they rightly show that absence due to illness also can gain partial control from employee attitudes (i.e., an employee with a hangnail takes sick leave; an employee with the flu remains at work and passes the virus to her coworkers). It would be remiss to exclude "involuntary absence" from our research into absenteeism causation. Clear criterion measures used in each empirical study would help to uncloud a foggy understanding and usage of these concepts in the current literature.

Smulders (1980) reviewed the Netherlands data on frequency and duration measures of absence and argues that they are conceptually distinct and only partially influenced by the same variables. Thus, in measuring absence behavior, investigators need to match samples for distinct variables depending upon the specific measures used. No studies have matched subjects in this manner or adequately controlled for factors of age, sex, task, etc. Such lack of control marks another confounding characteristic of the attitudinal research on absenteeism.

Hammer & Landau (1981) have identified the sample distributions as a significant flaw in this research. Most employees sampled have zero or low absenteeism rates. Due to the presence of large numbers of zero and low values in sample distributions of absenteeism the data become positively skewed and truncated. Hammer et al. (1981) looked at data from a 30-month study of absenteeism among factory workers and found frequency data to have fewer psychometric deficiencies, such as skewedness and leptokurtosis, than time lost measures for both voluntary and involuntary withdrawal. These authors summarize their findings, "The fragmented findings from studies that show little convergence on the causes of absenteeism could reflect inappropriate statistical analyses. The chances of coming up with no significant relationships are high when we keep fitting straight lines to curved data" (p. 580).

Statistical methods have assumed a normal distribution when that assumption has been erroneous. Baba (1990) used a field survey of 193 male aerospace professionals in Canada to compare the conventional use of the ordinary least squares (OLS) regression model (which most of absence research studies have used) versus the Tobit estimator method. The Tobit model explained more of the variances for both frequencies of absence and time lost measures. Significant predictors of time lost included number of children, job involvement, comparative absence, and life stress events for both OLS and Tobit regressions, but the Tobit analysis enhanced the explained variance from 17 to 21%. For frequency of absence, comparative absence, job involvement, age and life-events stress explained 28% of the variance using OLS regression and 33% using Tobit. Baba argues that the better Tobit method can fix the problem of low variance in absence research. His results show that the Tobit method takes the truncated data better into account and enhances the explained variance, but only by a small percentage, 4% for time lost and 6% for frequency of absence.

Besides variations of the criterion measurement of absenteeism and the flawed research methods or statistical procedures used in this body of research, dependent variables such as job satisfaction, job involvement, job commitment, supervisory satisfaction, intrinsic motivation, affective mood found to significantly covary with and predict absenteeism, lack a common operational definition. Investigators have used different labels, definitions, and survey instruments to identify and evaluate such key concepts. No one operational definition and diagnostic method has emerged in the literature to tap these key attitudinal variables of absenteeism.

Flaws in the empirical investigation of attitudes correlated with and predictive of absenteeism include a variety of design errors, lack of consistent operational definitions, and lack of clear criterion measures. Such flaws may partially explain the varied and often contradictory research results rampant in this literature.

CONTRADICTORY EMPIRICAL RESULTS

Empirical investigations of attitudes and absenteeism in the workplace have yielded mixed, contradictory, and fragmented results. However, a reasonable focus includes the variances in criterion measurement, operational definitions, survey tools, sampling distribution, and statistical methods. Still, the interaction of factors seems to affect each study differently so drawing reliable conclusions from the research proves difficult. However, trends in the data do emerge.

Hackett (1989) summarized and compared the results of three meta-analyses of the relationship of employee absenteeism to job satisfaction. He found significant low negative correlations between job and work satisfaction and absenteeism in each of the three data sets he studied (Hackett & Guion, 1985; McShane, 1984; Scott & Taylor, 1985). The most notable finding was the strong *positive* correlation between all the satisfaction and absenteeism relationships for both absence frequency and total time lost measurements for women. Hackett found that the greater the proportion of females in the sample, the stronger the link of absenteeism to job satisfaction such that absenteeism increases with job satisfaction.

Hackett (1989) found strong positive correlations of job satisfaction and absenteeism for women, a direction opposite to most other empirical results comparing absenteeism and job satisfaction. Hackett's findings cast doubt on the validity of much of the previous research. They suggest that the correlations between absenteeism and job satisfaction or job involvement may reflect a gender artifact of the sample distributions rather than a negative relationship between the two factors.

On the other hand, a study by Scott and McClellan (1990) looked specifically at employee characteristics and attitudes of secondary school teachers to find if men and women had different reasons for being absent. Although they found women to perceive some work related factors differently from men and to take more days off than men, women's absence occurrences were not significantly different from those of men. Women averaged 3.92 occurrences compared to 3.29 for men. The number of days absent, or the duration measures, was, however, found to be significantly higher for women (mean number of days taken by women is 6.92 in contrast with 4.83 for men). Scott and McClellan found striking absenteeism *similarities* between men and women: Role conflict, number of dependents, and job involvement were important factors in explaining levels of absenteeism for both men and women. These investigators found an employee's age and attitude toward pay to be the only two factors to exhibit a gender-related impact on absenteeism.

Somers (1995) studied the correlation of affective, continuance, and normative commitment and employee absenteeism among 422 staff nurses. This predominately female group showed affective commitment as the sole predictor of absenteeism and turnover.

Porter and Steers (1973) reviewed the literature on absenteeism, turnover, and job satisfaction. They found two studies about absenteeism and job satisfaction showing a significant inverse relationship. One study by Waters and Roach (1971) found a significant inverse relationship between satisfaction and absenteeism for a group of 160 female clerical workers. This is the same relationship that other studies have found for both men and women.

Melamed, Ben-Avi, Suz, and Green (1995) looked at the relationship of objective work conditions and subjective monotony to job satisfaction and sickness absence among 1,278 male and female workers. They found that job satisfaction was mainly related to subjective monotony whereas sickness absence was equally related to the work conditions and subjective monotony; however, sickness absence was related to the work conditions only in women subjects and not men.

Despite the variety of operational definitions, survey tools and occupational samples used, most empirical data (George, 1989; Hackman & Lawler, 1971; Herbiniak & Roteman, 1973; Newman, 1974; Rabinowitz & Hall, 1977; Smith, 1977; Waters & Roach, 1973) have shown significant low correlations between employee job satisfaction and absenteeism. Two studies (Cheloha & Farr, 1980; Saal, 1978) found that job involvement subsumes job satisfaction and mediates the negative correlation between absenteeism and job satisfaction. Unden (1994) found that of the 133 clerical workers studied, those who perceived that they had good social support at work had a lower level of absenteeism.

Several studies found no relationship between absenteeism and job satisfaction (Adler & Golan, 1981; Cordery, Mueller, & Smith, 1991; Hammer & Landau, 1981; Popp & Belohlav, 1982; Watson, 1981). Ivancevich (1985) and Breaugh (1981) found past absenteeism a better predictor of future absenteeism than work attitudes of job satisfaction, job involvement, or supervisory satisfaction.

Collectively, these empirical data seem perplexing. Still, it makes intuitive sense that people who find their work unsatisfying are less likely to come to work regularly and more tempted to take a break by using their sick leave. Yet, the research is equivocal about the relationship between taking sick leave and feeling dissatisfied with one's job.

Thus research needs to identify other factors that may account for this intuitive *truth*. The work of cognitive psychology may help to identify employee beliefs that cause avoidable absence-taking behavior. If we can clearly define and identify these beliefs, perhaps we can use the predictive cognitions to teach new skills and decrease unnecessary voluntary absenteeism in the workplace.

COGNITIONS AND ABSENTEEISM

Latham and Frayne (1989) have used self-management techniques to enhance employee self-efficacy—the belief that one can act and make a difference. These researchers examined job attendance rates with a sample of 40 unionized state government employees. They then trained them to develop self-efficacy in areas related to attendance with encouraging results.

Cognitive theorists such as Ellis and Knaus (1979), Ellis (1991), and Knaus (1979, 1982) have shown how erroneous beliefs-cognitions promote procrastination, depression, and self-concept disturbances. Whether these cognitions correlate with absenteeism remains an empirical question. However, if we can identify erroneous cognitions that promote unnecessary voluntary absenteeism, then we can find rational processes to help to disconfirm these irrational thoughts and replace them with functional alternatives. William Knaus (personal communication) has postulated eight cognitive categories that underlie unnecessary voluntary absences for empirical consideration:

- *Hookey:* Hookey players are like high school students who want to see if they can get out of class without consequence. Their cognitions often include: "Go ahead, take the day off. You deserve a break. You can get away with it." People who fit into this category routinely prioritize fun over work.
- *Drugging and drinking:* Cognitions center on several themes: "Life is too painful; What the hell, I'm not getting anywhere in life, so who cares; I need a high." People following any one of these cognitive patterns normally drink or drug to smother depression and anxiety. Some falsely believe that they can—or should—get high without consequence. As a byproduct, they are at risk of going absent from and losing their jobs.
- *Family obligation:* Here the obligation is to a group outside work. Cognitions include: "I must be near my children; I'm a bad mother (father) unless I pay more attention to the kids; I need to spend more time with my mate. I have family responsibilities and they come first." These individuals often make a hedonistic calculation and take time off to the level just below where they would receive a warning.
- *Resentment:* People in this category believe they have been treated unfairly. Resentment shows in rationalizations such as, "I used to be a hard worker until I found out that my boss was a jerk." Sometimes legitimate disappointments turn into resentment, "I lost the promotion because of nepotism. That is unjust and I can't stand injustice." Here unnecessary voluntary absenteeism is a reflection of rebelliousness—an "I'll get back at them" attitude.
- *Depressed pattern:* Depressed people have a higher incidence of absenteeism (Rieger, Boyd, & Burke, 1988). While some depressions reflect biochemical states, others involve the depressive triad: "Life is hopeless, I'm helpless, poor me!" These cognitions convey a sense of powerlessness and this attitude often reflects in the person's job performance efficacy and may correlate with below average attendance.
- *Neurotic anxiety patterns:* People who feel overwhelmed by their work often believe they can't manage. Some members of this class also

see themselves as incompetent, inferior, or disapproved of by their coworkers. One escape is through absenteeism.
- *Mental health day patterns:* Here the person looks for a temporary respite from job stresses. This is like an escape valve. Cognitions include, "I need a break"; "I've got to get away from this place." This pattern is common to people who stretch themselves. It serves, sometimes, as an insurance policy against burnout.
- *Self-indulgence:* People who fall into this category believe that the world owes them a living. They eschew responsibility and act on the impulsive thought that whatever they want they should have. So if they want a day off, they take it.

We need further research to operationalize and confirm or disconfirm these intuitive cognitive categories.

Once absenteeism evoking cognitions are identified and clarified, management can provide specialized training to counter such erroneous beliefs in employees who make valuable contributions but whose absenteeism patterns hinder production. This training may include cognitive restructuring methods appropriate to the workplace.

It is unfortunate that there is a dearth of research in the area of cognitions associated with absenteeism behavior. Nevertheless, this area holds promise for identifying and changing the underlying beliefs behind patterns of unnecessary voluntary absences. By working to correct these cognitive conditions, we might aid those who do not needlessly take time off by reducing the incidence of absenteeism among those who abuse the system. Such changes can contribute to higher morale and a healthier workplace.

REFERENCES

Adler, S., & Golan, J. (1981). Lateness as a withdrawal behavior. *Journal of Applied Psychology, 66*(5), 544–554.

Baba, V. V. (1990). Methodological issues in modeling absence: A comparison of least squares and Tobit analyses. *Journal of Applied Psychology, 75*(4), 428–432.

Breaugh, J. A. (1981). Predicting absenteeism from prior absenteeism and work attitudes. *Journal of Applied Psychology, 66*(5), 555–560.

Brooke, P. P. (1986). Beyond the Steers and Rhodes model of employee attendance. *Academy of Management Review, 11*(2), 345–361.

Chadwick-Jones, J. K., Brown, C. A., Nicholson, N., & Sheppard, C. (1971). Absence measures: Their reliability and stability in an industrial setting. *Personnel Psychology, 24*(3), 463–470.

Cheloha, R. S., & Farr, J. L. (1980). Absenteeism, job involvement, and job satisfaction in an organizational setting. *Journal of Applied Psychology, 65*(4), 467–473.

Cordery, J. L., Mueller, W. S., & Smith, L. M. (1991). Attitudinal and behavioral effects of autonomous group working: A longitudinal field study. *Academy of Management Journal, 34*(2), 464–476.

Dittrich, J. E., & Carrell, M. R. (1979). Organizational equity perceptions, employee job satisfaction, and departmental absence and turnover rates. *Organizational Behavior and Human Performance, 24,* 29–40.

Ellis, A. (1991). Using RET effectively: Reflections and interview. In M. E. Bernard (Ed.), *Using Rational–Emotive Therapy Effectively* (pp. 1–33). New York: Plenum.

Ellis, A., & Knaus, W. J. (1979). *Overcoming procrastination.* New York: New American Library.

George, J. M. (1989). Mood and absence. *Journal of Applied Psychology, 74,* 317–324.

Geurts, S., Buunk, B., & Schaufeli, W. (1994). *Journal of Applied Social Psychology, 24*(2), 1871–1890.

Hackett, R. D. (1989). Work attitudes and employee absenteeism: A synthesis of the literature. *Journal of Occupational Psychology, 62*(3), 235–248.

Hackett, R. D., & Guion, R. M. (1985). A reevaluation of the absenteeism-job satisfaction relationship. *Organizational Behavior and Human Decision Processes, 35,* 340–381.

Hackman, J. R., & Lawler, E. E. (1971). Employee reactions to job characteristics. *Journal of Applied Psychology, 55*(3), 259–286.

Hammer, T. H., & Landau, J. (1981). Methodological issues in the use of absence data. *Journal of Applied Psychology, 66*(5), 574–581.

Herbiniak, L. G., & Roteman, M. R. (1973). A study of the relationship between satisfaction and absenteeism among managerial personnel. *Journal of Applied Psychology, 58*(3), 381–383.

Ilgen, D. (1977). Attendance behavior: A re-evaluation of Latham and Pursell's conclusions. *Journal of Applied Psychology, 62*(2), 230–233.

Ivancevich, J. M. (1985). Predicting absenteeism from prior absence and work attitudes. *Academy of Management Journal, 28*(1), 219–228.

Klein, B. W. (1985, May). Missed work and lost hours. *Monthly Labor Review, 26*–30.

Knaus, W. J. (1992, January). A cognitive perspective on organizational change. *Journal of Cognitive Psychotherapy: International Quarterly, 6*(4), 277–299.

Knaus, W. J. (1979). *Do it now: How to stop procrastinating.* Englewood Cliffs, NJ: Prentice-Hall.

Knaus, W. J. (1982). *How to get out of a rut.* Englewood Cliffs, NJ: Prentice-Hall.

Latham, G. P., & Frayne, C. A. (1989). Self-management training for increasing job attendance: A follow up and a replication. *Journal of Applied Psychology, 74,* 411–416.

Latham, G. P., & Pursell, E. D. (1975). Measuring attendance from the opposite side of the coin. *Journal of Applied Psychology, 60,* 369–371.

Latham, G. P., & Pursell, E. D. (1977). Measuring attendance. *Journal of Applied Psychology, 62,* 234–236.

Lawler, E. E., & Porter, L. W. (1967). The effect of performance on job satisfaction. *Industrial Relations, 7,* 20–28.

McShane, S. L. (1984). Job satisfaction and absenteeism: A meta-analytic re-examination. *Canadian Journal of Administrative Sciences, 1*, 61–77.
Melamed, S., Ben-Avi, I., Suz, J., & Green, M. (1995). Objective and subjective work monotony: Effects on job satisfaction, psychological distress and absenteeism in blue-collar workers. *Journal of Applied Psychology, 80*(1), 29–42.
Newman, J. E. (1974). Predicting absenteeism and turnover: A field comparison of Fishbein's model and traditional job attitude measures. *Journal of Applied Psychology, 59*(5), 610–615.
Nicholson, N., & Johns, G. (1985). The absence culture and the psychological contract: Who's in control in absence? *Academy of Management Review, 10*, 397–407.
Patchen, M. (1960). Absence and employee feelings about fair treatment. *Personnel Psychology, 13*, 349–360.
Popp, P. O., & Belohlav, J. A. (1982). Absenteeism in a law status work environment. *Academy of Management Journal, 25*, 677–683.
Porter, L. W., & Steers, R. M. (1973). Organizational, work and personal factors in employee turnover and absenteeism. *Psychological Bulletin, 80*(2), 151–176.
Rabinowitz, S., & Hall, D. T. (1977). Organizational research on job involvement. *Psychological Bulletin, 84*, 265–288.
Rhodes, S. R., & Steers, R. M. (1990). *Managing employee absenteeism.* New York: Addison-Wesley.
Rieger, D. A., Boyd, J. H., & Burke, S. (1988). One month prevalence of mental disorder in the United States. *Archives of General Psychiatry, 45*, 977–986.
Saal, F. E. (1978). Job involvement: A multivariate approach. *Journal of Applied Psychology, 63*(1), 53–61.
Scott, K. D., & McClellan, E. L. (1990). Gender differences in absenteeism. *Public Personnel Management, 19*(2), 229–253.
Scott, K. D., & Taylor, G. S. (1985). An examination of the conflicting findings between job satisfaction and absenteeism: A meta-analysis. *Academy of Management Journal, 28*(3), 599–612.
Smith, F. J. (1977). Work attitudes as predictors of attendance on a specific day. *Journal of Applied Psychology, 62*(1), 16–19.
Smulders, P. G. (1980). Comments on employee absence, attendance as a independent variable in organizational research. *Journal of Applied Psychology, 65*(3), 368–371.
Somers, M. J. (1995). Organizational commitment, turnover and absenteeism: An examination of direct and interaction effects. *Journal of Organizational Behavior, 16*(1), 45–58.
Steers, R. M., & Rhodes, S. R. (1978). Major influences on employee attendance: A process model. *Journal of Applied Psychology, 63*(4), 391–407.
U.S. Department of Labor, Bureau of Labor Statistics (1981, March). Special Labor Force Reports—Summaries. *Monthly Labor Review.*
Unden, A. (1994). Social support at work. *Homeostasis in Health and Disease, 35*, 63–70.
Vroom, V. (1964). *Work and motivation.* New York: Wiley.
Waters, L. K., & Roach, D. (1971). Relationship between job attitudes and two forms of withdrawal from the work situation. *Journal of Applied Psychology, 3*(1), 92–94.

Waters, L. K., & Roach, D. (1973). Job attitudes as predictors of termination and absenteeism: Consistency over time and across organizational units. *Journal of Applied Psychology, 57,* 341–342.

Watson, C. J. (1981). An evaluation of some aspects of the Steers and Rhodes model of employee attendance. *Journal of Applied Psychology, 66,* 385–389.

9.

Changing People from Tender-Minded to Tough-Minded: A PATHWAY for Dealing with Chronic Pain

G. BARRY MORRIS, Ph.D.

Chronic pain is an issue of growing importance in the workplace. Workers' Compensation Boards throughout North America are grappling with definitions, adjudication categories, and prevention–intervention models (Association of Workers' Compensation Boards of Canada, 1994; Morris, 1995). Traditionally, chronic pain has been defined and treated within the framework of a biomedical model (American Medical Association, 1993). More recently, the biopsychosocial model has emerged as the most useful approach to understanding and managing chronic pain syndromes (Merskey & Bogduk, 1994). This model has stimulated the conceptualization of inclusive pain management programs that take into account psychosocial dimensions and contexts of chronic pain syndromes, both with respect to their etiology and their treatment.

The purpose of this chapter is to identify the critical components of a biopsychosocial approach to pain management, in which the psychosocial component is based on rational–emotive behavioral therapy (REBT), developed by Ellis (1962, 1971, 1985, 1995). These components constitute a seven-step pathway to a psychologically healthy orientation to chronic pain, i.e., they empower clients to regain and maintain control of this aspect of their lives.

DEFINITIONS OF CHRONIC PAIN

According to the *Medical Dictionary for the Non-Professional* (Chapman, 1984), pain is a "subjective unpleasant sensation resulting from stimulation of sensory nerve endings by injury, disease, or other harmful factors" (p. 207). In comparison, chronic pain, "almost always has no discernable pathophysical source" (Loeser, 1992, p. 10).

This distinction is supported by the definitions of pain and chronic pain adopted by the International Association for the Study of Pain: "Pain is that experience we associate with actual or potential tissue damage ... it is unquestionably an unpleasant emotional experience" (Merskey & Bogduk, 1994, p. xi). Moreover, the Association accepts the premise that, in the absence of tissue damage, the primary focus of chronic pain management must be the cognitive, emotional, and other psychological factors that underlie individuals' perception of pain. As there is no way of distinguishing this kind of chronic pain from that due to tissue damage, the Association contends that if clients "regard their experience as pain, and if they report it in the same ways as pain caused by tissue damage, it should be accepted as pain" (p. 210).

Several categories of chronic pain with strong psychosocial components have been identified: *Persistent chronic pain,* which has no pathogenic basis; *chronic pain syndromes,* in which there are acute mental and physical outcomes, with no discoverable organic pathology, such as Chronic Fatigue Syndrome, and Chronic Illness; *complex physical pain,* as in fybromyalgia and myofascial pain syndrome; and *unspecified physical pain,* a term used when the predominant features of the disability do not meet the criteria for any specific disability (Morrison, 1995). In addition, a number of stress-induced psychosomatic and somatoform disorders in which psychological factors play an important role in the onset, severity, exacerbation, or maintenance of symptoms, have been identified (Kellner, 1991; Maxmen & Ward, 1995).

PSYCHOLOGICAL CORRELATES OF CHRONIC PAIN

There is general agreement in the pain management literature that "beliefs about the etiology, diagnosis, and management of pain are critical determinants of the pain patient's experience that can facilitate or impede the recovery process" (DeGood & Kiernan, 1995, p.

153). Specifically, perception of fault "appears to be both a powerful correlate of self-reported mood and pain-related behavior, as well as a strong predictor of self-perceived response to treatment" (p. 157). Most importantly, pain patients who felt that their pain was caused by some other person's carelessness, lack of consideration, or irresponsibility, experienced significantly more concurrent emotional distress, had significantly lower expectations of treatment, and reported significantly more incidents of being made worse by a past treatment. This pattern of distress, expectations, and lack of satisfaction with treatment was particularly pronounced in those clients—about half of those with work related injuries or conditions—who blamed their employers for their pain. Such clients tend to develop beliefs about the need for revenge, restitution, and justice. Consequently, they are often unresponsive to treatment effort, and exhibit high levels of anger that weaken the therapeutic alliance.

Similarly, Wells et al. (1989) found that, given equal physical problems, pain patients with high levels of emotional stress are more disabled than those whose emotions are largely positive. Moreover, as shown in outcome studies, "psychological problems, rather than physical ones, predict outcome in chronic pain" (Gallagher et al., 1995, p. 304).

Williams, Urban, Keefe, Shutty, and France (1995) agree that "chronic pain patients vary in their reports of psychological stress. Some patients report only a few somatic symptoms of distress, while others report multiple symptoms of depression, anxiety, or more serious psychopathology" (p. 81). With respect to treatment outcomes, those manifesting high levels of psychological distress are most likely to benefit from general cognitive–behavioral interventions; those with moderate levels may require a more focused treatment for depression. These variations are noteworthy because subgroups of chronic pain clients may also vary in terms of their psychological characteristics, i.e., their pain beliefs, coping strategies, and the extent to which they believe they can control their pain. Finally, these differences may affect their interpersonal or social functioning, with highly distressed patients more likely to experience marital problems and difficulties in their relationships with family members, friends, and coworkers.

There is a high occurrence of depression in chronic pain patients (Haley et al., 1985; Magni, 1987). Pain and depression tend to co-occur, irrespective of disease severity, and of whether or not there is an organic basis for the pain. Anxious and/or depressed patients report more intense pain. Moreover, depression has been found to explain individual differences in pain better than health-related variables. In sum, both anxiety and depression contribute significantly to pain (Doan & Wadden, 1989; Haley, Turner, & Romano, 1985). The assumption in most of these studies is that affective states amplify the experience of pain (Hagglund, Kaley, Reveille, & Alarcon, 1989; Lichtenberg, DeVore Jognoson, & Arachtingi, 1992). As Casten, Parmalee, Kleban, Lawton, and Katz (1995) point out, however, "it is equally as likely that pain may precede anxiety and depression" (p. 275).

For the purposes of pain management, this issue of cause and effect is not of overwhelming importance. Whatever the premorbid personality, anxiety and depression are common in chronic pain clients, and must be addressed in therapeutic interventions. Eventually, research efforts to disentangle the complex relationships among psychological variables and chronic pain will enable practitioners to increase their effectiveness by tailoring pain management programs to the needs and concerns of clients with different levels and kinds of psychological distress, and different backgrounds with respect to the etiology of this distress (Klapow et al., 1995). At present, cognitive-behavioral programs tend to focus on the general relationship between pain and psychological functioning, and make adjustments to suit individual clients on the basis of professional clinical judgment.

A BIOPSYCHOSOCIAL APPROACH TO PAIN MANAGEMENT: THE PATHWAY MODEL

Pain management programs are designed to help individuals handle their pain, return to the workplace, and get on with their lives (Bonica, 1990; Caudill, 1995; Marcus, 1994; Phillips, 1988; Vasudevan, 1995; Von Baeyer, 1994). They tend to be recommended to clients who have not responded to the ministrations of medical doctors, physiotherapists, chiropractors, occupational rehabilitation counselors, and therapists; or who lack strategies that would enable them to sustain a specified or required level of physical functioning.

The biopsychosocial model has stimulated the development of holistic cognitive-behavioral approaches designed to help clients understand the interactive basis of their pain, and to use specific strategies drawn from each domain (Fordyce, 1995; Hendler, 1981; Vlaeyen,

Kole-Snijders, Boeren, & van Eek, 1995): physical, psychological, and social. These models tend to be predicated on the assumption that dysfunctional ways of thinking generate and sustain negative emotional states, which, in turn, not only contribute to the subjective experience of pain, but exacerbate and intensify the pain itself. Another assumption is that what has been learned can be unlearned, and that more effective ways of thinking, feeling, and acting in the face of chronic pain can be acquired and implemented. The final assumption is that, whatever purpose pain may be serving in the lives of clients who have become emotionally attached to their pain, they can learn more satisfying ways of meeting their need for attention, love, control, or power. Defining oneself in terms of one's pain is an expensive and ultimately self-defeating way of living out one's life.

Change is not easy, and initially may give rise to escalated levels of psychological distress. Effective pain management programs inform clients about the biopsychosocial dimensions of their chronic pain; assist them to initiate and sustain change processes; support progress toward a psychologically healthy orientation; and minimize backsliding.

Underlying the entire process is the conviction that in order to control something, you have to understand how it works. In this context, what has to be understood is how pain works, and how self-knowledge can give clients the power to control the thinking processes that determine the role that pain will play in their lives.

The purpose of pain management programs is to help the individual obtain an inner locus of control and a sense of independence. In effective programs, this sense of independence leads to a "redefinition of self," and to a new identity which incorporates both a revised body image and a strengthened and mentally healthy self.

Irrespective of what their premorbid orientation may have been, when people enter a pain management program, they tend to be externally oriented. They feel controlled by doctors, chiropractors, physiotherapists, spouses, lawyers, and well-meaning counselors who provide support and empathy, but do not provide their clients with the knowledge, insights, and skills they need to take charge of their pain. This dependency intensifies the feelings of frustration, helplessness, resignation, and despair experienced in direct reaction to the pain itself. In sum, prior to the intervention, clients tend to be "tender-minded."

THE PATHWAY: A HOLISTIC APPROACH

In this chapter, the management of pain is conceptualized as a pathway to psychological health. The word *PATHWAY* is used as an acronym for seven sequential components that constitute a powerful therapeutic intervention, and appear in one form or another in most cognitive–behavioral pain management programs. These components represent a distillation of the essential features of these programs. In addition, special attention is accorded to the physical bases of pain, and psychosocial dimensions of the biopsychosocial model are formulated in terms of rational–emotive behavioral therapy (REBT).

The PATHWAY comprises seven components or phases: P-Physical; A-Affect; T-Thinking; H-Health, W-Work; A-Achievement of Identity; and Y-Yardstick. The PATHWAY assists participants to develop an inner locus of control, become independent, and take responsibility for their pain. It enables them to achieve short- and long-term goals, and to reconceptualize their approach to life issues related to their condition. In short, clients become "tough-minded."

P-Physical

Helping clients to understand the physical dimension of their pain is an essential core of any pain management program. It is the physical domain that brings the client to the pain management program, and it is an understanding of this aspect of the presenting problem that lays the foundation for other elements of the intervention. Clients need to acquire a working knowledge of basic body processes, such as the functions of the central and autonomic nervous systems, the blood, bone, and muscle systems and the hormonal changes that occur when the body is under physical and psychological stress. More specifically, they need to understand the nature of chronic pain, how it manifests itself in common chronic pain syndromes, and how physical, psychological, and social factors interact in its genesis and treatment. At a more pragmatic level, clients need to learn how to use this information to deal with their pain through exercise, breathing, deep relaxation, and imagery.

A multidisciplinary approach is useful, as medical doctors or nurses, physiotherapists, chiropractors, and psychologists bring different but complementary perspectives to bear upon the physical dimensions of chronic pain. The integration of these perspectives within a clearly conceptualized holistic framework provides pain clients with both a general and specific knowledge base about the physical basis of their disorders, and equips them with strategies and techniques to attack and control their pain. The acquisition of a knowledge base is the first and critical step in assuming control, whereas the immediate positive results of the pain reduction techniques give discouraged clients a reason for hope, and motivate them to work on their particular symptoms.

A-Affect

The primary goal of this component is to help clients to relinquish their familiar old healthy body, and to reconcile themselves to its loss. This is a very difficult task, because the old body was strong, it was effective, and it did what the client wanted it to do. What each client is helped to do is grieve the death of the old body. This process, which has been called "living bereavement," has to be completed figuratively, of course, and that is what makes this portion of the program emotionally taxing and challenging.

The mourning process is usually done in solitude, and the accompanying emotions are turned inward. In some cases, however, grief is expressed through aggressive attacks against others. Clients in pain management programs have the advantage of working it out in the context of a support group, through guided interaction with other people with similar pain syndromes.

The mourning and grieving of the old body takes a variety of forms. Clients may cry, get angry, or become depressed. Some go through the classical stages of bereavement: denial, anger, appeal to a higher power or "bargaining," and acceptance. Others experience several emotions simultaneously.

In most cases, however, the primary emotion experienced by individuals as they acknowledge the chronicity of their pain is anger. This very natural emotional reaction to pain may be overt or covert. Women tend to internalize their anger, and are often diagnosed as chronically depressed. Males are more likely to externalize feelings of resentment, and may express them in violent outbursts and psychological or physical attacks on family members, coworkers, and even strangers.

Anger is used to block other feelings associated with pain, such as anxiety, fear, self-doubt, and confusion. Direct expression of anger does serve a ventilation function: tension is displaced, and temporary relief is obtained. Unfortunately, there is a concomitant negative effect, in that the anger triggers the release of hormones which enter into the muscle system and interfere with the healing process. Clients must, therefore, understand how anger affects the body, and learn how to control its expression.

Clients must also learn how to distinguish between constructive and destructive anger. Anger that is constructive can motivate a person to challenge unfair practices, overcome obstacles, and achieve goals. Destructive anger can result in loss of family, friends, and self-respect; therefore, clients are challenged to assume responsibility for their anger through acknowledging that it is their irrational thinking or lack of control, not the provocation, that creates a "breaking point," and leads to violent behavior.

Another common emotion in pain clients is guilt. Guilt is especially intense in males who cannot work and who, because of their religious beliefs, cultural conditioning, and moral orientation, define their self-worth in terms of their "work value." For females, guilt tends to be related primarily to family duties and marital responsibilities, and their roles in other relationships. Individuals who cannot work and discharge the responsibilities associated with their gender roles lose a critical aspect of the identity that they established as they negotiated the transition from adolescence to adulthood. They experience guilt because they cannot live up to societal expectations, and get caught in a spiral of self-downing, self-blame; feelings of self-worthlessness or "uselessness," self-doubt, and depression.

The third emotion that is very prominent among chronic pain clients is anxiety. Many clients become panicky, their time frames become constricted, and they spend more time worrying about the future than they do planning for it. In extreme cases, anxiety is transformed into a phobia, a fear of doing anything, because of an irrational fear of bringing further harm to their bodies. Such individuals are inclined to do nothing, rather than take a risk by doing something. Ultimately, they experience anxiety about their ability to cope and to survive.

Another focus of anxiety is personal and intimate relationships. Among individuals with chronic pain, the divorce rate is very high, relationships with children and other family members become strained, the loyalty of friends is severely tested, and the patience and tolerance of coworkers and employers cannot be counted on indefinitely.

Understandably, "of the psychological factors (other than depression) related to pain, anxiety is the most prevalent" (Casten et al.,

1995, p. 271). Unfortunately, however, anxiety produces tension, tension causes muscle tightening, and the muscle tightening increases the intensity of the pain. The more intense pain leads to an even higher level of anxiety, and the anxiety–pain relationship is perpetuated (Merskey & Bogduk, 1994).

Another factor that enters into the pain–anxiety–depression relationship, is that individuals with chronic pain often have too much time to think. When they think, old feelings and hurts, repressed conflicts from the past, unfulfilled ambitions, and self-doubts tend to dominate. Concerns that busy people are too busy to dwell upon become the primary content of the ideation of individuals with time on their hands. Feelings and conflicts that were not worked out in the past are catapulted into the present, and demand attention.

This negative ideation, which instigates and reinforces negative emotions, as debilitating as it may be, actually provides the therapist with an opportunity to implement the critical component of the PATHWAY—the cognitive restructuring that is at the center of the "T-Thinking" intervention.

T-Thinking

The conceptual framework for this component of the model is REBT (Ellis, 1995), and the focus is on the "demandingness" exemplified in the three basic neurosis- or disturbance-inciting "shoulds/oughts/musts" at the core of dysfunctional thought processes:

1. "I *absolutely must,* at practically all times, be successful at important performances and relationships—or else I, as a person, am inadequate and worthless!" (Ellis, 1995, p. 13). Given our own fallibility, the emotional consequences of this kind of self-pressure are feelings of severe anxiety, depression, despair, and worthlessness. Concomitant behaviors include withdrawal, avoidance, and addiction.

2. "Other people *absolutely must* practically always treat me considerately, kindly, fairly, or lovingly—or else they are no . . . good and deserve no joy in their existence!" (p. 13). Given other people's fallibility, this stance generates feelings of intense anger and resentment, and leads to psychological and physical attacks on others, strained or severed relationships, and social isolation.

3. "Conditions under which I live *absolutely must* be comfortable, pleasurable, and rewarding—or else it's awful, I can't stand it, and the world is just no good!" (p. 13). Clearly, the world is less than

perfect, and life is not always fair; therefore, self-pity, rage, and low frustration tolerance characterize individuals who subscribe to this belief. The behavioral consequences include withdrawal, procrastination, and addiction.

The goal of REBT is to replace these absolutist "demandingness" beliefs with rational appropriate expectations of self, others, and the world, thereby removing the cognitive underpinnings of the negative emotions that exacerbate chronic pain, and sabotage clients' efforts to manage it and incorporate it into a healthy, functional, redefined self.

Accordingly, there is a need to address not only the way clients think about their pain, but also how they think about life issues in general. Common dysfunctional, illogical, or irrational thinking patterns must be identified, challenged, disputed, and changed. The goal of this process of cognitive restructuring is healthy, appropriate thinking patterns.

The basic assumption is that irrational, self-defeating thought processes are the antecedents or roots of the client's negative emotions: depression, anger, guilt, and anxiety. Once these debilitating thought processes are identified and understood, the change process can begin.

As stated above, the most central irrational thought process characterizing chronic pain clients is demandingness. Clients may demand perfection of themselves, they may demand that others do what they expect them to do, and/or they may demand the world be just or fair.

Another debilitating thought process is "awfulizing." Individuals caught into this way of thinking have a tendency to catastrophize or exaggerate their feelings of pain, and conclude that there is nothing that can be done to help them. Their fear, tension, self-pity, helplessness, and inactivity exacerbate their pain, and make things worse than they would otherwise be.

A closely related negative cognitive stance is "low frustration tolerance" (LFT). Individuals may be convinced that they "cannot stand the pain," even though, in fact, they may have lived with it for many years. In other words, they need to learn that their pain is uncomfortable, not intolerable, and that they can, in fact, "stand it." Clients often express their LFT by claiming that their condition is too uncomfortable and too painful, that it hurts too much, and that it is too difficult to live with. In extreme cases this kind of thinking leads to suicidal ideation.

An important concomitant of awfulizing and LFT is self-downing. Not only do chronic pain clients tend to experience low self-worth and self-blame; they really believe that they are less than what they were before, that their disability is the central component of their identity, and that, whatever their value at one time, it can never be recaptured. Self-downing leads to negative self-evaluation, negative appraisals of challenges and opportunities, and depression.

These general, negative, and pervasive belief patterns are restructured by teaching clients the ABCs (activating event, beliefs about the activating event, and consequence) of REBT, and REBT methods (cognitive, emotive, and behavioral) of disputing self- and social-defeating beliefs. Other specific irrational beliefs, like those described below, are handled the same way.

Some clients have a tendency to blame themselves for their misfortune, and experience high levels of guilt. They believe that their pain is a punishment for some wrongdoing or transgression, and that they are, in fact, the authors of their pain. Blame proneness may, however, be directed toward others, with the client insisting that others accept his or her demands and do whatever the "victim" expects or wants them to do.

Other clients need to confront issues of dependency. Individuals with chronic pain tend to believe that they need someone stronger than themselves to support them. This orientation must be changed so that the client develops a sense of independence and an inner locus of control. Other beliefs such as unreasonably high expectations are also common, and these, too, need to be disputed and changed.

H-Health

Once clients have acquired an understanding of the physical bases of their pain, identified negative emotions, and learned how to control them, and acknowledged the fact that they can control the interplay among their thinking patterns, their emotions, and their physical pain, they may be said to have achieved a healthy psychological orientation. With this change in orientation, the focus of thinking shifts from negative ideation to the development of personal goals and objectives.

These long-range goals must be defined concretely in terms of a time frame, and broken down into short- and immediate-range goals. Moreover, clients need to learn how to deal with barriers and obstacles related to their particular condition, their social and work contexts, and their individual goals.

This healthy, appropriate orientation is rooted in rational, logical thinking patterns, and a recognition that these patterns lead to self-acceptance, acknowledgment of fallibility, and a high frustration tolerance characterized by ego strength, and ability to tolerate discomfort anxiety.

As clients move toward an integration of their chronic pain condition, their healthy emotions, and their new ways of thinking, they begin to redefine their "self," and make a conscious decision to adopt and implement a new orientation to their pain and their lives. At this juncture, they need to learn how to deliberately redesign their future. Whatever specific plan is adopted, the process remains constant: the development of realistic goals that are very concrete, clear, and attainable; a specification of what must be done each step of the way; and a commitment to try innovative ways of handling blocks and setbacks.

In addition, clients need to understand that there are many different life lines or goal lines: career and financial goals, social goals, love-line goals, family goals, and relationship goals. The relevance of each of these lines and the importance of incorporating all of them into a life plan must be emphasized. The identification of both short- and long-range goals along each line helps clients to keep things in focus, and to redefine themselves in an inclusive, holistic way.

W-Work

The self-definition and goal-setting exercises based on a psychologically healthy orientation to life and others is a necessary but not sufficient condition for living successfully with pain. The new orientation must be operationalized, usually in terms of work or action. Work may mean returning to work, or finding new work. New work may entail reevaluation of one's abilities and limitations, and retraining or reeducation.

The client must learn to take action, and to act in accordance with a new "philosophy." In the past, most clients probably used the strategy "ready, aim, fire." Now they are encouraged to adopt the position that they must get ready, fire, and then aim toward their goals. They must begin to implement concrete action plans, such as identifying specific employment opportunities appropriate to personal goals and abilities, and work toward finding employment consistent with a redefined self.

The concept of work in this framework is not confined to occupational decisions and changes. It includes working at maintaining the psychologically healthy ways of thinking that undergird the process of redefinition and reintegration. Obstacles, blocks, and barriers must be identified and dealt with if goals are to be achieved. Clients must learn to "Do and not stew," and must adopt the strategy of actively moving along the different life or goal lines, thereby reducing the probability of relapse or regression to an unproductive life-style. In sum, the client must keep moving, moving, moving, and firing, firing, firing.

Once concrete appropriate goals have been established, and the individual is moving toward their achievement, the stage is set for the achievement and consolidation of a new "self" and its affirmation in a restructured and strengthened identity.

A-Achieving Identity (Affirmation of New Self)

In the preceding phases of the PATHWAY, clients have gained an understanding of the manner in which physical, affective, and cognitive factors contribute singly and jointly to chronic pain; identified, acknowledged, and challenged their particular dysfunctional thought patterns; identified long- and short-term goals; and implemented an action plan. This process provides a basis for the redefinition of self. This new self incorporates a healthy psychological orientation, an internal locus of control, and a view of chronic pain as an integral, but not dominating or controlling, aspect of one's being.

Having worked through a crisis, and having gained control over the chronic pain that permanently altered the physical basis of their identity, clients are prompted to conduct a critical review of other aspects of their premorbid life-styles and the beliefs that shaped their personal and social functioning. In a sense, they have "the opportunity of a lifetime," a rare chance to achieve and affirm a new identity, and to implement and sustain it in the pursuit of clearly articulated, realizable, and rewarding lifeline goals. In the words of Ellis (1995), their pain has provided them with an opportunity to "effect a profound philosophical–emotional–behavioral change" (p. 2). What they need to do is use their new cognitive, emotive, and behavioral strategies "strongly and persistently" (p. 8) until they come into play automatically whenever their pain or some other life issue demands attention. If they regress, and overreact to negative stressors, they are at risk of allowing their pain to once again take ascendancy in their lives.

In the final phase of the intervention, the efforts of the therapist and client should be directed at inoculating the client against regression, by specifying the nature of the yardstick to be used in assessing progress.

Y-Yardstick

Therapeutic interventions have clearly defined temporal boundaries: they begin, and they end. The degree of success experienced by clients in maintaining the momentum generated by the program is dependent upon a number of factors, some of which are beyond the control of the therapist and the scope of the program. As indicated in the introductory section of this chapter, clients with a pronounced tendency to attribute their misfortune to employer negligence may be highly resistant to treatment, be it medical or psychological. Others develop such a strong emotional attachment to their pain that it has become the core of their identity, and change, even in the direction of a more rewarding life, is viewed as overwhelmingly threatening. For some, pain becomes a highly satisfying source of attention, concern, control, and power, and the prospect of giving it up and losing this "advantage" precludes genuine engagement in the intervention process.

Clients such as these may master the content of the physical and cognitive components of the program, and may even go through the goal-setting and develop an action plan. The problem is that they do not allow themselves to seriously challenge their dysfunctional thought processes, and do not put into practice what they have learned about the effect of negative emotions on their pain. The cornerstone of their identity is their pain, and redefining their "self" in a way that would relegate their pain to a minor component of their being is "unthinkable." In a sense, therefore, these clients cannot regress after the program, as they have never truly completed it. The best that one can hope is that, when a major life crisis occurs because of their reluctance to give up their pain, what they did learn will prompt them to reconsider their options.

For the majority of the clients who complete the program—those who were open to the treatment, internalized the basic paradigm of the model, and leave determined to implement their new identity—the issue is one of applying the rational thought processes that helped them to manage their pain to the management of the inevitable obstacles, setbacks, and disappointments that they will encounter as they implement their action plans. What they need is a yardstick which they can use to gauge their failures and successes.

This yardstick must be realistic. It must include a recognition that our fallibility precludes constant success. Backsliding is normal; what is not, is despair, and relentless self-downing. Moreover, backsliding does not necessarily lead to permanent regression. The mental yardstick clients use to judge their progress must be pliable. If it is not, the anxiety created by the confusion of a "slip" with a "fall" will once again initiate the debilitating pain/anxiety cycle.

It is equally important that the yardstick be flexible when it is used to measure success. Its calibration must permit recognition of small incremental gains as well as of major accomplishments. During the first 2 years after the intervention it is critically important that ways of sustaining momentum be put in place. In general, clients need to be encouraged to reinforce their positive behaviors, and to reward themselves generously for major achievements.

One of the basic premises of the PATHWAY model comes into play here. Information is power. Clients need to identify specific personal reinforcers, and know how to manage self-reinforcement schedules. They need to understand how to distinguish between positive and negative backslides; how to use a positive one to regroup and refocus; and how to get out of a backslide, and prevent it from turning into a down slide. They also need to be able to sense when temporary help is required, and when reading, physiotherapy, a discussion or support group, a follow-up or "booster" counseling session, or a refresher program may be in order.

CONCLUSION

The purpose of this chapter was to introduce the reader to the seven-step PATHWAY model for helping chronic pain clients understand the biopsychosocial dimensions of their condition, and internalize a psychologically healthy orientation to its management. In effect, the PATHWAY renders "tender-minded" people "tough-minded," capable of dealing with their pain.

Clients who successfully negotiate the difficult PATHWAY to empowerment and control achieve "tough-mindedness" through a "redefinition of self." Tough-minded people confront their pain, accept it, and integrate it into a new identity characterized by a strong ego, high frustration tolerance, resilience, independence, and an inner locus of control. They think rationally and logically; experience low levels of negative emotion; have clearly defined life goals; and work hard to bring them to fruition. Finally, they recognize that the pathway that they have adopted is not straight and narrow, are realistic with respect to their expectations of themselves and others, and use an objective, nonjudgmental measuring stick to monitor their progress. In sum, they live their lives and manage their pain in accordance with the basic principles of REBT.

REFERENCES

American Medical Association (1993). *Guides for evaluation of permanent pain.* Chicago: Author.
Association of Workers' Compensation Boards of Canada (1994). *A report on chronic pain and workers' compensation.* Edmonton, Alberta: Author.
Bonica, J. J. (1990). *The management of pain.* Philadelphia: Lea & Febiger.
Casten, R. J., Parmelee, P. A., Kleban, M. H., Lawton, M. P., & Katz, I. R. (1995). The relationships among anxiety, depression, and pain in a geriatric institutionalized sample. *Pain, 61,* 271–276.
Caudill, M. A. (1995). *Managing pain before it manages you.* New York: Guilford Press.
Chapman, C. F. (1984), *Medical dictionary for the non-professional.* New York: Barron's Educational Series.
DeGood, D. E., & Kiernan, B. (1995). Perception of fault in patients with chronic pain. *Pain, 64*(1), 153–159.
Doan, B., & Wadden, N. (1989). Relationships between depressive symptoms and descriptions of chronic pain, *Pain, 26*(1), 75–84.
Ellis, A. (1962). *Reason and emotion in psychotherapy.* New York: Institute for Rational Living.
Ellis, A. (1971). *Growth through reason.* North Hollywood, CA: Wilshire Books.
Ellis, A. (1985). *Overcoming resistance: Rational–emotive therapy with difficult clients.* New York: Springer.
Ellis, A. (1995). *Better, deeper and more enduring brief therapy: The rational emotive behavior therapy approach.* New York: Brunner/Mazel.
Fordyce, W. E. (Ed.). (1995). *Back pain in the workplace: Management of disability in nonspecific conditions.* Seattle, WA: IASP Press.
Gallagher, R. M., Williams, R. A., Skelly, J., Haugh, L. D., Rauk, V., Milhous, R., & Frymoyer, J. (1995). Workers' Compensation and return-to-work in low back pain. *Pain, 61*(2), 299–307.
Hagglund, K., Kaley, W., Reveille, J., & Alarcon, G. (1989). Predicting individual differences in pain and functional impairments among patients with rheumatoid arthritis. *Arthritis and Rheumatism, 32,* 851–858.

Haley, W. E., Turner, J. A., & Romano, J. M. (1985). Depression in chronic pain patients: Relation to pain, activity, and sex differences. *Pain, 23*(3), 337–343.

Hendler, N. (1981). *Diagnostic and nonsurgical management of chronic pain.* New York: Raven Press.

Kellner, R. (1991). *Psychosomatic syndromes and somatic symptoms.* Washington, DC: America Psychiatric Press.

Klapow, J. C., Slater, M. A., Patterson, T. L., Atkinson, J. H., Weickgenant, A. L., Grant, I., & Garfin, S. R. (1995). Psychosocial factors discriminate multidimensional clinical groups of chronic low back pain patients. *Pain, 62*(3), 349–355.

Lichtenberg, J. W., DeVore Jognson, D., & Arachtingi, B. M. (1992). Physical illness and subscription to Ellis's irrational beliefs. *Journal of Counselling and Development, 71*(3), 157–162.

Loeser, J. (1992, November/December). Managing chronic pain. *AHFMR Newsletter, 22.*

Marcus, N. J. (1994). *Freedom from chronic pain.* New York: Simon & Shuster.

Magni, G. (1987). On the relationship between chronic pain and depression when there is no organic lesion. *Pain, 31,* 1–21.

Maxmen, J. S., & Ward, N. G. (1995). *Essential psychopathology and its treatment.* New York: Norton.

Merskey, H., & Bogduk, N. (Eds.). (1994). *Classification of chronic pain.* Seattle, WA: IASP Press.

Morris, G. B. (1995). *Chronic disabilities: A proposed policy for adjudicating chronic pain and chronic stress claims.* Prepared for Saskatchewan Workers' Compensation Board, Regina. (Unpublished).

Morrison, J. (1995). *DSM-IV made easy: The clinician's guide to diagnosis.* New York: Guilford Press.

Phillips, H. C. (1988). *The psychological management of chronic pain: A treatment manual.* New York: Springer.

Vasudevan, S. V. (1995). *Pain: A four-letter word you can live with: Understanding and controlling your pain.* Milwaukee, WI: Montgomery Media.

Vlaeyen, J. W. S., Kole-Snijders, A. M. J., Boeren, R. G. B., & van Eek, H. (1995). Fear of movement/(re) injury in chronic low back pain and its relation to behavioral performance. *Pain, 62,* 363–372.

Von Baeyer, C. (1994). Chronic pain patients four years after brief treatment. *The Pain Clinic, 7,* 45–51.

Wells, K. B., Steward, A., Hays, R. D., Burnam, M. A., Rogers, W., Daniels, M., Berry, S., Greenfield, S., & Ware, J. (1989). The functioning and well-being of depressed patients: Results from the Medical Outcomes Study. *Journal of the American Medical Association, 262*(7), 914–919.

Williams, D. A., Urban, B., Keefe, F. J., Shutty, M. S., & France, R. (1995). Cluster analysis of pain patients' responses to the SCL-90R. *Pain, 61*(1), 81–91.

10.

How to Master Workplace Stress

ALBERT ELLIS and JACK GORDON

Mental health professionals need to be clear as to what they mean by *stress* before undertaking assessment and treatment strategies. As Wagenaar and La Forge (1994) observed, *stress* has become something of a catchall term. For some researchers *stress* is a noun, for others it is a verb, and for still others an adjective. Roskies (1983) is quoted as saying that stress has become the modern-day equivalent of the medieval demon—the universal explanation for a variety of mental and physical problems. Once a concept is stretched to mean anything one chooses, its usefulness in both science and philosophy is over. A workable definition must include not only everything that meets given criteria but tries to firmly exclude everything that does not. Taking our own advice to heart we shall use the term *stress* (or *distress*) to represent the result of several kinds of dysfunctional or irrational thoughts, feelings, and actions (Abrams & Ellis, 1994). The precise meaning of *irrational* will be made clear a little later. In other words, from a rational–emotive behavior therapy (REBT) treatment point of view we conceive stress as a particular kind of response to environmental irritants or stressors a person perceives and believes to be capable of reducing the quality of life and of threatening to overwhelm his or her capacity to achieve important goals effectively.

The kind of response we are talking about is really the physical and emotional distress that follows from, but is not just caused by, an environmental stressor perceived as particularly severe, or by a series of continuing stressors to which there appears to be no end.

WHAT IS AN OCCUPATIONAL STRESSOR?

In the past, stressors in the workplace were relatively few in number and commanded fairly general awareness. For example, people often had to work long hours in a tedious job with repetitive routines and with little time off. The threat of being fired and having no other means of financial support served to keep most people's noses to the grindstone.

Today, in the rapidly changing world of work, things are very different. Klarreich (1985) identified several occupational stressors that commonly lead to feelings of distress among today's workforce, but which were rare or unheard of not too many years ago. Today, geographical mobility is one kind of stressor that can trigger stress-related disorders. The opposite condition, being stuck in a dead-end job, working excessively long hours, or being incapacitated for a lengthy period can have a similar effect.

Work overload has long been known to contribute to a variety of stress-related symptoms, including hypertension, alcohol abuse, absenteeism, and poor work motivation.

Role ambiguity is another comparatively "modern" stressor. In management theory, roles can be clearly defined, but real life tends to be complex and not too easily split into rigid categories. Employees who expect precise, clear-cut job specifications may experience distress when they discover that the objectives and requirements of their position or role overlap with the responsibilities of that of a colleague. According to Kahn, Wolfe, Quinn, Snoek, and Rosenthal (1964), employees who experienced role ambiguity displayed a variety of distress symptoms, including lower job satisfaction, greater frustration, futility, lack of confidence, and increased job tension. A close cousin to role ambiguity is role conflict where an employee feels he or she is being "pulled" in different directions by conflicting job demands or is expected to perform tasks which are not part of his or her job specification. Again, lower job satisfaction and job-related stress symptoms are evident.

The relationship with the boss has always been a potential source of conflict for employees, as well as with colleagues and fellow employees. Perhaps more than in the past, conflicts between people in an organization arise nowadays for a variety of reasons, including new management concepts, fierce competition between "high flyers," dissatisfaction with "career development," the organizational structure, male–female relationships, and so on. All of these can lead to problems of relating which can trigger various stress symptoms such as rage, despair, jealousy, and depression.

Another category of stressors occurs outside the organization or workplace; events in the home, such as death of a spouse, divorce, marital separation, problems with children or other family members, can become stressors which lead to stress-related disorders which in turn interact with and exacerbate the stressors in the workplace. Holmes and Rahe (1967) developed a Social Readjustment Rating Scale each item of which had a stress value attached to it. Death of a spouse was accorded a rating of 100, for example; divorce rated 73; marital separation 65; jail term 63, and so on. While not everyone would agree with Holmes and Rahe's assessment, the major objection from the point of view of REBT is the implication that the external event, be it death of a spouse, or divorce, or anything else, is the direct cause of the individual's stress, and that since stressors appear to cause stress and illness, therefore we had better eliminate or change the stressors if we want to manage stress. In other words, Holmes and Rahe seem to imply that if the working environment is free of change from a hypothesized existing steady state, a "stress-free" existence will be achieved.

The difficulty with that view, apart from its implicit assumption that stressors directly cause stress, is that the creation of a working environment free of change would be quite impracticable, especially in today's business world where the very nature of work is rapidly being transformed and job security can no longer be assumed. The pace of technological change continues to gather momentum and will change the face of work in ways we can yet scarcely imagine (Toffler, 1971, 1980; Handy, 1985). We had better face the fact that change, even rapid change, is here to stay. If we are correct about this, it obviously has profound implications for the way we conceptualize stress and its treatment.

AN OVERVIEW OF RATIONAL–EMOTIVE BEHAVIOR THEORY

What Causes Stress?

Although REBT significantly stresses the cognitive element in stress and other kinds of self-defeating behavior, REBT maintains that thinking, feeling, and behavior are interrelated and mutually interacting processes. Moreover, these three fundamental human psychological processes almost always interact and often in complex ways (Ellis, 1985, 1991). Consequently, in the practice of REBT, counselors use not only cognitive restructuring methods to help people change their distressed feelings and behaviors, but they also frequently employ emotive–evocative and behavioral methods to help and encourage clients to change their thinking.

The key question for the rational–emotive behavior therapist then is: exactly how does the environmental stressor become a problem? What brings about the dysfunctional physical states and disordered emotional reactions we call stress? What do we mean when we say are experiencing stress? The core assumption of REBT is that what we label *stress* is determined not just by the unpleasant events or stressors that people experience in their working or personal lives, but mainly by their irrational cognitions or evaluations about what they perceive is happening to them. The goals of treatment and the primary task of the rational–emotive behavior therapist are: (1) to show clients that disturbed emotions and self-defeating behaviors, or their stress-related symptoms, usually arise from and are maintained by the philosophies, attitudes, distorted inferences, and irrational beliefs (iBs) they hold about the stressors in their lives; and (2) that by surrendering their irrational cognitions and replacing them with more rational philosophies they will help themselves to emote and behave in healthier and more constructive and self-helping ways.

The idea that life events themselves are stressful only if they are viewed that way is not new. Some 2,000 years ago the Greek philosopher Epictetus enunciated his famous dictum: "Humans are disturbed not by things, but by the views that they take of them."

Does stress then really exist? The short answer is, no. Like the fabled subatomic particle of the quantum physicists which goes in and out of existence depending on how you look at it, stress exists largely in the perceptions and reactions of the beholder (or stressee). There is practically nothing intrinsically stressful or assuaging but thinking makes it so (Ellis & Abrahms, 1978; Abrams & Ellis, 1994). Ellis, in the 1950s, and in his seminar work, *Reason and Emotion in Psychotherapy* in 1962, was the first to take this still revolutionary idea and make it a core concept of psychotherapy, and the foundation of rational–emotive behavior theory and its treatment for stress-related and most emotional disorders (Ellis, 1962, 1978, 1985, 1988, 1991; Ellis & Dryden, 1987). The real causes of stress are to be found mainly within the stressed individual, not in what is happening to him or her. Since REBT (or RET as it was then known) broke new ground with this new concept, several other investigators have come to the same conclusion (Bowers & Kelly, 1979; French, 1973; Goldberg & Comstock, 1976; Lazarus & Launier, 1978; McGrath, 1976). Stressors in themselves are not stressful until they are perceived as such, and

Ellis and Whiteley (1979) assembled research data that supported the basic clinical hypotheses of REBT.

We may note in passing that REBT therapists try to help people change the environmental stressors as a way of dealing with their stress. They first focus on people's *own* contributions to their distress and then often help them change their environment. Why? Because in the first place, as we noted above, stressors often cannot be changed. Even more important, dealing with them does not get to the root of clients' problems which basically lie in the manner in which they perceive and evaluate the stressors in their life.

Once clients reach the stage where they no longer "awfulize" and disturb themselves about the stressors and replace their previous irrational beliefs and attitudes with a more rational outlook, they may become sufficiently motivated to change the stressors if realistically they can be changed. People might, for example, decide to change their job, or even prepare themselves to take up new career, or leave a bad relationship. However, these changes are best contemplated *after* clients have stayed in the "stressful" situation, have worked through the process of uprooting their previously held iBs, have replaced their disturbed emotions and unconstructive behaviors with more appropriate or healthier responses, and are demonstrating more constructive ways of managing their working lives.

GOALS, PURPOSES, AND RATIONALITY

In REBT, rationality is not defined in any absolute sense. Rational–emotive behavior theory holds that human beings mainly strive to survive and to live happily in accordance with their own tastes. Furthermore, humans tend to be happiest when they choose important life goals and purposes and actively work to achieve them, so that they live a more fulfilling and pleasureable existence. Given that humans tend to be goal-oriented, and because REBT sees these goals as matters of choice rather than as absolute necessities, *rationality* in REBT theory means aiding or abetting people's basic goals and purposes, whereas *irrationality* consists of dysfunctional beliefs and inappropriate emotions that block or interfere with people's chosen goals and purposes. Thus, a working definition of rationality and irrationality might be expressed as follows:

Rationality

Beliefs, ideas, and attitudes that are:

1. Pragmatic—help people achieve their basic goals and purposes.
2. Logical—they make logical sense.
3. Realistic—they are empirically consistent with reality.

Irrationality

Beliefs, ideas, and attitudes that:

1. Prevent people from achieving their basic goals and purposes.
2. Are illogical (especially dogmatic) and foster magical thinking.
3. Are empirically inconsistent with reality.

THE ABCDE FRAMEWORK

As noted above, we tend to perceive, think, feel, and behave interactionally. It follows that to understand and eliminate stress, using a variety of cognitive, emotive, and behavior modification methods, we had better have an overall conceptual framework. The ABCDE framework is the cornerstone of REBT practice and the best way to conceptualize the REBT approach to stress.

The A stands for an Activating event, Adversity, or stressor that may be external or internal to the person. Here, A also stands for his or her inference or interpretation of the event.

B represents the person's Belief system or *Beliefs*. These are evaluative cognitions (or thoughts) that are either rigid or flexible. When such a belief is rigid, and takes the form of a "must," an "absolute should," or a dramatic "have to," it is called an irrational Belief (iB). When clients adhere to such rigid beliefs, they will tend to make irrational or ineffective conclusions from these irrational premises. Their irrational conclusions take the form of: (1) *awfulizing* (meaning more than 100% bad, worse than it absolutely should be); (2) *I-can't-stand-it-itis* or *low frustration tolerance* (the distressed person cannot envision being happy at all if what he or she demands must not exist actually does exist); (3) *damnation* (damning oneself, others, and/or life conditions); and (4) *always and never thinking* (people will insist, for example, that they will always fail or never will be approved by significant others).

When a person's belief is flexible, it is called a rational Belief (rB). A flexible belief takes the form of a desire, wish, or preference that the client does not transmute into a dogmatic "must," "should," "ought," or "have to." When clients adhere to such flexible rational Beliefs, they will tend to make rational, effective conclusions from these rational premises. These conclusions may take the form of evaluations of badness, whereby your client (if you are helping a person suffering from severe anxiety or stress) will conclude, "It's bad but not terrible," rather than, "It's disastrous," when faced with a negative activating event or stressor. A second type of rational conclusion is a statement of toleration. The client may say, "I don't like it, but I can bear it." A third type of rational conclusion is acceptance of fallibility, in which the client will accept himself or herself and other humans as fallible persons who cannot legitimately be given an overall global rating. Also, the client will accept the world and life conditions as complex, composed of good, bad, and neutral elements, and thus will also refrain from giving the world a global rating. A fourth type of rational conclusion is flexible thinking with respect to the occurrence of events. Here your client will refrain from thinking that something will always occur or will never happen. Rather, she or he realizes that most events in the universe can be placed along a continuum from "occurring very rarely" to "occurring very frequently."

C in the ABCDE framework stands for emotional and behavioral consequences of your client's beliefs about A. In REBT the Cs that follow from irrational rigid beliefs about negative As will be disturbed and are called unhealthy negative consequences and Cs that follow from rational flexible beliefs about negative As will be nondisturbed and are termed healthy *negative consequences* (Crawford & Ellis, 1989). Unhealthy negative emotions such as anxiety, depression, rage, shame, guilt, and self-downing are dysfunctional for any one or more of the following reasons: (1) they lead to the experience of needless psychic pain and discomfort; (2) they motivate people to engage in self-defeating behavior; and (3) they prevent people from carrying out behavior necessary to reach their goals.

Conversely, healthy negative emotions such as concern, sadness, annoyance, regret, remorse, and self-acceptance are effective for any one or more of the following reasons: (1) they alert people that their goals are being blocked but they do not immobilize them; (2) they motivate people to engage in constructive, self-helping behavior; and

(3) they encourage people in the successful execution of behavior deemed desirable to reach their goals.

THE THREE MAJOR MUSTS

In REBT the essence of emotional and behavioral disturbance consists of *demandingness* (Ellis, 1984). Unrealistic expectations tend to result from an absolutist perspective—of unrealistic demands as well as from magical thinking instead of rationally assessed preferences and desires. People hold innumerable variations of these core irrational Beliefs and clients will often express their own iBs in personally distinctive terms. However, practically all irrational Beliefs tend to be variations of three "Major Musts."

Major Must 1: Demands about Self

The first major *must* is often stated in these terms: "I *must* do well and be approved by significant others and if I'm not, then it's *awful. I can't stand it* and I am a worthless, damnable person to some degree when I am not loved or when I do not do well." These beliefs often lead to anxiety, depression, shame and guilt.

Major Must 2: Demands about Others

The second major must is often expressed as follows: "*You* must treat me well and justly, and it's awful and I can't bear it when you don't. *You* are rotten and damnable when you don't treat me well and you deserve to be punished for doing what you must not do."

Such beliefs are often associated with anger, rage, passive-aggressiveness, and acts of violence.

Major Must 3: Demands about World/Life Conditions

The third basic must often takes the following form: "Life conditions under which I live absolutely must be the way I want them to be and if they are not, it's terrible. I can't stand it. Poor me!" This belief is associated with feelings of self-pity and hurt, and problems of self-discipline; for example, procrastination and addictive behavior.

It is useful to bear in mind that virtually all iBs are variants of these three Major Musts.

STRESS AND OTHER KINDS OF EMOTIONAL DISTURBANCE

It will be helpful at this point to briefly outline the differences between severe stress reactions and other disturbances. One notable feature that distinguishes stress is the presence of various physiological disorders. These typically comprise disorders that develop or worsen as a direct result of stress, such as hypertension, migraine headaches, stomach ulcers, and lower back pain. A second feature of severe stress reactions is that they tend to follow from some unusually stark and harmful event such as rape, incest, or torture which overwhelms the average person's immediate cognitive resources so they are unable to cope, with the result that the person becomes severely disturbed and unable to live a normal life for some considerable time. Or a person may become physically incapacitated and unable to work for a long period resulting in loss of earnings and possibly loss of a job.

An apparently never-ending series of hassles, misfortunes, or conflicts may also trigger severe stress reactions. Thus, a person suffering from a severe stress reaction can usually identify some particularly noxious event or series of events as the impetus behind his or her particular stress-related syndromes. From the sufferer's point of view this has the disadvantage of encouraging and reinforcing the generally held belief that the stressor(s) in the person's life are the direct cause of his or her distress. The stressed person tends to conclude, "being forced into early retirement long before I'm due to retire gave me an ulcer," or "my boss's constant criticism of my performance is driving me crazy and that is what gives me my migraine headaches."

By contrast, people with strong anxiety-creating tendencies require relatively little in the way of activating events or stressors to trigger their anxiety stress. Their well-established beliefs that some "awful" consequence would ensue if some feared event out of many such possibilities were to actually happen, provides plenty of scope for these people's anxiety-creating tendencies to materialize. As we will show, one of the major aims of rational–emotive behavior therapy is to help the client to understand that the activating event or stressor he or she experiences does not by itself cause the psychophysiological distress, but rather the particular beliefs the person holds about the event.

It is worth mentioning that the stages in the process whereby irrational beliefs lead to the type of psychophysiological disorders discussed above often follow closely Selye's general adaptive syndrome. An activating event in the person's environment starts the process. The person then brings in his or her belief system and evaluates the event: "My life *must* not have so much hassle," or, "It's *terrible* that the company is shedding staff. I'll never find another job" or "I don't deserve to be passed over for promotion. I must get a promotion or else my life will be in ruins." Reiteration of these irrational beliefs causes arousal of the autonomic nervous system (ANS). If arousal of the ANS is continuously maintained, as will tend to happen if the stressed individual constantly recycles his or her irrational beliefs, the weakest systems in the body begin to break down as a result of the prolonged and unrelieved arousal of the ANS. Eventually, breakdown or weakening of the body's immune system can trigger a host of physical disorders and dysfunctional psychological reactions that may persist long after the activating events have ceased to exist (Esterling, Kiecolt-Glaser, Bodnar, & Glaser, 1994).

Finally, once people feel stressed, they may react poorly to the fact of feeling stressed and refuse to acknowledge that they can bear what they experience. They condemn themselves for their poor reactions to stress, make themselves anxious about being anxious, or depressed about their depression, or guilty about their anger. The upshot is that they distress themselves still further by condemning themselves for their "weakness," and create a vicious circle of self-denigration. These second order disturbances may be "discomfort disturbance" or "ego disturbance' " and frequently interact with and aggravate the client's primary disturbance (Ellis, 1994, 1995a).

AN EXAMPLE OF STRESS

Let us take a middle level executive whose work has been restructured following a takeover by a competitor, and who now finds himself grossly overworked. The executive has developed health problems. He cannot cope with the volume of work, he has migraine headaches, and his physician has told him he has hypertension and a suspected stomach ulcer. Nevertheless, this executive is reluctant to confront his boss about reducing his workload in case he loses his job. If according to REBT, the Activating Event or stressor (being overworked) did not directly cause this individual's emotional Consequence (suppressed resentment), what did? Answer: B: His beliefs about the Activating Event or stressor. This executive has two sets of Beliefs.

First, he has a set of rational Beliefs (rBs). These are mainly along the lines of:

> How annoying that my new boss is piling all this extra work on me! If this is the new management's policy I certainly don't think much of it. I don't like being so overloaded with work that I have no time to devote to my private life, and since my health is causing me problems now, I am determined to do something about this unpleasant state of affairs.

These particular Beliefs are rational because they state a desire to alter a state of affairs that is unacceptable. His aim of improving his working and personal life seems achievable and his determination to do so seems eminently sane and rational. As we have pointed out, this executive's feelings are appropriate in the circumstances; he feels annoyed and concerned rather than enraged and anxious. Now, if *he stays with these rational Beliefs* he would tend to act in a determined manner to change the Activating Events in his life if practicable, so that he enjoys a less pressured existence. If he cannot, for the time being, change the A he can learn to put up with it. He doesn't *have to* remain stressed and suffer poor health. However, we know that he feels resentment which he bottles up for fear of losing his job were he to express it, and suffers the consequences: continuing overwork, deteriorating health, and lower quality of life. According to rational–emotive behavior theory, resentment is an unhealthy emotion and springs from a set of irrational Beliefs which would mainly consist of such ideas as: "My boss *must* stop overloading me with so much work. It's *awful* that my health and personal life are deteriorating because of it, and *I can't stand it!* My boss is no good for treating me in this inconsiderate manner and he should be *damned* and punished for doing so!" REBT contends that these irrational Beliefs—the "musturbatory" premise followed by its three conclusions, and *not* the conditions of overwork itself—directly cause this executive's psychophysiological symptoms of resentment: hypertension, migraine headaches, and gastrointestinal problems.

The working conditions in this executive's life can justifiably be described as stressors. They truly exist. These stressors contribute to, but do not cause, his state of suppressed anger or resentment and the ensuing physical ills. Even if the stressors in his job continue to exist he could deal more sanely and satisfactorily with the "stress" he experiences. How? By Disputing his irrational Beliefs, at point D about the stressors he experiences at A.

Disputing Irrational Beliefs

Once your clients accept that the real cause of their stress is their set of irrational Beliefs about the stressors in their lives, the process of restructuring their beliefs can begin. Disputing is a logical and empirical process designed to help clients challenge the validity of their iBs and eventually reach the goal of internalizing a new rational philosophy. This is point E in the ABCDE framework.

REBT treatment strategies focus on teaching clients how to do the following kinds of disputing:

- *Dispute absolute musts:* "Why *must* I be successful and never experience hassles?" *Answer:* "I would very much *prefer* to succeed, but I don't have to. Because it is the nature of normal living today I do have to face many unfortunate hassles and difficulties because that is the way things are. Tough! But it isn't *awful* or *terrible.*"
- *Disputing low frustration tolerance:* "Where is the evidence that I *can't stand* the stressors in life?" *Answer:* "There isn't any! They will hardly kill me and I can be happy in spite of them. They are not *horrible*, merely bearably painful!"
- *Disputing feeling of worthlessness:* "Am I really and truly an inadequate, worthless person if I fail to handle stressful conditions well and even make them worse?" *Answer:* "No way. I am a person who may be acting inadequately or incompetently at this time in this respect but I am never a totally worthless (or good) person, just a fallible human being who is doing my best to cope with difficult conditions."

In the case of the overworked executive, his REBT counselor would show him that there is no reason why his boss *must not* overload him with work (he is the boss!) although it would be highly desirable to reduce the workload. Also, being overworked is undoubtedly a pain in the ass but it isn't a horror, and he can definitely stand it though he'll never like it. And the boss may be acting badly, or perhaps even trying to see how much he can get away with, but he is not a damnable person, merely fallible and ill advised. Once this executive has overcome the "horror" of being overworked, he can assertively request his boss to reduce or restructure the amount of work he is given.

Rational–emotive behavioral theory practitioners employ other cognitive methods as well as emotive and behavioral techniques. These are detailed extensively elsewhere (Dryden, 1987, 1990; Ellis, 1985, 1988, 1995a, 1995b; Ellis & Dryden, 1987). The following methods are used:

Cognitive methods:
Reframing, Referenting the Disadvantages of Dysfunctional Behaviors, Use of Rational Coping Statements, Modeling, Cognitive Distractions, Cognitive Homework, and Semantic Corrections.
Emotive Techniques:
Shame Attacking, Rational–Emotive Imagery (REI), Forceful Coping Statements, Forceful Self-dialogues, Use of Humor, Use of Group Processes and Exercises, Interpersonal Relationships, REBT Role-Playing, Reverse Role-Playing.
Behavioral Techniques of REBT:
In Vivo Desensitization, Remaining in "Awful" Situations, Response Prevention, Penalization, Medication, Skill Training (Assertion, Communication, Relationship, Sex).

Biofeedback and relaxation techniques may be used to reduce levels of tension in order to pave the way for more powerful cognitive and emotive techniques to address the irrational cognitions underlying clients' basic disturbances.

Rational–emotive behavioral therapy uses a considerable number of cognitive, emotive, and behavioral methods to help people make their lives less stressful, and equally important, to manage to live their lives in the face of stressors they cannot change. However, these techniques are used within a theoretical framework to help clients to change their irrational philosophies, and not in a hit-or-miss manner, or as ends in themselves.

Rational–emotive behavioral therapy encourages people to change or improve unpleasant social, work, and environmental conditions, but also to unwhiningly and unconditionally accept themselves, other people, and life conditions when these conditions cannot for the forseeable future be changed, and when tough environmental stressors persist. As Abrams and Ellis (1994) pertinently note, "severe stressors are often inevitable; undue stress about them is not."

REFERENCES

Abrams, M., & Ellis, A. (1994). Rational emotive behavior therapy in the treatment of stress. *British Journal of Guidance and Counselling, 22*(1), 39–50.
Bowers, K. S., & Kelly, P. (1979). Stress, disease, psychotherapy and hypnosis. *Journal of Abnormal Psychology, 88,* 490–505.
Crawford, T., & Ellis, A. (1989). A dictionary of rational–emotive feelings and behaviors. *Journal of Rational–Emotive and Cognitive–Behavior Therapy, 7*(1), 3–27.
Dryden, W. (1987). *Counselling individuals: The rational–emotive approach.* London: Taylor & Francis.
Dryden, W. (1990). *Rational–emotive counselling in action.* London: Sage.
Ellis, A. (1962). *Reason and emotion in psychotherapy.* Secaucus, NJ: Citadel.
Ellis, A. (1978). What people can do for themselves to cope with stress. In C. L. Cooper & R. Payne (Eds.), *Stress at work* (pp. 2209–2222). Chichester & New York: Wiley.
Ellis, A. (1984). The essence of RET. *Journal of Rational–Emotive Therapy, 2*(1), 19–25.
Ellis, A. (1985). Expanding the ABCs of rational-emotive therapy. In M.J. Mahoney & A. Freeman (Eds.), *Cognition and psychotherapy.* New York: Plenum.
Ellis, A. (1988). *How to stubbornly refuse to make yourself miserable about anything—Yes, anything!* Secaucus, NJ: Lyle Stuart.
Ellis, A. (1991). The revised ABCs of rational-emotive therapy. In J. Zeig (Ed.), *Evolution of Psychotherapy:* Vol. 11. New York: Brunner/Mazel. (Expanded version in *Journal of Rational–Emotive and Cognitive–Behavior Therapy,* 1991, *9*(3), 139–272.
Ellis, A. (1994). *Reason and emotion in psychotherapy.* (revised). New York: Carol.
Ellis, A. (1995a). *Better, deeper, and more enduring.* New York: Brunner/Mazel.
Ellis, A. (1995b). Fundamentals of REBT for the 1990s. In W. Dryden (Ed.), *Rational–emotive behavior therapy: A reader.* London: Sage.
Ellis, A., & Abrahms, E. (1978). *Brief psychotherapy in medical and health practice.* New York: Springer.
Ellis, A., & Dryden, W. (1987). *The practice of rational–emotive therapy.* New York: Springer.
Ellis, A., & Whiteley, J. M. (1979). *Theoretical and empirical foundations of rational–emotive therapy.* Monterey, CA: Brooks/Cole.
Esterling, B. A., Kiecolt-Glaser, J. K., Bodnar, J. C., & Glaser, R. (1994). Chronic Stress, social support, and persistent alterations in the natural killer cell response to cytokines in older adults. *Health Psychology, 13*(4), 291–298.
French, J. R. P. (1973). Person–role fit. *Occupational Mental Health. 3,* 15–20.
Goldberg, L., & Comstock, G. W. (1976). Life events and subsequent illness. *American Journal of Epidemiology, 104,* 146–158.
Handy, C. (1985). *The future of work.* Oxford, U.K.: Blackwell.
Holmes, T. H., & Rahe, R. H. (1967). The social readjustment rating scale. *Journal of Psychosomatic Research, 11,* 213–218.
Kahn, R. L., Wolfe, D. M., Quinn, R. P., Snoek, J. D., & Rosenthal, R. A. (1964). *Organizational stress.* New York: Wiley.

Klarreich, S. H. (1985). Stress: An interpersonal approach. In S. H. Klarreich, J. L. Francek, & C. E. Moore (Eds.), *The human resources handbook* (pp. 304–318). New York: Praeger.

Lazarus, R. S., & Launier, R. (1978). Stress-related transactions between person and environment. In L. A. Pervin & M. Lewis (Eds.), *Perspectives in interactional psychology* (pp. 59–86). New York: Plenum.

McGrath, J. E. (1976). Stress and behavior in organizations, In M. Dunnette (Ed.), *Handbook of industrial and organizational psychology* (pp. 58–79). Chicago: Rand-McNally.

Roskies, E. (1983). Stress management: Averting the evil eye. *Contemporary Psychology*, 28(7), 542–544.

Toffler, A. (1971). *Future shock.* New York: Bantam.

Toffler, A. (1980). *The third wave.* London: Collins.

Wagenaar, J., & La Forge, J. (1994). Stress counselling theory and practice: A cautionary review. *Journal of Counselling and Development*, 73(3), 23–31.

11.

Wellness in the Workplace: A Fourfold Path

F. MICHLER BISHOP, Ph.D., CAS

How can mental health professionals enhance wellness in the workplace? Those of us who practice cognitive–behavioral therapy or rational–emotive behavior therapy (REBT) utilize three types of techniques in helping people and ourselves better manage our lives. All of the techniques interconnect and interact, so focusing on one inevitably involves the others. People can work on themselves by using:

- Cognitive techniques—We can observe and work on the way we think. Unlike other organisms on the planet, humans have the unique ability to think about their thinking. We can work at uncovering the beliefs and ways of thinking which may be contributing to our emotional distress and which may be undermining our efforts to behave differently.
- Emotive techniques—We can work more directly on our emotions, learning to be more aware of what we feel both psychologically and physically, and learning to better express our feelings. Such techniques include methods to evoke emotions in those of us who have difficulty feeling what we feel.
- Behavioral techniques—And we can choose to work on practicing different behaviors from those we are conditioned or accustomed to perform. Naturally, the way we think and feel about a particular behavior changes as we practice it (or cease practicing it).

I have subtitled this chapter "A Fourfold Path" because many people also affirm that there is a fourth and essential way of working on oneself, a spiritual path, something that means many different things to different people, but which may significantly affect how we think and feel about ourselves, our lives, and our world and what we do, that is, how we behave. So I have included "spiritual techniques," although as I will discuss later, most "spiritual techniques" can be looked at as cognitive, emotive, and behavioral techniques.

The thesis of this chapter is that we can help people work on wellness in the workplace when we honor the interactiveness of our thoughts, feelings, and behaviors. The chapter focuses on the first three ways of working on ourselves. However, if spirituality or religious beliefs play a central role in our clients' lives and ways of thinking and believing, it is quite easy to show how spiritual beliefs are not necessarily in conflict with cognitive, emotive, and behavioral approaches to wellness (cf. Ellis, 1992, 1994b; Robb, 1993; Young, 1989).

During training workshops, I use the following diagram to talk about the way our thoughts, feelings, and behaviors interact:

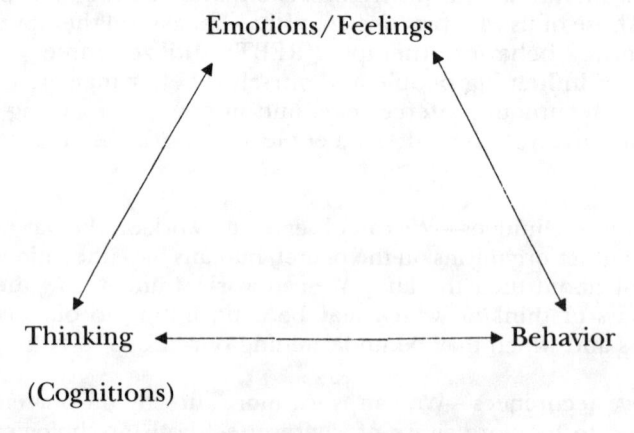

Emotions/Feelings

Thinking ←——————→ Behavior

(Cognitions)

For example, stop for a moment and think about something sad that has happened recently in your life. If you dwell on that event long enough, you will notice that you begin to feel sad as well. If you continue this exercise for very long, you may also change your behavior. You may begin to stare out the window or you may get up, stretch, get a cup of coffee, or make a telephone call. This is just a simple example that demonstrates ways in which what we think about immediately affects our feelings which subsequently affects our behaviors.

Similarly, if the telephone rings and we answer it and talk a long time, when we hang up, this change in behavior may lead us to think,

"I didn't want to talk so long," and as a result, we may find that we feel annoyed or discouraged.

A little reflection and observation reveals that we cannot think about anything without feeling something and that such feelings (and thoughts) usually lead to new behaviors, about which we will have some thoughts and feelings. Recent work by Rauch and his associates (Rauch, Jenike et al., 1994; Rauch, Savage et al., 1995) using positron emission tomography (PET) with people suffering from simple phobias and from obsessive–compulsive disorder (OCD) reveals significant changes in cerebral blood flow upon, in some cases, touching a "provocative" object, or, in other cases, simply thinking about it. In the case of the OCD patients, once provoked they remained aroused for several hours. This research adds support to the notion that thinking can cause dramatic changes in blood flow in the brain and that these changes (and the feelings that patients experience at the same time) can endure for hours. Such feelings, of course, often cause further changes in thinking and behavior. Hence, all thoughts, feelings, and behaviors appear intimately and inextricably interactive and interwoven. If you want further evidence, get yourself hooked up to a biofeedback machine which shows your level of relaxation (or tension and anxiety) as a line on a computer screen. As you try to relax, have someone say to you: "Can I ask you something personal?" The line reflecting your internal state will instantly jump. Merely asking such a question creates a dramatic change in your neurological and physiological system.

Ellis (cf. 1994a), for the past 40 years, has been one of the strongest advocates of the idea that our thinking affects our emotions and behavior. Rational–emotive behavior therapy (REBT), which he (1994c) recently renamed to reflect each of its three components, encourages people to use a variety of cognitive, emotive, and behavioral techniques to lead fuller, happier lives. Having worked with REBT for the past 10 years, I have been convinced of the usefulness of using all three types of techniques and this chapter reflects that work.

THE ROLE OF CHEMICALS

Chemicals clearly affect the way we think, feel, and act. So are chemicals a fifth way of working on oneself? Some religions use chemicals for a variety of spiritual purposes. In the late 1960s, LSD and other chemicals were championed as "mind expanders" and "consciousness raisers," but many religious groups and esoteric schools eschew the use of chemicals, including, for some, even the use of mild stimulants like tea and coffee.

However, most of us routinely turn to chemicals to change the way we feel. We eat snacks and meals to keep our energy flowing. We use coffee, tea, alcohol, sugar, betel, coca leaves, tobacco, and other substances for an added boost. In fact, some clients who have used chemicals so often to affect the way they feel have rarely practiced other techniques. The cognitive, emotive, and behavioral techniques discussed in this chapter and elsewhere take longer to work, take practice, are harder to use, and don't always appear to work. Hence, chemicals will always have considerable appeal.

On the other hand, while routinely using chemicals may impede our development, under some circumstances they may be helpful while we are learning new techniques, and such chemicals as Prozac, Xanax, etc., are widely used. Although some people report benefits from using LSD, peyote, and other drugs, many others appear to benefit little if at all, and some are undoubtedly harmed. Therefore, I have not included chemicals as another or fifth way of working on oneself.

INDIVIDUAL VS. ORGANIZED GROUP EFFORTS TOWARD WELLNESS IN THE WORKPLACE

Returning to our initial question, How can mental health professionals work to improve wellness in the workplace? it is clear that this chapter will focus on how individuals can work on themselves. However, unquestionably there are powerful economic, social, and political factors which also have as large if not a larger impact on wellness.

In the United States, the land of the "self-made man," the notion of individual responsibility is often taken to an extreme, downplaying the impact of social, political, and economic factors. As the United States moves toward an even more conservative political stance, the message is broadcast everyday: Responsible men and women take care of themselves, finding ways to make a new living when they are downsized. This is, of course, partly true, but it does not take into account that many people may not be, by nature, so proactive, creative, and entrepreneurial, and even if they are, the opportunities simply may not exist.

Do mental health professionals who are truly interested in wellness have an ethical responsibility to become more aware of the historical, cultural, political, economic, and social factors which have had a dramatic impact on workplace wellness? Historically, there is evidence that our beliefs about who is responsible for worker wellness have been systematically manipulated in the media (cf. Rowland, 1983). Have we as mental health professionals—especially psychologists who routinely focus on individuals over groups (with the exception sometimes of family systems)—accepted the belief that responsibility for wellness ultimately resides in the individual? Where did this assumption come from? Historically, whose end did it (does it) serve, and to what extent is it valid? At the end of the 19th century and in the early 20th century, considerable time and effort were expended to place the responsibility for wellness on the individual. If an accident occurred, it was because the individual broke a rule or behaved carelessly. It was not the company's responsibility. However, the advent of white lung, repetitive motion disorders, and other diseases that directly result from working conditions have raised questions about such an attitude.

Ignoring such questions and encouraging people to take on sole responsibility for their health may cause us to collude with forces which have little if any interest in wellness, except in terms of productivity. Politically and economically, many white collar workers in the 50 years following World War II took health insurance and pensions for granted, totally unaware that such benefits were unheard of for both white and blue collar workers until blue collar, unionized workers demanded them. Subsequently, white collar managers also demanded them, and those benefits, which had an indisputably positive effect on wellness, became the norm. Now, at the end of the 20th century, white collar workers in many parts of the country are being forced to accept jobs without such benefits, resigned to the fact that they have no options, and believing that this added stress to their current life (for example, in the form of no health insurance) and their future life (no pensions) is unavoidable—and unwilling to object in any organized manner about such added stresses to their lifestyle. Yet just the thought of losing one's job increases anxiety and affects one's behavior and has an impact on wellness, as a series of *New York Times* articles (1996) has highlighted.

On the other hand, just as some modern psychologists see the cause of many mental and emotional problems as stemming from underlying irrational beliefs, schemas, or cognitive distortions, similarly our ability to affect political, social, and economic change is also heavily impacted by our beliefs. If we believe that we cannot affect change, we will not try to affect change—in our workplaces or within ourselves. Currently, in Manhattan, the pressure on white collar employees to work every evening and on weekends is so pervasive that some people are beginning to take it as the norm, even if it is unhealthy for them. In the late 19th century and early 20th century, those working in coal mines in areas with no unions thought of themselves as practically powerless to affect their wellness. The first task faced by union organizers was to change workers' perceptions of their ability to effect change.

Because wellness results from a number of interacting factors, some internal to the individual and many external, maintaining our wellness in the workplace cannot solely be a function of working on ourselves. It is also a function of our willingness to work to change the larger systems in which we work and live.

COGNITIVE APPROACHES

It is interesting to note that much of what is espoused under the rubric of cognitive behavioral therapy is not new. Over 2,500 years ago, the Buddha also primarily relied on working on one's thinking and behavior, and Ellis (1994a) has based his work on stoics such as Epictetus and Marcus Aurelius. Buddhism was not a religion in the traditional sense; it was a path out of suffering and, ultimately, to a new spiritual place (Conze, 1959). The Buddha is quoted as saying (Int. Buddhist Inf. & Res. Ctr., 1993):

> Our life is shaped by our mind; we become
> what we think. Suffering follows evil
> thought as the wheels of a cart follow the oxen
> that draw it.
> Our life is shaped by our mind; we become what we think.
> Joy follows a pure thought like a shadow that never leaves.
>
> "He abused me, he beat me,
> he defeated me, he robbed me,"
> in those who harbor such thoughts
> hatred is not brought to an end.
>
> "He abused me, he beat me,
> he defeated me, he robbed me,"
> in those not harboring such thoughts
> hatred is brought to an end.

For hatred never ceases here
by means of further hatred.
By love alone does hatred cease—
this is an eternal law. (p. 2)

This fickle, unsteady mind, difficult to guard, difficult to control, the wise man makes
straight, as the fletcher straightens the arrow.
Hard to control, unstable is this mind; it flits wherever it list. Good is it to subdue the
mind. A subdued mind brings happiness.
Difficult to grasp, exceedingly subtle is this mind. It is ever in quest of delight. Let the wise man keep watch over it. A guarded mind brings happiness.
Whatever harm a foe may do,
or one enemy to another,
a wrongly directed mind can do
far greater harm than that.

Neither mother nor father
nor other relative can do so much good;
a rightly directed mind can do
far greater good than that. (pp. 2–3)

But the notion that we can work on our thinking and change and, to some extent, control our thinking is new to many people. They have accepted what modern psychology textbooks tell them: "The brain does this . . . , the brain does that . . . " No doubt our brain *does* function in many important ways outside of our awareness or ability to affect it. However, such people do not see that they can, to some extent, control some of the ways their brain functions, and thereby, affect the way they feel and behave.

I have found in my work that convincing people that they *can* affect the way they think and feel is often *central* to the problem of change. Miller and his associates (Miller & Rollnick, 1991) have focused on the motivational aspects of change, and the model of change developed by Prochaska, DiClemente, and Norcross (1992) provides an effective tool for mental health workers and their clients, suggesting that change is a recursive process involving many steps forward and back. But the main problem as we help people help themselves often centers on motivating them to start and to continue. While we may be convinced that cognitive, emotive, and behavioral techniques are very effective, we must convince our clients, as well, of their efficacy.

As Prochaska, DiClemente, and Norcross have suggested, many people do not start working on changing because they do not believe they can change and/or they do not know how to begin.

Helping people understand why they behave the way they do often helps them begin to take the first steps toward changing such behavior. Hence, all good therapy sessions or workshops focus on three factors: (1) motivating for change; (2) examining the "why"; and (3) teaching the "how"—cognitive, emotive, and behavioral techniques. Even psychoanalysis, which places so much value on understanding the "why," was very popular at one time (and, in many countries, continues to be embraced with great enthusiasm) partly because it offered hope (i.e., motivated people) as well as techniques.

Building on the Known

The basis of cognitive therapy is that we can change our thinking and that by changing our thinking, we can change the way we feel and act. But, as noted above, the very idea of manipulating one's thinking is new to some people. Nevertheless, they could not have gotten through life without using and manipulating the way they think. They are just unaware that they can do it intentionally and also get better at it with practice.

We can quite easily and quickly make people aware that they routinely manipulate their thinking—often for the purpose of planning, but also sometimes with the specific goal of altering their feelings. Most people are familiar with figuring out in their head what they intend to say to someone—or what they wished they had said! All of us use daydreaming to alter our feelings; for example, for a few minutes at our desks during the cold winter, we may stop to think about a vacation on a warm island in the Caribbean. It immediately affects our mood. In one case, when I was working with a telephone installer who was about to get fired because he frequently lost his temper on the job, we discovered that as the pitcher on his baseball team, he used self-talk and a variety of other cognitive strategies to "concentrate" when he was on the mound. Once aware that he controlled his thinking and feelings on the mound (so as to control his pitching), he was more open to and motivated to use cognitive, emotive, and behavioral techniques to help himself on the job.

Deconditioning Knee-Jerk Thinking

That we can be conditioned is obvious. As a result, many of our reactions are in effect conditioned responses. In the face of a challenging situation, our heart rate increases and our belly tenses without our hardly noticing it. The first feelings that rush through and over us happen like a blush—quickly, with little noticeable thinking. Cognitive processing that occurs so rapidly that I have labeled it "knee-jerk thinking" highlights the fact that it happens with seemingly no possibility of intervention to slow it down or stop it, like the knee jerk stimulated by a doctor hitting our knee with a hammer during a routine physical.

How can we change such thinking if it occurs so fast? Techniques such as desensitization, progressive relaxation, and hypnosis help people decondition such reactions and learn to respond differently. But the likelihood is that many people may still initially respond in the same way. Therefore, it is helpful to focus on *time*. Even if conditioned responses occur, we can learn to accept them while learning to reduce *their duration* (for example, in minutes), and while learning new, more helpful responses.

Recently I was working with a woman who has always had extramarital affairs and spends a great deal of time and energy ensuring that she has more than one man in her life. When one of them stopped returning her calls, she at first immediately felt "hurt," "abandoned," and "anxious," but then she told me she said to herself: "I don't have to feel this way. That's just my 'knee-jerk thinking' kicking in—with the feelings that go with it. There may be lots of reasons that he is not calling. He *is* married and has other obligations. It may not just be because I'm not pretty enough. I don't always have to feel hurt and rejected. I *do* have other friends in my life, so I don't *have* to have his attention." Then she said she not only felt better—"less at the mercy of all the bad things in life," but also more hopeful that she would be able to be less obsessive and dependent in the future.

Using Analogies with Other Organs

In workshops and in session, to heighten people's awareness of their ability to affect the functioning of various organs in their body, I ask them to speed up their heart rate. Most people look blank. But if they simply raise their arms or talk, their pulse will increase.

Lungs may be the best analogy for the brain. In India, breathing has been studied and used in many different exercises for a variety of behavioral, cognitive, and spiritual reasons. But most of the time we breathe without thinking about it. Nevertheless, many of us have learned to change our breathing for a variety of reasons. For example, as a child, I practiced many hours learning to hold my breath so that I could stay under the water while swimming for longer time periods. Later in life, I learned deep diaphragmatic breathing in order to relax when I was tense.

Similarly, most of the time we pay little attention to how our brain is functioning. We just drive the car or watch the television or write the chapter of the book. But when some of us get stuck we stare out of the window for a few minutes because we have learned that this state—staring—somehow has a beneficial effect on the way we process information; new ideas will come which if they are actively sought after, do not. Similarly, we "consciously" sit and think (imagine) ways we might develop new aspects of our businesses or use our time more effectively. Some of my acquaintances use meditation to help themselves cope with the stresses of everyday life in New York City, and others used guided imagery, visualization, or rational–emotive imagery (Maultsby, 1971) to work on problems in their lives. In each of these cases, we intervene and purposely, intentionally, guide the use of our mental powers or abilities.

Using Our Internal VCR

Playing Different Videotapes

The invention of the television and especially of the VCR provides us with a powerful analog. It is obvious to most people that if they watch a horror film, they may feel tense, scared, and perhaps even horrified. And if they watch the comedy channel, they feel lighter, more cheerful, "better," and if they watch pornography, they feel titillated or disgusted. It is not so obvious to them that they sometimes play the same "videotapes," for example, of an argument they have had with their boss, repeatedly, and then complain that they are still upset.

Can we choose to play different videotapes and thus manipulate the way we feel? Clearly, when we plan a vacation we think about various trips, and about various places we could visit. We imagine the beaches or cities we might visit, and we begin to get excited about the trip.

But at other times, we seem to get stuck playing the same videotapes over and over again. Why do we get stuck? There are several possible answers. As noted before, some people do not conceive of their thinking as something that can be manipulated, so they do not attempt to intervene. Or some people think it would be fraudulent or phony to play other videotapes. They deeply believe that what they are thinking about they *should* be thinking about. That is, many people ruminate and worry because deep down they think it makes sense. They have a big problem, and they have learned to think to solve problems.

Recently I was working with an attractive, 40-year-old man who had had a problem with alcohol but had stopped drinking, was going to AA, and was beginning to live a less anxiety ridden life. He worked for one of the major New York networks and frequently got himself very depressed over the "slimy" programming that he had to help produce. He kept thinking about the things his equally "slimy" boss had said and "looking" at various scenes from recent past shows in his head. Everything he was thinking about or imaging was negative.

I suggested that humans have an immense capacity to stress and ignore various stimuli both internal and external to them. At the time he was only playing the negative videotapes—he was only looking at the negative in his life. "But thinking about positive things seems really stupid, even fraudulent to me," he objected. I could see his point. He had a serious problem and to not focus on it seemed irresponsible to him. "Is dwelling on this problem helping?" I asked. "No. I'm driving myself insane. I'm going to crack up soon," he responded. "Will playing these videotapes repeatedly help?" He agreed they would not. "I am not urging you to think only of the positive aspects of your life, but isn't it clear that the balance is out of whack. You are just looking at horror films and feeling horrible! What could you put your mind on or become engaged in that might 'change the channel'—to mix metaphors?"

Slot Machine Thinking

When we ruminate about "slimy" working conditions, crazy bosses, or "insane" corporate rules, we may also do so because we believe that if we run the problem through our heads once more, we will come up with a solution. (And we may also be secretly holding tightly onto some of our favorite irrational beliefs: "I have to find a solution. I should be able to find a solution. If I can't find a solution, there's something wrong with me.") Like slot machine players, we believe that ruminating will eventually pay off. And we may be right—if we ruminate long enough! If we sit in front a slot machine long enough, it will pay off. But what are the odds and what are the costs?

Helping people see that ruminating may work but at a very high cost helps motivate them to seek other paths to solving a problem. When they can see that they are using "slot machine thinking" to solve a problem, they often begin to be open to other problem-solving techniques. Such techniques will not be as easy or as well practiced, but they offer better odds—better payoffs for less cost.

Other Factors

It is also helpful to point out the possible evolutionary, historical, and developmental factors which may underlie various behaviors and make them more resistant to change.

Evolution

Those of our ancestors who worried all of the time and remained hypervigilant even while others were relaxing around the fire at the end of the day, may have survived longer. They heard the snap of a twig that signaled the approach of danger and they stored up more grain to protect against hunger in the future. When clients are attempting to understand their constant worrying and vigilance, they may stop putting themselves down so much when they recognize that such behavior may have had value for survival at some point in the past. And if such behaviors are programmed into us, it makes sense to be patient as we try to overcome 4 million years of genetic programming! But, of course, that is what is wonderful about humans and what makes working to help people change so enjoyable. We are not solely determined by genetic factors. (In fact, even height is not solely determined by genes, otherwise the sons and daughters of immigrants to this country would not have been consistently taller and bigger than their parents.) Unlike other organisms on this planet, we are conscious that we are conscious and therefore can transcend some of our genetic givens.

Historical

Historically, most people never had to manage their lives in anything but the simplest ways (many of us carry around the idea that we needn't learn how to manage it now). Only a very small minority of people could actually steer the course of their lives. The vast majority had only very limited options. Once having chosen a path, if they had a choice at all, they had to stick to it for the rest of their lives. Most people's fathers and mothers were peasants or farmers and they became peasants or farmers. Some people chose the military or the clergy to escape such a fate, but once having chosen it, they had few opportunities to change their mind. There were always, of course, some people who pulled up stakes and moved on to what they hoped would be greener pastures, but they were the minority, and once having moved, they often had to stick with their choice or die. There were some wealthy people who had some choices, but even in their case, who they married and what they did with their lives was largely determined for them. And even today many people outside the economically developed countries do not have many, if any, options available to them.

So this fact of being able to manage one's life, to change course if one is not happy, is a relatively new phenomenon and one unique to advanced economic development. Ironically, it can have two effects: People have many opportunities throughout their lives to try to live a better life. But they can also easily upset themselves with the range of opportunities available and their perceived failure to take advantage of them or to have decided correctly.

Humans are unique in the sense that they can imagine or envision alternative futures and alternative pasts. This is our great power, enabling us, for example, to create works of art, conceive of and build libraries, study for 6 to 10 years in order to practice a profession, etc. But like most other human qualities, our ability to imagine alternatives is a double-edged sword. We can lie awake at night creating waves of anticipated anxiety—"What if I pick the wrong thing and fail?" or depressive thinking, "I should be more like Jack. He takes the initiative. I never do. What's wrong with me?"

So wellness can be affected by the diversity of our options—or at least from the running commentary in our heads about how we are dealing or not dealing with the opportunities that life presents us with.

Development

Clients are also helped to become more accepting of their behaviors when they see that the behaviors that seem dysfunctional at their current point in life had significant value at another stage in their development. A woman I treated once was very submissive and quiet. When she saw that such behaviors had helped her survive in a violent, alcoholic household, she was more accepting of herself, and more willing to do the long hard work to learn new, more assertive ways of interacting with people, especially authority figures.

Similarly, the way we think at 40 is not the way we think at 25. If we lose a job at 25, it is easy to be hopeful and to say to ourselves, "I'll get another one soon," or "Maybe I'll change my mind about my career." But at 40 it is not easy to think in a similar fashion. It is much more common to think, "Oh, my god, what am I going to do. I'm doomed."

EMOTIVE APPROACHES

People do not readily accept the idea that they can to a large degree take responsibility for their emotions, for their emotional life. For many, their emotions are like the weather—outside of their control. They just have to bear with the "sunny" days and the "Monday morning blues." They do not believe that they can change their emotions or that they can choose to feel differently.

Selling them on such a radical idea requires just that—selling. They may resist. They may suspect that if they are responsible for how they feel, then they are responsible for all of the feelings they have ever felt—and the things they have done because of those feelings. They will not quickly want to embrace such an idea! It is also clearly easier to just emote and not have to think about whether we, in fact, *have* to emote this way or that. And, of course, it is much easier to blame someone or something else for how we feel. We can use a four-step process to help people take more responsibility for their emotional life.

Step 1: Note I:

We cannot begin to change something that we are unaware of. Many people have to begin the process of taking more responsibility for how they feel by observing more carefully what they are feeling, and to what degree, as they move through the day. (Of course, this is not a new concept. "Awareness workshops" were very popular in the 1960s but soon lost their appeal and were finally buried with the "touchy feely" epitaph.) Men and women who are unaware of how they feel are more vulnerable either to not being able to express themselves, or to passive–aggressive behavior which usually antagonizes people, and to emotional outbursts. Because they cannot feel how they feel, they miss the fact that they are, for example, becoming more and more angry—until it is too late and they explode. Two exercises are particularly helpful:

Taking Our Emotional Temperature

Between 0 and 10, where 0 is suicidal and 10 is euphoric, how do you feel right now? On average, we would expect to find the answer cycling around 5; that is, 5 would be the norm. But sometimes, because of various changes in hormonal secretions and because of the vicissitudes of life, we may find that the answer is 3 or 4 or 6 or 7. And on occasion, we may experiences 0's, 1's, and 2's and 8's, 9's, and 10's.

Some people, for a variety of reasons, may be lucky to feel most frequently in the 6 and 7 range. Other people, unfortunately, come up most frequently with 3's or 4's. Those people may be suffering from dysthymia, that is to say, chronic, low grade depression.

Some people strive continually for 9's and 10's, ignoring the fact that life is always in flux. Research (cf. Goleman, 1992) suggests that on average, people feel blue about 3 out of 10 days. Refusing to accept the ups and downs in one's moods is a surefire formula for more depression and anxiety, and may lead to a greater use of drugs to change, moderate, and modify what is thought of as unacceptable.

Evocative Techniques

Most of the people who come to the Institute for Rational–Emotive Thinking in New York are overemoting. That is, they are having panic attacks, are very depressed, or are getting angry at many things and people in their lives. But some people are what I call "underemoters." Computer operators, engineers, and lawyers sometimes fall into this group. Kets de Vries (1993) suggests that corporate culture may value and promote such people, and that there is a connection between alexithymia and the "organization man" mentality. Men are often oversocialized to express anger when they actually feel (but deny feeling) ashamed, guilty, anxious, or depressed. In contrast, women, many of whom have been oversocialized against anger, may report feelings of depression, anxiety, and guilt when, to an outsider, it would seem more reasonable to feel angry. But they cannot or will not feel (or report) that emotion. For underemoters, we need to employ emotional evocative techniques, such as shame attacks (cf. Ellis) and emotional awareness exercises as discussed by Farrell and Shaw (1994).

Step 2: Name It

The problem at this step is that many people use a very limited emotional vocabulary. They say they feel "bad" or "upset" or "frustrated" when they may mean angry, depressed, anxious, tense, etc. However, they do not use those words. In addition, they do not use more moderate terms such as *irritated, annoyed, concerned,* etc. We can help them by giving them techniques to expand their emotional vocabulary.

Pick a time of day, for example, when you are waiting for a telephone call to go through or when you are waiting for an elevator. Ask yourself: How am I feeling? But don't accept a "head answer." For example, when you ask "How am I feeling?" don't accept, "I feel that they should have given me that promotion." That is a *thought,* not a *feeling.* In fact, whenever you start with "I feel that ... ," you will probably come out with a thought not a feeling.

Carry a card around with you with healthy negative and positive emotional states on one side—like *irritated, angry, concerned, alert, calm, pleased, happy, disappointed, sad,* and on the other side, emotional states that frequently make matters worse like *rageful, anxious, ashamed, humiliated, depressed, hopeless, helpless.* If you cannot tell how you feel, look at the card.

Usually we feel a stew of emotions; that is, it is not normal to feel just one pure emotion. We may, for example, experience a "bittersweet" feeling when our child goes to school or daycare for the first time: We are happy that he or she is maturing and moving ahead as we want them to, but we are a little sad to see them growing up so fast and a bit apprehensive about what the future in school holds for them.

Ronald Levant (Levant & Kopecky, 1995) suggests sitting down and writing as many emotional words as you can think of in 2 minutes, repeating the exercise every day until emotional terms come to you quickly and easily.

Step 3: Choose It

Many people make themselves feel very bad when they do something wrong, and they berate themselves inside their heads—"I'm such a jerk! How could I have been so stupid?! I always get things wrong" —creating feelings of shame, anxiety, depression, hopelessness, anger, etc. They know they do not like these emotions, but do not know what they *would* like. So I ask people that question in my office. I suggest that not knowing what they would like to feel is a little bit like starting off on a trip without knowing where you are going. Occasionally someone in my office says "calm" or "serene," and I point out that being calm or serene is pretty difficult in New York City! We can then discuss what might be more reasonable and reachable. For example, recently a client was going for a job interview. His firm was being downsized and he was looking for a way to get out before being asked to leave. He wanted to be "calm" in the interview; we worked toward feeling "concerned, alert, and engaged," because "calm" seemed inappropriate in something as important as a job interview.

Step 4: Practice It

Lastly, we have to practice to become more aware of how we feel and change how we have been conditioned to feel. Many books on cognitive–behavioral therapy and REBT (e.g., Burns, 1980; DiMattia & Mennen, 1990; Ellis, 1995; Ellis & Becker, 1982; Ellis and Harper, 1975; Ellis and Vega, 1990) outline such techniques, so I will not discuss them here.

BEHAVIORAL TECHNIQUES

So far, we have discussed the possibilities and benefits of wellness for teaching people to change the way they think about situations and take more responsibility for their emotional life. Now we turn to behavioral approaches.

Deep Diaphragmatic Breathing

It often surprises me how few people know deep diaphragmatic breathing, and among those who know how to do it, how few actually do it. Yet, in my office, whenever I ask them to do it, they immediately feel "better"—calmer, more at ease, less tense physically, less neurologically agitated.

It is helpful to point out to clients two facts. First, once we have learned deep breathing, we can do it in less than a minute at our desk, or waiting for the elevator, or sitting on the subway. It does not have to be something that we have to add to our already crammed schedule. Yet the results of three to five deep, diaphragmatic breaths is dramatic. Second, we can do these exercises without other people noticing. That is, it is possible to take one or two deep, slow breaths while we are sitting in an interview or in a tense business meeting or waiting on a stage to give a speech. Once people realize that they can use this technique surreptitiously, easily, and quickly, they may be motivated to do so.

Progressive Muscle Relaxation

It is also surprising that so many people do not know or use any progressive muscle relaxation techniques. Here again, the exercises are easy to learn and easy to use. While it may be preferable to take 20 minutes at some point during the day, that is completely unnecessary to reap significant benefits. Simply stopping for one minute at one's desk, raising one's shoulders slowly as high (and as close to one's ears) as possible and then releasing (slowly and gently) can relieve the tension that almost always builds in people's necks and shoulders as they work at the computer or on the telephone. Such chronic tension, if never relieved, can lead to intense lower back pain, pinched nerves in the neck, and other debilitating ailments.

Over the past 10 years, we have been bombarded by media campaigns (newspaper and magazine articles, TV and radio news programs, etc.) urging us to stop drinking while driving, to stop smoking, to eat less fatty foods, and to exercise more. And many people have made dramatic changes in their behaviors because of these public relations campaigns. In fact, millions more people have stopped smoking because of the media and legislation than have done so as a result of individual or group therapy. Consequently, if we truly want to increase wellness in the workplace, we need to pay attention to these examples. How can we increase the number of people who take three deep breaths while they are waiting for the elevator? How can we convince bosses that 15 minutes of sleep in the afternoon at one's desk or in a special "power nap" room increases productivity in the afternoon (and may also reduce accident rates) (cf. Markels, 1995). How can we convince people to do one minute of progressive muscle relaxation exercises at their desks every 2 hours?

Clearly many people are eager to learn, otherwise the popularity of self-help books of all kinds would not be so great. *The 7 Habits of Successful People* (Covey, 1989), containing many cognitive, emotive, and behavioral ideas, has remained for years on the best-seller list. But while many people believe in taking courses in better management techniques and go to a gym regularly, they are still resistant to the idea of better managing their emotional life.

Time Management

Most of us realize sooner or later that our most valuable resource is our time, and, as a result, we begin to try to figure out how to improve the way we use time. However, courses and books on time management often fail to address one of the key underlying problems: the irrational beliefs that prevent people from continuing to study how to become better at time management. To learn how to manage our time wisely is difficult, requires practice, and most irritating of all, takes time! Many people have told me that after an initial phase of great enthusiasm, they have stopped using the techniques. Is this because the costs outweigh the benefits? My experience suggests that it is because they are telling themselves something like: "It shouldn't be this hard. It won't work anyway. I have too much to do."

Coming to work and just starting to work without prioritizing our time is not surprising. Humans learn patterns or groups of behaviors which we can run off with little conscious attention, freeing our minds for other work. Hence, upon sitting down at our desks, it is not surprising that we begin to make telephone calls or write memos, etc., without first stopping to think about how to organize our day. It is even less surprising that we do not interrupt our chain of behaviors to reprioritize. Many of us, once we get going, keep going, as long as we are at our desks. Once people recognize this phenomenon—what I call "psychological momentum"—they may be more willing to take the attention and energy required to interrupt their activity, to pause and rethink the use of the time remaining in the day.

Recently I was helping a 32-year-old man who works for a brokerage firm. He constantly feels as if he is overwhelmed. Despite twice promising to use 5 minutes at least three times per day to rethink and restrategize his use of the day, he had not done so. We used the ABC technique and his heightened awareness of how he was feeling (as the result of some emotive homework exercises) to ferret out the problem.

Activating event: Entering the office; intends to prioritize the day.
Consequences: Tight feeling in stomach. Feelings of hopelessness and helplessness.
Beliefs: This is pointless. I won't keep at it *(as I must)*. I've never succeeded at this in the past *(so I won't succeed at it now or in the future)*. I don't have time. I can't stand this feeling of discomfort.

In the past, he had abused alcohol and later Xanax to cope with his feelings of anxiety and discomfort. He has not used those chemicals for 4 years and has developed a much greater ability to stand frustration and discomfort than in the past, but he believes that it is the feelings of discomfort that ultimately derail his intent to plan the day. If he reaches for the phone and starts working, the discomfort goes away along with the self-downing and self-doubting thoughts. He starts to roll!

He further reports that he often seems to simply forget about his goal. He just enters his office and starts working. In order to break that pattern, just before he leaves in the evening, he now puts his telephone in the middle of his desk as a mnemonic device; he has to move it to start work. He has also used rational–emotive imagery (Maultsby, 1971) and guided visualization: After moving the telephone, he sits and visualizes a dial, a dial that is "connected" to his anxiety, tension, and discomfort. He slowly turns down his anxiety and tension. Then he begins his planning for the day.

Reducing Alcohol and Substance Use/Abuse/Dependency

Many mental health practitioners cling to the idea that alcohol and substance abuse is a disease and therefore outside their purview; their main role is to get people into treatment and into attending AA or NA meetings. Currently from 3 to 7% of adults in the country are severely dependent on alcohol (Sobell, Sobell, Bogardis, Leo, & Skinner, 1992). But 15 to 35% are "problem drinkers," people who are not severely dependent but who create problems for themselves by overdrinking. These people are not severely dependent and may not have a "disease." Hence, while the dependent group may be beyond the help of mental health professionals working outside of clinics, those who are "problem drinkers" can benefit from practical suggestions to help them cut down. And with useful suggestions, we may prevent their moving into the "dependent" category. Several new programs such as Toronto's Addiction Research Foundation's (1994) *Motivational Strategies for Promoting Self-Change: Dealing with Alcohol and Drug Problems* and Hester's (1995) new computer program *Behavioral Self-Control Program for Windows* look especially promising. In the future, newer programs may be accessible over the Internet and people may be able to get help via their desktop computers. But in the meantime, mental health professionals can increasingly get the message out that not everyone has to stop; some people can (and better) slow down, and that we have techniques that help.

Workshops

Finally, mental health professionals can run workshops at lunch on a wide variety of subjects such as "How to Change Your Boss," "Learning How to Be More Assertive but Not Aggressive," "How to Ask for a Raise," "How to More Effectively Handle a Mistake." And each of these workshops can provide suggestions for handling both the practical and the emotional side of each issue: When I have made a mistake, what am I telling myself? If I am feeling panicky, my palms are sweating, and I can hardly breathe, what am I doing that is turning realistic concern into panic? Is that helping? What would be helpful to think and to feel? What have I learned that I could try but am not? Why not? What am I telling myself to convince myself not to try those techniques?

On the practical side, what *would* help? What is keeping me from doing that? What am I telling myself? What have I learned that would help? Having people in the workshop do ABC's and then role-play situations is very valuable. Having group members take turns being the "minitherapist" and the "client," and having group members assign homework to each other, helps transfer the responsibility for learning from the group leader to the participants.

SPIRITUAL "TECHNIQUES"

I have put quotation marks around the word *techniques,* but it is useful to note that for thousands of years in all parts of the world, various forms of spiritual exercise and rituals have been used in the belief that they helped one move along one's spiritual path, but many spiritual activities were, in effect, combined cognitive, emotive, and behavioral techniques. In the East, it is especially common to use imagery techniques, breathing techniques, etc., to work on one's spiritual development, and throughout the world, it is still common practice for people to pray—at the very least, a behavior which causes them to change their focus from self-absorption to something outside of themselves. It also changes what they are saying inside their heads, and what they are thinking about themselves, their world, and how they fit into it.

Until very recently in the United States, many people did not eat meat on Friday. This simple behavioral change (or "technique") reminded them—made them think about—their religious affiliations and perhaps made them reexamine and reflect on their beliefs. Those readers who have fasted, if only for 24 hours, know very well that the small behavioral change, not eating for 24 hours, causes a person to think, feel, and act differently, and not only during those 24 hours but afterwards, as well. Fasting when not done to excess, may help people understand their low frustration tolerance better—and develop higher tolerance for frustration and discomfort. The broker mentioned above, while he was working on maintaining his sobriety, went to a Zen monastery in the Catskills that Alcoholics Anonymous uses for weekend retreats. He believed that sitting for one hour from 5 A.M. to 6 A.M. without moving had helped him more to change his thinking about discomfort, and his ability to stand it, than any CBT technique. Of course, for me, it was a CBT technique!

I also include in "spiritual," from the Latin root *inspirare,* meaning to breathe, anything that inspires us or helps us "lift our spirits" (excluding chemicals, although, as noted earlier, some groups on the planet use chemicals for spiritual development). It is interesting to note that the opposite of to inspire is to expire, or to die. For many people, finding something meaningful at work beyond the obvious objectives of their job inspires them, that is, helps them feel more alive. One person I know while working to make his division grow and be profitable has always tried to help his subordinates also develop and advance in the business. In fact, without this other focus away from the mundane goals of his job, he believes he would not have been able to continue working. Most people in the helping professions work there because, despite the insurance forms they have to fill out in their private offices or the political machinations in their institutional settings, they find their work inspiring.

Other people find beauty inspiring. A client of mine keeps her spirits up for weeks after looking at a piece of beautiful artwork in a museum. She also lifts her spirits through singing and playing the piano. Many people garden, go hiking, skiing, or sailing, and travel for similar reasons. Looking at the views from the top of a mountain is one of the most uplifting experiences I have.

One of the most important aspects of REBT is its focus on moderation and balance. People are urged to moderate their thinking, specifically to think in preferences and not demands, and to balance their short- and long-term interests. Demandingness, low frustration tolerance, "I-can't-do-it-itis" and self-downing—are all seen to contribute to opting for short-term solutions and pleasures at the expense of long-term solutions and pleasures. In addition, Ellis (e.g., 1988, 1994a, 1995) sends out a clear message in all of his writings and presentations: it is fine to try to get what you want and to pursue happiness. But if people start thinking that they are entitled to what they want and thereby turn their "wants" into demands, they will frequently experience psychological and physical distress. Thus like the stoics and the Buddha before them, modern cognitive behavioral therapy, and especially REBT, urges working on our thinking, feelings, and actions—on our mental and physical wellness—and on accepting what we cannot change while working on what we can change, both within ourselves and within the systems that so dramatically affect all of us.

WHAT DOES THE FUTURE HOLD?

This chapter has focused on a sampling of cognitive, emotive, behavioral, and even spiritual techniques which may be helpful to mental health professionals trying to improve wellness in the workplace. When these techniques are combined and used in an interconnected and artful manner, people can learn powerful ways to work on themselves. However, as I noted above, such a focus on the individual, while very healthful, may not be sufficient. We may also want to work with various professional and political organizations or vote for political candidates who seem to be sensitive to the manner in which labor laws and laws affecting working conditions and working environments affect the physical and psychological well-being of us all. Just as people have become increasingly convinced that managing their diet and exercising are important for overall wellness, they may also become equally concerned about other factors affecting their combined cognitive, emotive, behavioral, and spiritual well-being.

REFERENCES

Addiction Research Foundation (1995). *Motivational strategies for promoting self-change: Dealing with alcohol and drug problems.* Toronto, Ont: ARF.
Burns, D. D. (1980). *Feeling good: The new mood therapy.* New York: William Morrow.
Conze, E. (1959). *Buddhism: Its essence and development.* New York: Harper.
Covey, S. R. (1989). *The 7 habits of highly effective people.* New York: Fireside.
DiMattia, D. J., & Mennen, S. (1990). *Rational effectiveness training: Increasing personal productivity at work.* New York: Institute for Rational–Emotive Therapy.
Ellis, A. (1988). *How to stubbornly refuse to make yourself miserable about anything—Yes, anything!* Secaucus, NJ: Lyle Stuart.
Ellis, A. (1992). My current views on rational–emotive therapy (RET) and religiousness. *Journal of Rational–Emotive and Cognitive–Behavior Therapy, 10*(1), 37–40.
Ellis, A. (1994a). *Reason and emotion in psychotherapy* (rev. ed.). New York: Birch Lane Press. (Original non-published, 1962).
Ellis, A. (1994b). My response to "Don't throw the baby out with the holy water": Helpful and hurtful elements in religion. *Journal of Psychology and Christianity, 13,* 323–341.
Ellis, A. (1994c). Changing rational–emotive therapy (RET) to rational emotive behavior therapy (REBT). *The Behavior Therapist, 16*(10), 257–258.
Ellis, A. (1995). *Better, deeper, and more enduring brief therapy: The rational emotive behavior therapy approach.* New York: Brunner/Mazel.
Ellis, A., & Becker, I. (1982). *A guide to personal happiness.* North Hollywood, CA: Wilshire Books.
Ellis, A., & Harper, R. A. (1975). *A new guide to rational living.* North Hollywood, CA: Wilshire Books.
Ellis, A., & Vega, G. (1990). *Self-management strategies for personal success: A workbook.* New York: Institute for Rational–Emotive Therapy.
Farrell, J. M., & Shaw, I. A. (1994). Emotional awareness training: A prerequisite to effective cognitive–behavioral treatment of borderline personality disorder. *Cognitive & Behavioral Practice, 1*(1), 71–92.
Garson, B. (1975). *All the livelong day: The meaning and demeaning of routine work.* New York: Penguin.
Goleman, D. (1992). Strategies for lifting spirits are emerging from studies. *New York Times,* Dec. 30, 1992, C6.

Hester, R. (1995). *Behavioral self-control program for Windows.* Albuquerque, NM: Alcohol Self-Control Computer Program.

International Buddhist Information and Research Centre (1993). *The path to inner peace and happiness, selected verses from the Dhammapada and other sayings of the Buddha.* Toronto, Canada: Buddhist Centre Toronto Maravihara.

Kets de Vries, M. F. R. (1993). Alexithymia in organizational life: The organization man revisited. In L. Hirschhorn & C. K. Barnett, (Eds.), *The Psychodynamics of Organizations* (pp. 203–215). Philadelphia, PA: Temple University Press.

Levant, R. F., & Kopecky, G. (1995). *Masculinity reconstructed.* New York: Dutton.

Markels, A. (1995, June 26). Shhh! Napping is trying to tiptoe into the workplace. *The Wall Street Journal,* A1.

Maultsby, M. C., Jr. (1971). Rational emotive imagery. *Rational living, 6*(1), 24–27.

Miller, W. R., & Rollnick, S. (1991). *Motivational interviewing: Preparing people to change addictive behavior.* New York: Guilford.

New York Times (1996, March 3–9). The downsizing of America. A1.

Nielsen, S. L., & Ellis, A. (1994). A discussion with Albert Ellis: Reason, emotion and religion. *Journal of Psychology and Christianity, 13,* 327–341.

Prochaska, J. O., DiClemente, C. C., & Norcross, J.C. (1992). In search of how people change: Applications to addictive behaviors. *American Psychologist, 47*(9), 1102–1114.

Rauch, S. L, Jenike, M. A., Alpert, N. M., Baer, L., Breiter, H. C. R., Savage, C. R., & Fischman, A. J. (1994, January). Regional cerebral blood flow measured during symptom provocation in obsessive–compulsive disorder using oxygen 15-labeled carbon dioxide and positron emission tomography. *Archives of General Psychiatry, 51,* 62–70.

Rauch, S. L., Savage, C. R., Alpert, N. M., Miguel, E. C., Baer, L., Breiter, H. C. R., Fischman, A. J., Manzo, P. A., Moretti, C., & Jenike, M. A. (1995, January). A positron emission tomographic study of simple phobic symptom provocation. *Archives of General Psychiatry, 52,* 20–28.

Robb, H.B. (1993). Using REBT to reduce psychological dysfunction associated with supernatural belief systems. *The Journal of Cognitive Psychotherapy, 7*(4), 281–289.

Rowland, A. (1983). Tanning leather, tanning hides: Health and safety struggles in a leather factory. In J. Green, (Ed.), *Workers' struggles, past and present: A "radical America" reader* (pp. 362–378). Philadelphia, PA: Temple University Press.

Sobell, M. B., Sobell, L. C., Bogardis, J., Leo, G. I., & Skinner, W. (1992). Problem drinker's perceptions of whether treatment goals should be self-selected or therapist selected. *Behavior Therapy, 23*(1), 31–42.

Young, H. (1989). *Howard Young: Rational therapist: Seminal papers in rational–emotive therapy.* Loughton, Essex, U.K.: Gale Centre.

Part II

Programs for Organizational Renewal in a Changing Environment

This section examines programs that are significant for organizational renewal given a climate of change. If change is indeed a constant, then organizations will need to adopt new approaches.

Backer and Porterfield in their chapter point out that to help employees understand and respond to change at work employers need to encourage development of new strategic skills in their workforces. Workers already deal with much change in today's complex, ever-changing work environments. However, few go beneath the surface to respond to change in a more strategic way, using state-of-the-art approaches from behavioral sciences, management sciences, and the emerging complexity sciences. Organizational health psychologists can help employers provide a number of support structures for their workers' efforts to understand and respond to "the changing nature of change," both in response to transformational change interventions (e.g., reengineering or total quality improvement), downsizings, or unplanned change such as those coming from rapidly shifting marketplaces.

Klarreich emphasizes in his chapter that many programs have been initiated to come to grips with the changing environment and the highly competitive marketplace. Whether it be operational programs such as continuous improvement or total quality management, or efforts to improve the people side of the equation such as change management or change master programs, the results are similar. Either people find these efforts enjoyable but not meaningful, or they find them a burden that complicates an already complicated working life. The anticipated solutions quickly become more problems to add to an already long list. He further indicates that before any programs are attempted we need to uncover that which will sustain drive, determination, and effort in the face of change. The characteristic is resiliency. Klarreich proceeds to describe the concept and outlines a training program to enhance this powerful competency.

Stockman indicates that reengineering was not intended to be what it has become today. Corporate leaders and thinkers in North America had seen what the emphasis upon information systems and quality management had produced so positively and profitably in Japan and a few Scandinavian and European nations. Consequently, the reengineering process began in earnest in North America during the early 1980s. North American companies, state, provincial, and federal organizations have laid off nearly 4 million workers since 1989. Unfortunately, some Wall Street and business analysts began praising reengineering, identifying the key component as downsizing of personnel. The process snowballed.

Today, some 15 years later, the downsizing continues. The process of serious and thorough reengineering has become problematic. Oftentimes the results are: personnel cuts which are too severe, cutting deeply into a needed workforce; heavy stress and morale issues for the employees who remain; and a company which has downsized but not rightsized. Investor pressure on corporations to increase earnings is driving the downsizing. Wall Street honors the downsizing with multipoint, value-added stock increases. Short-term gains are impressive.

What is critical, and so often lacking, in this process is that the reengineering process continues. Stockman's chapter attempts to challenge and assist executives to confront these reengineering problems head on, and to establish within the reengineered environment a dedication to participative design with self-managing teams.

Dixon discusses organizational transformation and how action based, experiential programs can facilitate this process. The conceptual distinction between task and maintenance team behaviors is used to illustrate three progressively more sophisticated levels of team learning sought through an experiential intervention. Next, concepts behind transformative learning are examined in connection with the role of the experiential facilitator as a change agent. Finally, the components of group development theory are used as a framework to explore the literature on how experiential programs have been used as a catalyst for organizational renewal.

Finally McLachlan summarizes the importance of outcome management. In his chapter he specifies that if an organization is to remain on a course of renewal, outcome management is essential to check whether the "right" direction and suitable objectives are being realized. He presents an approach for managing a business in real time through tracking the attainment of important organizational goals.

12.

Change at Work: Why It Hurts and What Employers Can Do about It

THOMAS E. BACKER, Ph.D. and JOHN PORTERFIELD, M.A.

> As citizens of the 20th century, we have witnessed more change in our daily existence and in our environment than anyone else who ever walked the planet. (Cascio, 1995)

INTRODUCTION

Making the workplace healthier requires that organizational psychologists help both employers and employees look more critically than ever before at the patterns and consequences of change at work. At one level, this seems a banal and unnecessary proclamation. In a time of rapidly advancing technology, waves of corporate downsizing, increases in the diversity of the workforce, growth of telecommuting, and a thousand other waves of change, no one at work could possibly deny that change is with us at every level of public and private sector work.

But simple acknowledgment of this reality is not enough. Employers and workers need to be helped to understand change at a deeper and more complex level, especially in terms of the psychological and spiritual aspects of change as we near the year 2000. And workers and employers need to respond to the changing nature of change in ways not even contemplated just a few years ago.

This is true not only for the many thousands of workers at AT&T or IBM, being downsized for the first time in the history of their huge, paternalistic corporate organizations. It is equally true for the workers who remain after these downsizings, and for the many millions of workers whose employment security has not been directly affected by the current wave of changes. It is true for entrepreneurs and self-employed professionals whose work opportunities are thriving and growing, and it is true for workers in the government and nonprofit sectors, whether they have been affected by the current tight resources in these arenas or not.

In other words, what will contribute to healthier life at work is for *every* worker to become a "change expert." Increased understanding of the complex nature of change, and how this impacts on life at work at the end of the 1990s, is part of being a change expert. So is increased skill in responding to the many changes affecting work life (and often related to changes in family, personal, and community life as well). Part of the skill for responding comes from more actively integrating personal spirituality into the workplace.

The purpose of this chapter is to present briefly some basic strategies by which organizational psychologists can support private and public employers in their efforts to help their workers develop greater ability for understanding and responding to change at work. It is based upon a model for workplace change developed by the authors through observation, clinical and consultation practice, review of the behavioral and management science literature on this subject, and clinical interviews with a wide range of workers in the public and private sector, whose lives have been altered by their encounters with change at work (Backer & Porterfield, in press).

The more strategic way of thinking about change emerging from this model centers on what hasn't changed—*human nature.* Our psychological responses to change or the anticipation of it haven't altered significantly in thousands of years. Thus, much of this approach is grounded in behavioral science, supplemented by concepts from organizational development and management sciences, and from the emerging complexity sciences. Finally, our strategic approach integrates spirituality, not in the sense of any one particular approach to religion or spirituality, but rather in encouraging each worker to bring spirituality to work in whatever way that makes sense for him or her. In essence, it means bringing a personal sense of meaning to the many changes happening at work so that they can be viewed in a larger context.

The approaches presented here can be applied by employers and their workers both in everyday work life and in systematic, large-scale organizational transformation programs. Employers may need to create significantly improved training programs and other information–skill development interventions at the workplace. In fact, Paul

Kennedy (1993), in *Preparing for the Twenty-First Century*, says that "the forces of change facing the world could be so far reaching, complex and interactive that they call for nothing less than the reeducation of humankind" (p. 2).

For workers themselves, the methods for understanding and responding to change reviewed here can become part of a "portfolio" that can be used every day on the job or taken from job to job in this postmodern era of employment. Employers benefit from supporting workers in developing these portfolios. This is true even if the employee subsequently leaves to work in another organization.

The price of inattention to the human dimensions of change is high. In a 1995 *Harvard Business Review* article called "Why Transformation Efforts Fail," Harvard Business School professor John Kotter reports the results of a decade-long study of more than 100 companies which have engaged in significant organizational transformation. The change programs Kotter studied included efforts at implementing total quality management, reengineering, rightsizing, restructuring, organizationwide cultural change, and corporate turnarounds. Kotter notes in his summary: "A few of these corporate change efforts have been very successful. A few have been utter failures. Most fall somewhere in between, with a distinct tilt toward the lower end of the scale" (p. 59).

In another recent study, Arthur D. Little (1994) conducted in-depth interviews with 350 executives in 14 industries. They found that in attempting to implement change, from work redesign to organization culture, many firms had not learned from their past mistakes. As many as 70 to 80% of the change initiatives had failed outright. Some 40% of the executives surveyed were very unhappy, finding change too slow, and seeing little significant benefit from the change initiatives. Finally, 80% of the companies expected to be going through other major changes within a few years. Those leaders who *were* successful in implementing change were able to help managers and employees fundamentally change the way they think about and approach change.

In a third study, the Wyatt Company in 1993 surveyed executives of 531 companies that had restructured their operations. The most cited barriers to effective change were employee resistance and "dysfunctional corporate culture"; that is, culture at odds with long-term organizational health (Stewart, 1994).

The individual consequences of these rapid, multiple changes can be just as intense, from difficult-to-manage, illness-inducing stress (Backer, 1983) to lessening of individual creativity (Backer, 1992b), to substance abuse (Backer & O'Hara, 1991), to disrupted careers and personal lives (Backer & Porterfield, in press).

WHAT CHANGE MEANS

As we end the 1990s, human history is at a crossroads we have never faced before (Drucker, 1994). We are at the end of a decade, the end of a century, the end of a millenium, the end of a zodiacal age of about 2,000 years, and the end of a "yin-yang" energy cycle of about 5,000 years (Vash, 1995). Also at the world level, we are seeing extraordinary changes of a more practical sort:

1. The end of communism as a viable political system;
2. Advancing globalization of economic activity;
3. Increasing influence of environmental issues on all work-related decisions;
4. Changes in the nature of the job market and work itself;
5. Changes in structure and design of work organizations (focus on core competencies and outsourcing of everything else; movement to temporary systems and virtual organizations);
6. Changes in role of the manager at work;
7. Changes in self-perception of workers (empowered workers, more diversity in the workplace);
8. Increased importance of information technology in all areas of work.

Management scientist Peter Vaill (1989) describes this poetically when he says, "We're all living in permanent white water." Today it seems we are unable to even partly recover from one wave of change before another is upon us. Twenty years ago, management science literature was filled with references to "planned change," but now the best we can do is somehow manage all the change thrust upon us by an increasingly chaotic environment.

Innovation production is constant in today's world—more innovative programs and products, of more sophisticated nature, are emerging constantly (Backer, 1992a). Moreover, advances in information technology make sharing of what's new easier and faster than ever before. And the larger environment of change in the world is fundamentally different today from 10 or even 5 years ago, in at least three significant ways:

- *First, the pace of change is increasing.* For instance, Peter Drucker (1994) says most jobs we'll be managing after the turn of the century haven't been conceptualized yet, and depend on technology not invented yet. And frequently change "sneaks up on us" without our realizing how profound its implications are; for example, there are now more English speakers in China than in the United States, forcing business to redefine what is a "market" just as they've had to with the emergence of the "universal teenager."
- *Second, an increasing amount of change involves both destabilization and diminishing resources.* Just as one example, 850 of the Fortune 1000 corporations have downsized in the last 3 years, and few public organizations remain unaffected by repeated cycles of budget cuts and decreasing stability, such as staff layoffs even for civil servants and tenured academic faculty.
- *Third, the nature of change itself is changing.* Tom Peters in *Thriving on Chaos* (1987) talks about a paradigm shift not just from an old to a new set of rules, but to a world in which at least some rules are changing all the time, and in increasingly unpredictable ways. Hazel Henderson, the economic futurist, says that the fundamental logic error of our times is to assume that anything will ever go back to the way it was (quoted in Backer, 1993, p. 3).

Yet our skills for surviving and thriving in the face of change are mostly based on a linear, slow change and return to equilibrium model of the world. We want to be able to tweak the system, maybe take our medicine of sacrifice and hard work, and then have things go back to the way they were. As recently as the 1950s, the models used by economists set annual growth in the Gross National Product as a fixed number! Problem solving based on such outdated and inaccurate models is not likely to be effective in today's rapidly shifting world of work.

WHY CHANGE HURTS

Many changes at work, as described above, hurt for obvious reasons: we *lose* something (a job, a meaningful activity, a status symbol such as a corner office, etc.). Loss, or the anticipation of it, is the root of the hurt of change. Change also can reduce real or perceived security about the future, increasing anxiety even though the pain of actual loss is not present. In an uncertain environment, future losses are simply more likely even if one cannot judge precisely when or where they will happen.

And this is not only true for changes of negative valence. Even neutral or positive change reminds us of the fear of loss, particularly in an unstable, rapidly changing environment where we have become suspicious that the most ballyhooed, seemingly positive change can actually have negative outcomes. As a result, to some extent, all change is painful. Says writer Anne Fisher (1995) in a recent *Fortune* article, speaking about recent transformational efforts in the private sector: "Pushed to change the way they work, most people push back. Every change, no matter how innocuous or even beneficial it may seem on the surface, costs somebody something."

As Fisher emphasizes, the next stage in the loss–fear–anxiety cycle is *resistance*, a specific or generalized unwillingness to undertake, permit, or "go along with" the workplace change (Marshall & Conner, 1996). Beginning with psychologist Kurt Lewin in the 1940s, resistance to change has been documented as a ubiquitous phenomenon in work organizations, and with predictable consequences of lost productivity, lowered morale, etc. (Backer & Porterfield, in press). At the least, resistance creates an uneasy atmosphere of tension and anxiety, and uses up energy that cannot then be used for productive work.

Moreover, fear, anxiety, and resistance associated with change lead to *stress*, which in large amounts can cause psychological symptoms or even physical illness (Backer, 1983), and tempt workers to abuse alcohol or drugs (Backer & O'Hara, 1991). Stress often reduces workers' innovativeness and creativity on the job as well (Backer, 1987, 1992b).

Given all these psychological realities, it should not be surprising that most people are fundamentally ambivalent about the many changes taking place in their workplaces. In a Roper Starch survey (Waldrop, 1994), 60% of respondents agreed that most changes happening today may "turn out for the best in the long run," but that change is truly difficult in the here and now, and that changes are now happening faster than ever before.

RESPONDING TO CHANGE

How can organizational psychologists help employees cope better with the ocean of changes described above, and secondarily with the fear, anxiety, and resistance that result from these many changes? The first step is to build employees' *understanding* of change. The concepts just presented about what change is and why it hurts can form the basis for workplace educational seminars (in person or by video), group support sessions, or printed materials that can be disseminated to workers (Backer & Porterfield, in press; Bridges, 1991). Special programs might be designed for change agents within a work organization, who have more focused responsibilities to manage the change process (Sherman, 1995).

Understanding how we learn about change also is vital, beginning with the models for change we observed from our parents and siblings, classmates and teachers, and in the communities where we grew up. Opportunities for workers to study their own history of learning about change, so that they may be able to challenge the assumptions they have always lived by, can be provided by employers in a variety of educational settings, formal and informal. And workers can be encouraged to self-diagnose their own "personal profiles" for reacting to change, and those of their coworkers, subordinates, and bosses. Finally, the organizational "profile of response to change" may yield valuable insights about organizational culture and how it provides a context (supportive or unhelpful) for individual workers to respond to change.

The second step for organizational psychologists is to increase each worker's individual ability to respond to change. That can include changing the dimensions of workers' "personal profile" that are dysfunctional (e.g., a "knee-jerk" reaction that any suggestion for change is to be ridiculed and torpedoed). Individual counseling by organizational psychologists, supervisors, or EAP staff can help with this task.

It also can include using the many methods now available for assessing *readiness for change,* so that both employers and workers themselves can deal with potentially troublesome readiness issues up front (Armenakis, Harris, & Mossholder, 1993; Backer, 1994; Stewart, 1994). Learning about some of the basic concepts of readiness for change, e.g., that gathering information about the context and potential consequences of change can significantly enhance readiness, may be guided through seminars, print materials, and other interventions. And it can include understanding better how both worldview and personal *spirituality* interface with response to change. For instance, there are common messages coming from management science and the world of organized spirituality that may have a significant bearing on how workers respond to change in the workplace:

1. *Nothing is separate—everything's connected, with no boundaries.* This is a common concept of Eastern and Western esoteric spiritual traditions, and is becoming increasingly so in management circles (for instance, the theme of the Western Academy of Management's 1993 conference in Los Angeles, California, was "Managing the Boundary-less Organization"). This larger perspective often helps to make better sense of seemingly unconnected change, and thus to reduce the fear, anxiety, and resistance it generates.

The attention to interconnectedness is everywhere in the business community. For instance, Charles Garfield, who writes about peak performance in individuals and organizations, talks about the end of the era of the lone pioneer, and the rise of strategic alliances, partnerships, which interconnect every aspect of business today (discussed in Baker, 1993, p. 4). A quote from "A New Age for Business," a 1990 issue of *Fortune* magazine, reflects the emerging points of view in the business community: "The new paradigm takes ideas from quantum physics, cybernetics, chaos theory, cognitive science and Eastern and Western spiritual traditions to form a world view in which everything is interconnected . . . what has emerged is a host of management theories and practices befitting an age of global enterprise, instantaneous communication and ecological limits" (Rose, 1990, p. 157).

2. *Self-awareness is the key to growth, and adverse experience in particular can increase self-awareness.* This again is a common element of spiritual belief systems which has found a place in management sciences recently, especially through the focus on self-development in leadership training models, such as those of the Center for Creative Leadership, and the philosophies if not always the practices of empowerment and the quality improvement movement. The focus of case studies in business training on failure experiences, and crisis management debriefings in industry, are just two of the trends toward positive use of adverse experience.

Much of what is presented in this chapter to you, the organizational psychologist, concerns increasing understanding and self-awareness in workers with respect to change and how they react to it. Coping with today's kind of change requires open acknowledgment that much change will continue to be uncomfortable, even negative, and that we can learn from adverse experience. Joseph Campbell says: "Dig where you stumble, that's where the treasure is."

3. *Human consciousness, expressed in deeply held values and emotions, inspires and influences reality.* Deeply held values are of course the core of spirituality, but recently we have come to recognize their central importance in business, as well, from the crisis of ethics to

the failure of many efforts to promote organization development (OD). The latest empirical research on OD shows that most conventional OD training (team development, problem solving, etc.) does *not* have long-term impact. Only basic restructuring, stemming from changes in the organization's core norms and values, has significant effects on organizational performance. And again, values provide a context for understanding and guiding change; individual and group experiences can help workers to see how both their own personal values and the values of the work organization do so.

4. *Balance is the key to harmony.* The Eastern traditions in particular hold strong to this, and now companies like Ford are looking more at "wholeness" in management development, where there is a deliberate balancing of work and personal goals, work and family life, to create a healthier work environment.

One of the important balances is between what in life changes, and what doesn't change. There is a need to search for islands of stability—even lab rats are more likely to survive stress if they have some little corner of the cage in which shock doesn't happen. Employers can help workers cope with massive, rapid change more satisfactorily if they provide these islands of stability in the workplace, and encourage workers to find their own (e.g., work assignments that encourage connection with well-known, comfortable activities, or quiet, interruption-free "time-out" rooms where workers can recover lost resilience from the onslaught of change).

Constant change blurs our view of what is stable, and perhaps of the wisdom of George Bernard Shaw's comment—"If it is not necessary to change, it is necessary not to change." Employers need to identify, announce, and symbolize activities and aspects of the work environment that are *not* going to change, to help give workers a sense of stability.

APPLICATIONS TO ORGANIZATIONAL TRANSFORMATION

Transformational change interventions often fail, or at least do not have the hoped-for impact on organizations and systems. A main reason is that these interventions frequently do not strategically address the complex human dynamics of change. This happens despite awareness of and commitment to intervening at this level by top management and change leaders. The wisdom of "systems don't change, people change" is widely acknowledged, but insufficiently implemented (Burke, 1995; Arthur D. Little, 1994; Mirvis, 1988; Nadler, Shaw, Walton, & Associates, 1995; O'Toole, 1995; Porras & Robertson, 1992; Price Waterhouse Change Integration Team, 1996).

Dealing with the human side of change is especially important when transformation is undertaken in a highly bureaucratic, tight-resources environment; when existing culture and prior experiences with change suggest that major change will be resisted by some within the system; and when there are many other changes happening simultaneously, within the system and in the larger environment. For instance, the U.S. Department of Veterans Affairs is undertaking a major transformation of its $17 billion a year hospital system, one of the largest health care systems in the world. Many challenges and opportunities related to the human side of change await in this vast effort (Backer, 1996). Similar difficulties and successes have surfaced in the private sector; two recent examples are given below.

Example One: Reengineering

"Reengineering," a highly visible transformational intervention in the private sector, involves analyzing every aspect of business process. First, the organization learns how to increase efficiency and quality (often through high technology applications). Then a total redesign of the way in which the company functions can implement these improvements. Many corporations have implemented reengineering interventions in the last five years.

However, MIT's Michael Hammer (the leading guru of this influential movement; Hammer & Stanton, 1995) acknowledges that two thirds of reengineering interventions have failed, mostly due to staff resistance. Human beings' innate resistance to change is "the most perplexing, annoying, distressing, and confusing part" of reengineering, says Hammer. Resistance to change "is natural and inevitable. To think that resistance won't occur or to view those who exhibit its symptoms as difficult or retrograde is a fatal mistake.... The real cause of reengineering failures is not the resistance itself but management's failure to deal with it" (p. 17).

This is true even when the implementation was exemplary, people knew their jobs were on the line, and there was strong top management support. Reengineering interventions have often cost corporations millions of dollars, and many are now seen as at least partial disappointments, even by the consultants who implemented them. For instance, reengineering expert Thomas Davenport (1995) writes that "once out of the bottle, the re-engineering geni quickly turned ugly. So ugly that to most businesspeople in the U.S., re-engineering has become a word that stands for restructuring, layoffs and too-often failed change programs" (p. 18).

Davenport reaffirms Hammer's analysis of why this widespread failure occurred: "The rock that re-engineering has foundered on is simple: people." A 1994 report on reengineering by one of its leading consulting firm implementers states that 50% of participating companies find that the most difficult part of reengineering is dealing with fear and anxiety in their organizations. In this study, 67% of corporate reengineering interventions were judged as producing mediocre, marginal, or failed results by the corporations in which they were based (Davenport, 1995).

Hammer and Stanton (1995) offer some remedies for this low success rate, which begin by simply acknowledging the profound importance of the human side of such enormous change. For instance, they advocate getting workers involved in the reengineering effort, so they are criticizing from the inside rather than resisting from the outside.

Example Two: Jaguar

There are some private sector organizations in which transformational change has succeeded. For instance, after being purchased by Ford Motor Company, Jaguar of North America responded in 1991 to falling sales and profits by implementing a complete reorganization (Fisher, 1995). North American operations were split into three units, and 33% of staff were let go. Survivors lost company cars, titles, and other rewards, and had to work harder under the new regime. This created a stressful environment in the head office, paralleled by negativity amongst American Jaguar dealers.

In going out into the field to implement these changes, Vice President of Customer Care Dale Gambill asked for honest feedback from dealers. They told him they felt the company was inefficient, served customers poorly, and was insensitive to dealers' needs. In implementing the corporate transformation, Gambill put the loudest dissenters in charge of solutions, then "got out of their way" so they could implement some important changes in the Jaguar operation.

Employee involvement groups helped to surface complaints, offer a way to discuss possible solutions, and then provide feedback about subsequent improvements. This effort since has corrected many of

Jaguar's shortcomings. Jaguar now ranks in the top 10 of J. D. Power's survey of customer satisfaction with automakers, up from 24th place 4 years earlier. Problems and tensions remain, but dealers report they are happier because "someone was listening," and allowed them to find their own mechanisms for an effective response.

CONCLUSION

This chapter has only touched on the many issues involved in understanding and responding to change in the workplace. It has laid out a bare architecture for organizational psychologists to use with employers who might want to help their workers with this important task for the new millenium. Many resources have been left unexplored.

For instance, *complexity sciences* (Backer & Porterfield, in press; Waldrep, 1992) may provide many useful concepts about how individual people, who are each "complex adaptive systems" (a central notion of complexity sciences), can most productively interact with other complex adaptive systems—communities, workplaces, the many units or groups within them, etc.

Paying attention to the human side of change may help to increase the resilience of these systems in responding to the demands of change. And it may promote what complexity scientists refer to as "spontaneous self-organization"—swift movements to much higher levels of complexity that facilitate adaptive response to externally changed circumstances. As Kiel (1994) points out in a book designed to promote uses of complexity sciences in government organizations, "increased complexity tends to increase responsiveness to the environment; decreased complexity leads to decreased responsiveness." But the definitions of "complexity" are changing. The old complex forms—the modern corporation—don't work so well anymore. New complex forms are needed—temporary systems (exemplified by the motion picture production team), or the virtual organization which exists only in cyberspace (groups that work together via telephone, e-mail, etc.).

Kiel goes on to say that "At the deepest level, public managers may learn that it is the level of freedom in systems, not of control, that will determine their success as managers. . . . Chaos includes a deeper order . . . more important than control . . . recognizing the fluidity and shifting order that are generated by dynamic systems" (p. 12).

Understanding the nature of complex adaptive systems and the rules that govern them, helps us learn new skills. Complexity sciences, combined with understanding about the psychobiological bases of stress and adaptation (especially the central concept of "resilience" as a measure of the individual's or system's continuing ability to respond to change) can provide that understanding.

In his book, *Managing in a Time of Great Change* (1995), Peter Drucker observes that:

> society, community and family are all conserving institutions. They try to maintain stability and to prevent, or at least slow, change. But the modern organization is a destabilizer. It must be organized for innovation, and innovation as the great economist Joseph Schumpeter said, is "creative destruction" . . . it must be organized for constant change. (1995, p. 12)

Thus work organizations have played their own part in gearing up the cycles of change that now require enhanced skills for understanding and responding. This suggests that public and private workplaces have a responsibility to their workforce and to their communities: to provide training, counseling, and other kinds of support designed to help workers improve their understanding and responding.

Such support also has a payoff for employers, of course. Workers who understand and respond better to the onslaught of changes that are now affecting virtually every workplace are also likelier to be healthier, and to function at a higher level of effectiveness. Thus it is in the self-interest of employers of all types to encourage and underwrite these activities, since "change expert" workers are also likely to be more productive, and better able to cope with the changing demands of today's work environments. Organizational psychologists are clearly faced with a significant opportunity!

REFERENCES

Armenakis, A. A., Harris, S. G., & Mossholder, K. W. (1993). Creating readiness for organizational change. *Human relations, 46*(6), 681–703.

Arthur D. Little, Inc. (1994). *Managing organizational change: How leading organizations are meeting the challenge.* Cambridge, MA: Author.

Backer, T. E. (1983, February 14). Beating the stress syndrome. *ADWEEK,* 20.

Backer, T. E. (1987). How health promotion programs can enhance workplace creativity. In S. Klarreich (Ed.), *Health education and fitness in the workplace* (pp. 325–337). New York: Praeger.

Backer, T. E. (1992a). Getting management knowledge used. *Journal of Management Inquiry, 1*(1), 39–43.

Backer, T. E. (1992b). Workplace creativity: Psychological, environmental and organizational strategies. *Creativity Research Journal, 5*(4), 439–443.

Backer, T. E. (1993, August). Managing innovation and change—Common messages from business and spirituality. Address to California State Univ., Long Beach College of Health and Human Services Convocation.

Backer, T. E. (1994). *Readiness for change, educational innovations, and education reform.* Washington, DC: U.S. Department of Education, Office of Educational Research and Improvement.

Backer, T. E. (1996). Managing the human side of change in VA's transformation. Background paper. Washington, DC: U.S. Department of Veterans Affairs.

Backer, T. E., & O'Hara, K. (1991). *Organizational change and drug-free workplaces: Templates for success.* Westport, CT: Quorum Books.

Backer, T. E., & Porterfield, J. M. (in press). *Understanding and responding to change: The worker's portable guide.* San Francisco: Jossey-Bass.

Bridges, W. (1991). *Managing transitions.* Reading, MA: Addison-Wesley.

Burke, W. W. (1995). Organization change: What we know: What we need to know. *Journal of Management Inquiry, 4*(2), 158–171.

Cascio, W. F. (1995). Whither industrial and organizational psychology in a changing world of work? *American Psychologist, 50*(11), 928–939.

Davenport, T. H. (1995). Why re-engineering failed. *Fast Company, 1*(1), 70–74.

Drucker, P. F. (1985). *Innovation and entrepreneurship.* New York: Harper & Row.

Drucker, P. F. (1994, November). The age of social transformation. *Atlantic Monthly,* 53–80.

Drucker, P. F. (1995). *Managing in a time of great change.* New York: Truman-Talley Books/Dutton.

Fisher, A. B. (1995, April 17). Making change stick. *Fortune,* 121–130.

Hammer, M., & Stanton, J. (1995). *The re-engineering revolution.* Cambridge, MA: MIT.

Kennedy, P. (1993). *Preparing for the 21st Century.* New York: Random House.

Kiel, L. D. (1994). *Managing chaos and complexity in government.* San Francisco: Jossey-Bass.

Kotter, J. P. (1995, March–April). Leading change: Why transformation efforts fail. *Harvard Business Review,* 59–67.

Marshall, J., & Conner, D. R. (1996, Winter). Another reason why companies resist change. *Strategy and Business,* 4–7.

Mirvis, P. H. (1988). Organization development: Part 1: An evolutionary perspective. In W. A. Passmore & R. W. Woodman (Eds.), *Research in organizational change and development* (Vol. 2). Greenwich, CT: JAI Press.

Nadler, D., Shaw, R. A., Walton, E., & Associates (1995). *Discontinuous change.* San Francisco: Jossey-Bass.

Nadler, D. M., & Tushman, M. L. (1990, Winter). Beyond the charismatic leader: Leadership and organizational change. *California Management Review,* 77–90.

O'Toole, J. (1995). *Leading change.* San Francisco: Jossey-Bass.

Peters, T. (1987). *Thriving on chaos: Handbook for a management revolution.* New York: HarperCollins.

Porras, J. I., & Robertson, P. J. (1992). Organizational development: Theory, practice and research. In M. D. Dunnette & L. M. Hough (Eds.), *Handbook of industrial and organizational psychology* (2nd ed.). Palo Alto, CA: Consulting Psychologists Press.

Price Waterhouse Change Integration Team (1996). *Paradox Principles.* Chicago: Irwin.

Rose, F. (1990, October 8). A new age for business. *Fortune,* 156–164.

Sherman, S. (1995, December 11). Wanted: Company change agents. *Fortune,* 197–198.

Stewart, T. H. (1994, February 7). Rate your readiness to change. *Fortune,* 106–110.

Vaill, P. (1989). *Managing as a performing art.* San Francisco: Jossey-Bass.

Vash, C. L. (1995). *The gods were growing old again and it was time for another shakeup.* Speech to the annual conference of the Council of State Administrators of Vocational Rehabilitation.

Waldrep, M. (1992). *Complexity.* New York: Simon & Shuster.

Waldrop, J. (1994, September). Change is good unless it happens. *American Demographics,* 12–13.

13.

Resiliency: The Skills Needed to Move Forward in a Changing Environment

SAM KLARREICH, Ph.D.

INTRODUCTION

As organizations wrestle with changes such as restructuring, downsizing, realigning, merging, rightsizing, and reinventing, change management solutions have evolved. The people side of the solution has involved numerous human relations/resources programs that suggest the only way to manage change is to "work through it." This means going through the various "stages" of change until you arrive at "acceptance," then and only then can you move forward and make the adjustments necessary to become productive once again. However, moving through a series of stages suggests that handling change is a unilinear process that moves from "denial" or "endings" to "acceptance" or "new beginnings," depending on the theory and program that is applied. But people do not necessarily move in a unilinear fashion as they grapple with change, but seem to be more haphazard in their approach. Their emotions overwhelm them and a seemingly logical methodology to handle change gets tossed aside. The immediacy of the problem and the associated feelings rule the day and formula solutions are placed on the back burner. For this reason and others I am certain, change management programs have not met with meaningful success. Although participants typically enjoy the experience, there is usually no transfer to the workplace situation. So many people wander through numerous change management programs enjoying themselves while the experience lasts and return to work only to quickly find that they are once again overwhelmed and unprepared for the onslaught.

On the technical side, many programs have been initiated to help people come to grips with the abundance of change by offering solutions that modify the processes of work. Continuous improvement, total quality management, and reengineering, to name a few, have been hailed as the methods to simplify work processes, remove redundancies, eliminate waste, enhance work flow, and obviously contribute to the bottom line. People would find these methods so helpful that they would no longer be overwhelmed by change, because they would now be working smarter but not necessarily harder. However, the anticipated successes have not materialized. These technical programs have not only failed to simplify people's lives, but in fact have made them more complicated. To organize these programs, more committees have sprung up, more meetings have been arranged, more paperwork has been created, and thus more time and energy have been consumed. Additionally, the bottom line has not improved. The solutions quickly become more problems and suddenly the frustration levels of people escalate and the organization is once again wrestling with even more problems than when it started.

Before any programs are attempted, we need to ask ourselves what do people require in order to sustain determination, drive, commitment and productivity? It would appear that "resiliency" is that characteristic which above all others will allow people to recover, bounce back, and indeed sustain renewed effort no matter the change or setback.

DEFINITIONS OF RESILIENCY

Masten, Best, and Garmenzy (1990), refer to resilience as good adaptation despite stressful situations. Gordon and Song (1993) identify it as a defiance of negative predictions of success. Rigsby (1990) argues that resilient people are those who succeed in spite of the fact that they are members of high risk groups for whom adaptive success is given low probability, have endured stressful experiences, and suffered trauma. Bartelt (1990) postulates that resilience as a component of the self enables success in the face of adversity. McCord (1990) indicates that a mark of personal resilience is the degree to which a person changes in response to altered circumstances; resilience implies that a person thrives in spite of adversity or because of it and as well involves successful engagement with risk not the evasion of it. Taylor (1990) suggests that resilience be viewed as a study of adaptation and the attainment of various psychosocial milestones and developmental tasks. Finally, Anderson (1990) points out that resilience requires demonstrable evidence of consistently good performance.

In summary, resilience seems to involve successful adaptation in spite of any adversity to the point where there is a defiance of possible negative outcomes and an ongoing engagement of risk.

Given this definition, how do we then explain resilience? It can be seen as an idiosyncrasy that some people possess and others do not. Or it can be viewed as a specific characteristic or trait that has strong genetic links and can neither be influenced nor nurtured. The explanation that I prefer and the one that I will adopt throughout the course of this paper is that resilience is a complex behavior in response to interactions with the external environment that includes others, situations, and opportunities.

To explore whether a concept of resiliency has application in the workplace and whether resiliency training has utility, a number of key executives from major companies were interviewed.

THE CORPORATE LANDSCAPE

Numerous executives from organizations that were in the midst of change were interviewed (see Appendix A for the Resiliency Interview Schedule). Three case studies will be described. The respective executives were assured of the confidential nature of the interview and were encouraged to be open and honest in their responses to a variety of questions. The first category of questions focused on the changes that the company was experiencing and the second category focused on resiliency, ranging from its meaning, to a description of resilient people, and a discussion about the value of resiliency training for the organization.

Case Study 1—Telecommunications Manufacturing Company

The Director indicated that his company had to make a major shift in its direction due to the fact that the Canadian market was saturated. So it decided to globalize its operations. With this globalization came numerous joint venture projects in China and other countries that were interested in his company's technology. However, with expansion came relocation and restructuring in order to streamline operations and reduce fixed costs. These steps were necessary to remain more globally competitive. So the company moved and expanded part of its operations into the United States. Many of the senior executives were transferred across the border and as such families and homes were uprooted. This has caused considerable hardship and stress and the company is struggling with the fallout. Shifting all of the manufacturing operations to the United States, meant that the Canadian plant would only be needed for research purposes and would require considerably fewer employees. To date 900 people have been laid off with the prospect of another 2,000 being let go.

The company has always prided itself on providing a secure and stable place of employment. Over the years it has nurtured a family environment where employees were supported and "looked after." But the changes have left many people shell-shocked. The layoffs, the early retirements, and contractual work with no benefits to replace full-time employment, have driven most into a profound state of disbelief. To counteract this phenomenon, the company has gone out of its way to provide career transition/outplacement counseling and has made available up to $35,000 to each affected employee for retraining. But the resentment still exists.

Because many of the employees have remained in a state of denial regarding the recent changes, resilient behavior does not appear to be present. Over the years people developed such a strong state of dependence, this has prevented them from seeking out ways to improve their working lives. They have simply spawned an "entitlement" attitude that has now left them reeling. People have given up being responsible for their lives in favor being cared for and looked after. Resilience has been replaced by considerable moaning, whining, and a profound absenteeism problem. To add to their lack of resilience is a neglect of the future and the promise that it might hold. Management and employees alike have simply given up and are too preoccupied with survival and the pains of change. Because they believe their life-styles are at risk, they have become apathetic in the face of a different future.

However, there appears to be a new breed on the horizon. Some of these people are already working in this organization. They expect contract work. They are always updating and upgrading their resumés with the expectation that their time here might be short-lived. These people are not dependent but are responsible for their own working lives. They are the first to "put their hand up not a hand out." These are the resilient individuals and will be the new breed of tomorrow. They are preoccupied with persevering through the day no matter the obstacles.

To currently help people in the organization, there is a need to teach them that change is a challenge that can be survived. In essence, people need to shift their mindset. A way to do this would be to create working "partnerships" between employees and management. Employees would work with management not on the basis of guarantees or security, more on the basis of a delivery of services and expertise. Management would reward, recognize, appreciate, and support employees as they continue to put forward their best efforts. All would realize that changing market needs and demands could at any time impact the partnership and change the existing working arrangement. Is this possible to do now? This question invites considerable speculation.

Resiliency training for this organization would be a great idea. A great deal of training has come through this organization, so it would need to be unique and not a "quick fix." If the program could offer a long-term return, there would be an overwhelming amount of interest.

Case Study 2—Cable Company

The Director indicated that a recent merger had taken place, driven by the need to consolidate various operations. The company has a history of acquiring smaller companies, but this was the first merger, and although it was a sound move, there was considerable risk attached to it because there was a need to leverage the financing.

The merger quickly surfaced a great deal of redundancies which meant that many senior managers were forced to leave and the bulk of middle management were also given their "pink slips."

Adjusting to the merger has been a major effort because the cultures of the two organizations are so different. The one company was more traditional with a "family atmosphere" and prided itself on excellent job security. Employees felt empowered to make their own decisions and to take more responsibility. Change was introduced slowly and was carefully processed before decisions were rendered on which direction to take.

The other company is considerably more aggressive and thrives on the fast pace of change. It is very entrepreneurial and seems to delight in creating deals and the chaos and turmoil that comes with this frenzied deal making. Making money is not the objective, rather creating growth, assets, and shareholder value seem to drive the organization. But this strategy may not be sufficient in light of stiffened competition which is very customer focused, whereas the other organization is not.

The Director expressed his belief that humans are not intrinsically able to foresee change, let alone accept and deal with it effectively; although, if people could learn to accept the existence of constant change, they would be better prepared and undoubtedly more resilient. A trend that he did notice was self-preservation among some employees and maybe this is what resilience is about. People simply aren't as loyal as they used to be. The company is spending inordinate sums of money to train them, yet they easily leave for better opportunities elsewhere; sometimes they are carrying out their job search on company time. It seems that self-interest and the prospect of expanding their portfolio of training and experience from numerous companies is their ultimate goal.

Resiliency nonetheless is a tough concept to work with, given that the prospect of downsizing weighs heavily on everyone's shoulders. People are simply living day to day with the threat that they, including the Director, might be let go. And yet in this environment, we are still expected to produce at least 100%. On top of this is the added problem of poor communication. The CEO barks out commands and expects everyone to jump to attention. There is very little input into his decision-making process, yet we are expected to be motivated and perform to our potential and as well outperform the competition. How can people in this environment remain dedicated to the organization?

If there is a key to resiliency, it is clearly attitude. What we need to do is remind ourselves that change is here to stay; that change can be managed; that each day presents new challenges that will test our abilities; that one must thrive on the challenge and that we have people outside of work who love and care for us and want us to succeed.

Attitude adjustment might simply be too much to ask of people and for that reason resiliency training could prove to be most enriching. The concept of resilience is no doubt an intriguing one and would certainly have a place in this organization. The caveat is to make certain that this just isn't another "training program." It is too important and too timely a topic to offer another "flavor of the month."

Case Study 3—Computer Sales Company

The Director indicated that this organization had, over the past number of years, been through numerous merger attempts, none of which came to fruition. The most recent merger effort stalled for about one year. During that time everything was in limbo. People simply put work "on hold" because no one knew what was going to happen. Productivity suffered and customers complained. However, the deal was consummated, then the downsizing began, due to the redundancies, and over 400 people lost their jobs. Most of the losses came from the middle management ranks; although many other people also left, because they saw no future in being with a company going through this major transition. The communication to employees could have been better throughout the course of this merger and that partially explains why so many people left. They were enraged at the way they were treated throughout.

Now that the dust has settled, there is a hiring freeze. Because there are fewer people to do work, the workload has dramatically increased. Everyone seems to be stretched to the limit. However, the leaders have begun to show some compassion. Training and development dollars have increased to improve the employee skill base. Management has begun to develop a new mission statement, including considerable input from everyone. As well, senior management have become highly visible and begun to make themselves available and accessible. The numerous closed door, secretive, behind the scenes, meetings and planning escapades, have been replaced with openness and a willingness to listen to all. The company has also made a point of improving and expanding its technological capability to keep pace with the competition, but more importantly to serve its clients' needs more effectively.

The Director went on to state her belief that most people have an innate capacity to be resilient. Most want to be successful and will often do what it takes to get there. Where that does not happen is the big puzzle that needs to be explored and resolved. Those who lack resiliency seem to underestimate the amount of change and often are overwhelmed by its impact. The organization can help people who are struggling by being open, supportive, communicative, and psychologically minded, in the sense that it is sensitive to people's unique reactions.

Resilient people are willing to "make mistakes." By making mistakes, you are essentially breaking new ground and can learn from it. In being resilient, it is essential to see problems as challenges and opportunities; to regard rejection from customers as valuable data; to remain flexible yet persistent in all business dealings; to believe that the goal will be achieved no matter what. It is also crucial to understand your limits and know when to seek assistance and support and have the courage to delegate, or as a last resort turn the issue over to someone better qualified in the organization. These core components will improve confidence and increase energy.

Resiliency training would be an invaluable service, especially for the "walking wounded." A case in point is a valued employee to whom we devoted a considerable amount of training dollars. She had problems adjusting to the new environment and the heavier work demands. In turn she hid her inadequacies and lost her credibility. Unwilling to speak to management and resolve matters, she remains unproductive, and there is a real possibility that she might lose her job. With this person and others similar to her in the organization, resiliency training would be a godsend!

CORE COMPONENTS OF RESILIENCY

It is obvious from the case examples that there is a real need for resiliency skills training. These examples just scratch the surface of a corporate landscape that is replete with companies struggling to come to grips with the many damaging consequences of change. Before a training program can be described, it would be essential to specify the core components of such a training module.

INTERNAL LOCUS OF CONTROL/PSYCHOLOGICAL COMPETENCE

Resilient people seem to be very psychologically competent and demonstrate a large measure of internal locus of control. This is a critical component of resiliency training.

Kobasa (1979) points out that psychologically competent people are "hardy" individuals who have a clear sense of their values, goals, and capabilities and a fundamental belief in their importance. Furthermore, they possess a strong tendency toward active involvement and engagement with their environment and are not a victim of change but rather welcome it or bring it about. Bandura (1977) referred to this pattern of behavior as self-efficacy. Rachman (1978) indicates that psychologically competent people have the confidence that they have the skills and knowledge to overcome realistic threats and do not dwell on unrealistic ones. Furthermore, these individuals readily admit concern and fear, yet they know that they are capable and have the resources for coping effectively with changes that come their way. Orr and Westman (1990) suggest that competent people believe in themselves and in the importance of what they are doing; they believe and act as though they can influence their environment within reasonable limits, without the manipulation of others; and most importantly they believe that change rather than stability and predictability is the norm. Antonovsky (1990) postulates that these people have a strong will, a strong sense of commitment, a powerful conviction that the principles they have adopted and follow are important, and they possess a unified conception of the world and its workings. Scheier and Carver (1987) relate competence to dispositional optimism and a generalized expectancy for favorable outcomes no matter what obstacles are encountered. Rather than engage in denial these people deal directly with the problem at hand and see the best in the situation. When the predicament seems out of control, they resort to an adaptive process of acceptance in order to facilitate adjustment to this hardship. Finally, Werner (1982) described competence and control as a more positive self-concept and a more nurturing, responsible, and achievement oriented attitude toward life. There was also a strong element of self-improvement and continued psychological growth evident.

MINDFUL BEHAVIOR

Resilient people seem to demonstrate mindful behavior and this is another important component of resiliency training.

Peterson and Bossio (1991) refer to this as becoming aware. When obstacles, roadblocks, or unpleasant surprises are encountered, mindful people focus their attention and efforts on the task at hand and how it is being managed. They act with their minds and make conscious decisions as to whether their behaviors were appropriate. Joseph (1993) talks about the fact that people ordinarily are on automatic pilot and are not too concerned about the appropriateness of their actions until the desired outcome does not occur. Then suddenly they engage in active thought. Ellis (1988) emphasizes that people had better become aware of their reactions, to actively rid themselves of what doesn't work, and replace these with more productive responses.

It would appear that resilient people actively engage in mindful behavior and pay close attention to what they are doing and the results of their efforts. Furthermore if the outcomes are not satisfactory, they go inside themselves to seek out a more effective strategy and are not prone to blame others nor avoid the problem altogether.

REGULATING COGNITIONS-BELIEFS

Resilient people seem to have regulating cognitions or beliefs that are healthy and helpful, allowing them to freely explore a variety of behavioral options. This is a critical part of the resiliency training program.

Rosenbaum (1990) describes regulating cognitions as necessary for self-control behavior. First the individual notices a disruption in his or her habitual way of thinking; next, evaluates this disruption as important to his or her well-being; then, believes that a special course of action will lead to a desirable outcome; finally, expects that he or she will be capable of self-change. Ellis (1962, 1988; Ellis & Harper, 1975) discusses the importance of rational and logical beliefs as the key to a productive life-style and resiliency. People tend to trouble themselves with illogical and counterproductive beliefs such as the need for approval, the need for perfection, the need to control others, and be in control themselves and the dire consequences that will occur should these not be achieved. It is important to challenge and dispute this line of reasoning in favor of less demanding, more flexible, more tolerant thinking. This ultimately leads to behavior that is more rewarding and achieves better results. People who conspire against themselves through crooked thinking and misdirected beliefs, do not deal with obstacles well and may end up either anxious, depressed, or angry. These reactions make for considerable misery in the face of workplace change. Ellis indicates that the building blocks and the foundation to dealing successfully with change are reasonable beliefs based on fact and scientific inquiry. Once people challenge their "stinking thinking" and replace it with helpful and logical thinking, it is possible to achieve resilience.

EXPLANATORY STYLE-PERCEPTIONS

Resilient people have a particular explanatory style that could best be described as optimistic. This allows them to disengage from the hardships of struggling with obstacles and to persist in the pursuit of their goals. This is a key part of the resiliency training.

Seligman and Schulman (1986) discovered that salespeople who had an optimistic explanatory style dealt with setbacks better, sold more, survived change well, and were more productive. Individuals who perceived that bad events were internal, stable, and global were less persistent after failure than those who saw these events as external, unstable, and specific. Seligman, Nolen-Hoeksema, Thornton, & Thornton (1990) noted that a pessimistic explanatory style leads to poor performance because of the expectation that bad events will reoccur in a variety of different areas. As the performance deteriorates, achievement declines and people are then less likely to initiate new activities. Colligan, Offord, Malinchoe, Schulman, & Seligman (1994) indicate that how changes are experienced but more importantly how they are explained, is crucial to change being managed effectively. When people experience change that they have no control over, "Why did this happen to me?" is a common question that is asked. How these people in turn explain the cause of the change will determine how they are affected by this event. If they personalize the issue and see it as stable and global, they are at risk for becoming depressed, especially if the issue is bad and harmful. On the other hand, if they externalize the cause and view this harmful issue as transient and specific, these people will cope effectively. Finally, Schroeder and Costa (1984) point out that it is not life events that are important, rather it is how people perceive these. If people perceive situations as not exceeding their ability to cope, then they will handle these well, minimize stress, and improve their health and well-being.

STRUCTURED CONVERSATIONS

Resilient people seem to make a point of carrying out task-oriented, problem-focused conversations. They seem to structure their conversation in such a way that conflict is minimized and achieving results are maximized.

Frederick (1990) discusses, in his article on the resourcefulness of coping, the importance of conversation that is task oriented and focused, because it heightens the ability to cope with extreme trauma. Self-expression that is directed at achieving a better result, rather than blaming or condemning, leads more rapidly to problem resolution. Norman (1984) points to the importance of structured talk rather than random conversation. Discussion free of self-pity, "bitching," and moaning, but focused on a purpose and a result to be achieved at the end of the conversation, allows people to quickly bounce back from adversity. Ellis (1988) makes reference to the importance of straight talk and structuring conversations so they are no longer unclear, defensive, or shy in their quality. Rather, talk that is direct, clear, and indicates what is wanted, creates more productive relationships and improved results.

SOCIAL SUPPORT

Resilient people seem to have a strong and broad social support network that includes coworkers as well as friends and relatives. This is a powerful protective factor against unrelenting change.

Werner (1982) indicates that resilient people seem to draw on a large number of sources of support. These sources would include spouse, colleagues at work, parents, siblings, friends, in-laws, and would also incorporate faith and prayer. Although internal locus of control, mentioned earlier, is an important component, the role of external support in the form of emotional support from work, family, church, friends, etc., plays a critical role in sustaining resilience and minimizing vulnerability. Zimmerman (1990) argues that supportive, community based activities that include problem solving and recognizing factors that influence decision making can often have a payoff for people in the workplace because of skill and knowledge transfer. Rottenberg (1985) suggests that social support is crucial because it heightens moral and spiritual development and provides a caring community that enhances the ability to survive almost any significant setback. Finally, Beardslee (1989) points out that cognitive development, self-understanding, self-esteem, coping behavior, and a sense of being effectual, can all be improved through social support.

It would appear that resilient people indeed seek out social support and as well seem to know "the right people to speak to," who are capable of offering meaningful input.

VIGOR

Resilient people seem to take an extremely vigorous approach to life. They appear to be actively engaged in a variety of activities and energized by the mix of involvements.

Richardson (1985) points out that if people stay fit and healthy, they can approach tasks and opportunities with more energy and resolve. Furthermore, with added vigor, stressful situations can be handled more effectively and change can be managed more successfully.

RESILIENCY SKILLS TRAINING

From the description of the core components, this training will be cognitive and behavioral in its approach. To date no formal training has taken place; however, there is a pilot project scheduled with an organization in the near future. The program will then be evaluated and possibly offered throughout the company.

The key elements will now be described. In this skills based program, participants will get involved in experiential exercises, individual and small-group paper-and-pencil exercises, small- and large-groups practice and discussion sessions. The program will probably run 3 to 4 days.

Glean Resiliency Trends from Those Who Have Achieved
Remarkable Results as Patients or Athletes

After proper introductions, a discussion of the key objectives and a tabulation of what people hope to gain from this workshop, this exercise will be introduced. First, the facilitator defines the meaning of resiliency. The participants in small groups record and summarize on their flipcharts what psychological competencies were demonstrated by patients and athletes who overcame adversity and "insurmountable" odds. The facilitator conducts a debriefing and summarizes the key psychological competencies.

Isolate Personal Experiences of Resiliency That Will Lay the Groundwork for Resiliency in the Workplace

Participants individually record competencies that helped them to overcome personal hardships. Then, these are summarized in the small groups and recorded on flipcharts for discussion in the larger group. A debrief is conducted by the facilitator who suggests that these same competencies can be applied to workplace obstacles with the potential for significant gains.

Distinguish between Resiliency and Vulnerability

Participants detail the differences between resiliency and vulnerability in the large group. The facilitator captures the information on a flipchart and summarizes the data under cognitive and behavioral categories. The cognitive domain includes: mindful behavior, regulating cognitions-beliefs, explanatory style/perceptions. The behavioral domain includes: structured conversations, social support, and vigor. The facilitator then promotes the idea that becoming skilled in both the cognitive and behavioral domains can enhance psychological competence and internal locus of control. Although people have a greater or lesser degree of psychological competence, this can be considerably improved upon with cognitive and behavioral skills training.

Recognize the Biological Underpinnings of Resiliency and Vulnerability

A brief lecture and discussion is carried out by the facilitator, reminding participants that all are not created equal. Some seem to be inherently more resilient, whereas others seem to be more vulnerable. Yet with knowledge and practice improvements can be made to lessen vulnerability and heighten resiliency.

Assess the Key Workplace Barriers and Changes That Can Get In the Way

Participants individually record and discuss in their small groups the key changes/barriers that they need to be mindful of. Summaries are recorded on flipcharts and debriefed in the larger groups. This now sets the stage for the cognitive and behavioral strategies that will be described, discussed, and rehearsed, to heighten participants' resiliency.

Determine the Distinct Mental Frameworks That Create Resiliency or Vulnerability

The facilitator lectures at length on the key mental frameworks, i.e., mindful behavior, regulating cognitions-beliefs, and explanatory style-perceptions. Then a distinction is made between those cognitive procedures that create vulnerability versus resiliency. A discussion with the larger group takes place to clarify points and heighten understanding. Returning to the small groups, participants individually record personal, not work-related examples, where they were vulnerable and resilient and the cognitive procedures they used to create each scenario. Each small group through discussion summarizes the examples and presents to the larger group a case study of vulnerability and resiliency, capturing the different cognitive procedures that produced each. A debrief follows. The key message is that knowing and practicing the strategies that produce resiliency can improve one's cognitive skills and make it possible to transfer these to the workplace.

Acquire Cognitive Resiliency Skills

Participants refer to the workplace changes-barriers earlier recorded and begin to individually map out their cognitive resiliency strategies and record these in response to these changes. Discussion in the small groups centers on the effective use of mindful behavior, regulating cognitions-beliefs, and explanatory style-perceptions. Each small group creates a case study that demonstrates the use of the cognitive strategies to heighten resilience in the face of change and presents this to the larger group for discussion and feedback. To enhance learning and acquisition the facilitator demonstrates the effective use of these cognitive strategies. Individual participants are encouraged to conduct role-plays to demonstrate these strategies. A debrief is then conducted.

Acquire Physical Resiliency Skills

The facilitator discusses vigor, energy, and the physical side of resiliency. Fitness, diet, relaxation breaks, and the research by Rossi (1991) on ultradian rhythms are discussed. Participants then prepare individual programs to heighten their vigor and energy. They are encouraged to present their program to the larger group for feedback. A debrief is then conducted by the facilitator, who subsequently proceeds to conclude the cognitive component of the program and introduces the behavioral component.

Acquire the Skills of Structured Conversations

The facilitator demonstrates how to conduct a structured conversation. The key elements are then broken down and carefully described. Afterwards, the large group is divided into triads. Each member of the triad has an opportunity to carry out a structured interview. In addition each will have an opportunity to play the role of a person in the workplace who is creating roadblocks-changes-problems for that member doing the structured conversation; each will also play the role of the observer and monitor and provide specific feedback to the interviewer on his or her ability to conduct the structured interview with the interviewee. More demonstrations by the facilitator are provided as needed. A debrief is then completed.

Acquire the Skill of Building Meaningful Relationships

The importance of social support in the form of meaningful relationships is discussed. Relationships with colleagues, relatives, siblings, friends, etc., are recognized as being important to preserve health and well-being and maintain resilience. Participants proceed to record the key people in their lives who could be considered supports. These supports are ranked according to the depth of relationships they have with the participants. Next the participants record steps that could be taken to strengthen the ties with those people who are important in their lives. The small groups summarize these methods and present them to the larger group for discussion.

Create a Resiliency Network that Supports Initiatives and Better Results

The facilitator discusses the importance of establishing a supportive workplace network that will bolster personal resilience. The difference between workplace "mentors," "confidants," "advisors," and "boosters" are described and their importance to the support network discussed. Participants then individually record names of people who could fulfill those categories and strategies that could nurture these relationships. The small groups then summarize the strategies and present these to the larger group for discussion. A debrief follows. The facilitator points out that these cognitive and behavioral strategies are only effective if applied and regularly practiced, which sets the stage for the next section on how to make it happen.

What Needs to Get Done and How to Get There

The facilitator emphasizes the importance of planning and arranging a timetable of activities that will ensure the practice of the cognitive and behavioral strategies and the perpetuation of resilience. Participants individually complete and record a timetable of activities by answering the questions who, what, when, where, and how, as they apply to the use of these strategies with specific workplace changes. Participants are then encouraged to share their plans with the large group. A debrief follows.

Develop Symbols of Resiliency That Will Endure No Matter What

The facilitator lectures on the power of symbols as reminders of what was learned and the importance of continuing to apply the newly acquired skills. Participants are encouraged to draw a symbol-logo or write an expression that has meaning for them, that will endure, and will inspire them to remain resilient. Drawings need not be works of art! Then participants are encouraged to share their accomplishments with the large group. Each presentation is applauded. The facilitator summarizes and closes the workshop.

SUMMARY

Organizations are wrestling with change and in the process the people seem to be having considerable difficulty maintaining their determination, drive, commitment, and productivity. Cookie-cutter solutions have not lived up to their billing, as organizations continue in their struggle to find a way to assist people to renew their efforts. Resiliency appears to be that characteristic above all others that relates to the ability to recover, bounce back, and sustain renewed effort no matter the changes that have taken place. This paper has described the concept of resiliency, extracted its key cognitive and behavioral components, and then detailed a resiliency skills training module that can be applied to any organization whose people are in the throes of change. In the near future a pilot program will begin and its results will be evaluated to determine its utility.

Resiliency skills training holds considerable promise as a powerful mechanism to mobilize people's internal resources so that they engage workplace change rather that avoid or resist it.

APPENDIX A

Resiliency Interview Schedule

Change

There has been considerable change inside your organization.

- In your own words how would you describe these changes?
- What brought about these changes?
- What has happened to your people as a result of these changes?

Resiliency

Some people are better than others in their capacity to bounce back and overcome the hurdles associated with change and sustain their focus in the drive toward the achievement of their objectives. This is what we mean by resiliency.

- How resilient have your people been during these recent changes?

- Do particular people stand out as being more resilient?
- What are the key qualities of these resilient people?
- In your opinion how do people in general achieve resiliency?
- How would you assess your own resiliency throughout the course of your company's changes?
- What advice would you give to other companies going through change?
- Would your company benefit from a resiliency training program?

REFERENCES

Anderson, L. (1990). Effectiveness and efficiency in inner-city public schools: Charting school resilience. In M. C. Wang & E. W. Gordon (Eds.), *Educational resilience in inner-city America: Challenges and prospects* (pp. 140–151). Hillsdale, NJ: Erlbaum.

Antonovsky, A. (1990). Sense of coherence. In M. Rosenbaum (Ed.), *Learned resourcefulness: On coping skills, self control and adaptive behavior* (pp. 34–62). New York: Springer.

Bandura, A. (1977). Self-efficacy: Towards a unifying theory of behavior change. *Psychological Review, 84,* 191–215.

Bartelt, D. W. (1990). On resilience: Questions of validity. In M. C. Wang & E. W. Gordon (Eds.), *Educational resilience in inner-city America: Challenges and prospects* (pp. 94–108). Hillsdale, NJ: Erlbaum.

Beardslee, W. R. (1989). The role of self-understanding in resilient individuals: The development of a perspective. *American Journal of Orthopsychiatry, 59,* 267–277.

Colligan, R. C., Offord, K. P., Malinchoe, M., Schulman, P., & Seligman, M. E. P. (1994). CAVEing the MMPI for an optimism scale. *Journal of Clinical Psychology, 50,* 71–90.

Ellis, A. (1962). *Reason and emotion in psychotherapy.* Secaucus, NJ: Lyle Stuart.

Ellis, A. (1988). *How to stubbornly refuse to make yourself miserable about anything—Yes anything.* Secaucus, NJ: Lyle Stuart.

Ellis, A., & Harper, R. A. (1975). *A new guide to rational living.* Hollywood, CA: Wilshire.

Frederick, C. J. (1990). Resourcefulness in coping with severe trauma: The case of the hostages. In M. Rosenbaum (Ed.), *Learned resourcefulness: On coping skills, self control and adaptive behavior* (pp. 150–171). New York: Springer.

Gordon, E. W., & Song, L. D. (1993). Variations in the experience of resilience. In M.C. Wang & E. W. Gordon (Eds.), *Educational resilience in inner-city America: Challenges and prospects* (pp. 26–43). Hillsdale, NJ: Erlbaum.

Joseph, J. M. (1993). Resiliency and its relationship to productivity and nonviolence. In V. K. Kool (Ed.), *Nonviolence and psychological issues* (pp. 143–169). Lanham, MD: University Press of America.

Kobasa, S. C. (1979). Stressful life events, personality and health. An inquiry into hardiness. *Journal of Personality and Social Psychology, 37,* 1–11.

Masten, A. S., Best, K. M., & Garmenzy, P. (1990). Resilience and development. *Development and Psychopathology, 2*(3), 425–444.

McCord, J. (1990). Resilience as a dispositional quality: Some methodological points. In M. C. Wang & E. W. Gordon (Eds.), *Educational resilience in inner-city America: Challenges and prospects.* Hillsdale, NJ: Erlbaum.

Norman, G. (1984). *How a heroic band of POWs survived Viet Nam.* Boston: Houghton Mifflin.

Orr, E., & Westman, M. (1990). Does hardiness moderate stress and how: A review. In M. Rosenbaum (Ed.), *Learned resourcefulness: On coping skills, self control and adaptive behavior* (pp. 63–86). New York: Springer.

Peterson, C., & Bossio, L. M. (1991). *Health and optimism.* New York: Free Press.

Rachman, S. J. (1978). *Fear and courage.* San Francisco: W.H. Freeman.

Richardson, L. D. (1985). Surviving captivity: A hundred days. In B.M. Jenkins (Ed.), *Terrorism and personal protection* (pp. 380–415). Stoneham, MA: Butterworth.

Rigsby, L. C. (1990). Americanization of resilience: Deconstructing research in practice. In M. C. Wang & E.W. Gordon (Eds.), *Educational resilience in inner-city America: Challenges and prospects.* Hillsdale, NJ: Erlbaum.

Rosenbaum, M. (1990). The role of learned resourcefulness in the self-control of health behavior. In M.Rosenbaum (Ed.), *Learned resourcefulness: On coping skills, self control and adaptive behavior* (pp. 4–39). New York: Springer.

Rossi, E. L. (1991). *The twenty minute break.* New York: Tarcher/Putnam.

Rottenberg, L. (1985). A child survivor—Psychiatrist's personal adaptation. *Journal of the American Academy of Child Psychiatry, 24*(4), 385–389.

Scheier, M. F., & Carver, C. S. (1987). Dispositional optimism and physical well-being. *Journal of Personality, 55*(2), 169–210.

Schroeder, D. H., & Costa, P. T. (1984). Influence of life stress on physical illness. *Journal of Personality and Social Psychology, 46*(4), 853–863.

Seligman, M. E. P., & Schulman, P. (1986). Explanatory style as a predictor of productivity and quitting among life insurance sales agents. *Journal of Personality and Social Psychology, 50*(4), 832–838.

Seligman, M. E. P., Nolen-Hoeksema, S., Thornton, N., & Thornton, K. M. (1990). Explanatory style as a mechanism of disappointing athletic performance. *Psychological Science, 1*(2), 143–146.

Taylor, R. D. (1990). Risk and resilience. In M. C. Wang & E. W. Gordon. (Eds.), *Educational resilience in inner-city America: Challenges and prospects* (pp. 122–130). Hillsdale, NJ: Erlbaum.

Werner, E. E. (1982). Vulnerable but invincible: A longitudinal perspective. In M. Brambring, F. Losel, & H. Skowronek, *Children at risk* (pp. 161–176). Germany: de Gruyter.

Zimmerman, M. A. (1990). Toward a theory of learned hopefulness. *Journal of Research in Personality, 24*(4), 71–86.

14.

Experiential Training for Organizational Transformation

TIM DIXON

An experiential training program can assist in the process of organizational renewal. Such an organizational transformation is but one level of intervention, albeit the most sophisticated and challenging level, that these action-based programs can facilitate. As a means of introducing the potential for experiential training to serve as a catalyst to organizational renewal, below I have provided testimonial accounts of the key insights gained by participants from two different programs. Note the connection in Janet's case between learning on a personal level and her role in a work team. Whereas, Harvey points out the power that this type of training can have in surfacing the emotional issues which organizations tend to avoid in work environments.

> Reflecting back to her own outdoor training program with Colorado Outward Bound's Corporate Development Program, Janet Long (1984, p. 65) drew an analogy between dynamics in the workplace and her group's experience while getting everyone up and over "The Wall." She recounts how "I've never been good at making my needs known, but in this situation I felt a responsibility to the group. I thought back to the office and wondered how many projects I had avoided or contributed less than I could have because I didn't give someone the chance to fill in my weak spots."
>
> Harvey Peters, chairman of Minerva Training, explained how successful experiential trainers focus upon the group process rather than the adventure task, "Organizations are generally focussed on task and

are lacking in skill areas of human emotions. Consequently, teams can often sabotage their own effectiveness because of emotional issues. The outdoors deals highly effectively with emotional issues by helping them surface and then processing constructively." (Williams, 1990, p. 16)

Renewal Benefits Found in the Literature on Experiential Training

From the above examples, one gets the sense that the learning outcomes about team issues or group dynamics from an experiential training program can be both powerful and diverse. Janet saw how her personal weak spots could be filled in by the group, while Harvey found that "outdoor" programs deal directly with the emotional issues which can sabotage team effectiveness. Whether taking place indoors or outdoors, an experiential training program is designed to help employees perform more effectively at work. The action–reflection cycle inherent in these interventions begins with a facilitator introducing a series of group initiatives. After participants attempt to solve each challenge, the facilitator asks debrief questions which invite participants to link their team behaviors exhibited in the problem-solving process to their workplace issues. Corporate adventure training is a type of experiential training program which utilizes perceived risk and natural consequences as crucial elements of the sequenced activities and usually occurs outdoors. One group of researchers investigating the phenomenon of corporate adventure training suggested that during these programs "leadership and personality styles, decision making models, problem-solving strategies, conflict management, creativity, risk taking skills, and mutual instruction all come into play and become potential topics for discussion" (Wagner, Baldwin, & Roland, 1991, p. 54). Although some of the outcomes identified by Wagner and his associates represent learning on an individual level, much of the literature on this type of training highlights group or team related benefits. Yet, significant organizational transformations have come about through the use of experiential training methodologies.

It is the opinion of this writer that organizational renewal in a changing environment must begin with an awareness building process on an individual level. Such personal learning should then be followed by an organized commitment on the part of the composite team members to alter the behaviors they use in team problem solving. By using an experiential learning approach in which the actions of program participants are discussed in a reflective debriefing process, these programs invite the reformation of each participant's perspective to allow a more inclusive, discriminating, and integrative understanding of one's experience. Team learning requires acting on these insights.

Crucial to achieving organizational renewal following an experiential intervention is that action occurs back in the workplace, so that critically positioned teams within an organization attempt to transform the way in which individuals and work groups come together to solve organizational problems. In short, the discovery process begins with the individual through self-reflection and the awareness generated on a personal level must be shared and applied on a team level for organizational transformation to occur. "Personal experience can only be the necessary point of departure for gaining socially valid knowledge: it cannot itself constitute the whole universe of such knowledge" (Hart, 1990, p. 67).

Thompson (1991, p. 47) declared that outdoor experiential training is most often used to create metaphors with learning outcomes in the area of "teamwork (in other words, cooperation, collaboration, trust)." Thompson also claimed that according to both clients and sponsors of wilderness trips, one style of adventure-based training programs, "team communication and group process skills are cited as inevitable byproducts." Furthermore, a research study which included experimental and control groups found participation in this type of action-oriented training led to significant improvements on measures of teamwork such as group goals, genuine concern, effective listening, decision making, respect for diversity, high standards, recognition of ideas, and encouragement for feedback (Bronson, Gibson, Kichar, & Priest, 1992).

It seems as though this type of training can address a wide range of team related training needs. Yet, Buller, Cragun, and McEnvoy (1991) stated that not all training needs can be addressed with sequenced outdoor activities or initiatives. According to these authors, this training methodology:

> is an appropriate vehicle for addressing the process issues that frequently get in the way of goal accomplishment and group effectiveness: developing self awareness, risk taking, communicating support, giving and receiving feedback, problem solving, decision making, assessing and using resources, managing conflict and team building. (Buller, Cragun, & McEnvoy, 1991, p. 59)

Perhaps these writers would suggest that facilitators of such programs should delve into team process issues (such as processes for information sharing), but steer clear of specific business issues (such as restructuring job functions within a department). Based on my experience facilitating such programs, and the information shared within an international community of practitioners who utilize experiential methods—the Experience Based Training and Development professional group—this approach can be used to address both general group process issues, as well as specific business systems and problems.

Content of the Chapter

How can adventure-based programming impact so many diverse group dynamics, and yet fall short of "fixing" all organizational problems? Are certain types of experiential training programs more effective at addressing specific organizational issues? Do all employees need to do the same activities to learn the same lessons or contribute to the renewal of an organization's problem solving approach? Answers to such questions will be sought in this chapter. One premise throughout this chapter is that a wide variety of program models are not being clustered as experience-based training and development (EBTD) because of the program locations (i.e., in the wilderness versus at a hotel) nor because of the activities utilized (i.e., a high ropes course versus a river rafting experience). Rather, for the purpose of this chapter, it is the common goal of "enhanced teamwork" that unites these types of experiential training programs under the umbrella term of EBTD for organizational transformation.

The conceptual distinction between task and maintenance team behaviors will be used in this chapter to illustrate three progressively more sophisticated levels of team learning through an experiential intervention. Next, concepts behind transformative learning will also be examined in connection to the role of the experiential facilitator as a change agent. Finally, the components of group development theory will be used as a framework to explore the literature on how experiential programs have been used as a catalyst for organizational renewal.

EXPERIENTIAL TRAINING AND LEVELS OF TEAM LEARNING

As an intact work team participates in one of these programs, individuals may learn more about the way the composite team members interact together. The awareness that is generated during an EBTD session may provoke the development of new behaviors. This expanded repertoire of effective team behaviors can, in turn, carry a team into the next stage of group development. Through an experiential intervention with sustained organizational support (i.e., follow-up sessions and coaching on the use of new skills), teams with a significant realm of influence within an organization can develop a process for solving problems and working together which by example may lead to a change in organizational norms. However, a single EBTD session cannot take a group through all developmental stages and resolve every critical issue for each stage. Yet, it is possible for an EBTD provider to design a training process that does help a team to accelerate the transition from one stage to the next.

All the more powerful in the opinion of this writer, is that given the right conditions, a series of EBTD sessions can significantly decrease the amount of time necessary to evolve a newly formed group into a high performance work team. These conditions would include a receptivity to and support for change within the team's organization, as well as the requisite level of sophistication on the part of the EBTD provider in both program design and facilitation. Within the confines of a single EBTD session, at the very least, a team can be provided with awareness building opportunities which illustrate the interpersonal dynamics characteristic for teams at each stage in the development cycle.

Awareness is the foundation upon which a team change can be initiated. Furthermore, within an organization a critical mass for organizational transformation can be achieved if significant behavioral change occurs within influential teams (such as a senior management group or a human resource department). For an overview of the three levels of EBTD program outcomes, ranging from awareness building to functional understanding through to organizational implementation, refer to the Miller–Dixon EBTD Levels of Intervention model (Miller & Dixon, 1994) outlined below.

Miller–Dixon EBTD Levels of Intervention

The Miller–Dixon EBTD model (Miller & Dixon, 1994) was created to provide a consistent set of terms for defining the types of training outcomes EBTD programs can achieve. Without a simple language to conceptually represent the possible levels of EBTD programming, a great danger exists for clients and facilitators to perceive different desired outcomes from an EBTD relationship or session. The model contains three levels, which are outlined below: awareness building, functional understanding, and organizational implementation. A basic premise of this model is that all three levels of programming represent equally valid training outcomes.

Awareness Building

Awareness level programming seeks to facilitate a basic, intellectual understanding of team related concepts by debriefing around issues such as leadership, communication, or trust. These programs tend to be less concerned with provoking individual behavioral change, and more with fostering within the team a shared level of conceptual awareness of generic group dynamics. Such programming can be done with minimal needs assessment and often can be accomplished in a day or even less. Because these programs are more "educational" than "developmental," generally the outcome will not create any significant or long-term impact on an organization. Finally, the facilitator need not have a sophisticated understanding of the subtle organizational dynamics at play, nor mastery over the concepts behind organizational behavior.

Functional Understanding

Functional understanding level programming seeks to facilitate behavioral change on an individual level by debriefing around issues specific to that team and helping participants formulate action plans to implement their new behaviors. These programs tend to focus on the transfer of learning to each individual team member's organizational situation. It is this change on an individual level that transforms the team environment. Such programming can usually be accomplished in a single multiday intervention with a follow-up component. Because these programs are more developmental than educational, generally the facilitator assumes a basic awareness among participants of the concepts behind group dynamics. Finally, the facilitator needs an understanding of the subtle interpersonal dynamics at play within the team, which is obtained through an in-depth needs assessment.

Organizational Implementation

Organizational implementation level programming seeks to facilitate organizational change by debriefing around specific business issues or long-range organizational goals. These programs must result in concrete, importable action plans for the team that add value to their organization. It is this change on a team level that transforms the organizational environment. Such programming typically requires multiple interventions over a period of time and may necessitate partnering with other organizational development (OD) consultants. Because these programs are intensely developmental in nature, generally the facilitator assumes participants understand the function of various group dynamics within their own teams and throughout the organization. Finally, the facilitator needs a deep understanding of the context of the organization's business environment and the organizational dynamics at play, which is continuously modified through an on-going needs assessment process.

Task and Maintenance Discrimination and the Role of a Facilitator

One role of the EBTD facilitator is to help teams identify growth opportunities related to group task needs and group maintenance needs. To effectively nurture growth in teams, facilitators should be able to recognize within each client group the team's repertoire of roles for fulfilling both task related needs and group maintenance needs. If a given facilitator cannot recognize the expression of distinct team roles, then the facilitator is unlikely to serve as an effective catalyst for helping the teams expand their range of available roles. Let us first examine the distinction between task and maintenance team issues, from there we can explore the types of debrief questions an experiential facilitator could employ depending upon the level of training outcome desired.

Does promoting team development simply require a facilitator to ask task and maintenance related debrief questions? The answer to this question could be yes; if the client was only expecting awareness building as a program outcome. Given such a training objective, then a series of debrief questions, which bring clarity to the difference between group task behaviors and group maintenance behaviors, may be sufficient. The distinction between group maintenance and task behaviors dates back to the early work by Parsons (1951). (For a comparison of task related group behaviors and maintenance oriented behaviors which often manifest during EBTD programs, refer to the table below.)

Should the EBTD facilitator strive for more than a basic awareness of these group behaviors, then a different type of debriefing needs

TABLE 15.1
Group Task and Maintenance Behaviors

Group Task Behaviors	Group Maintenance Behaviors
Initiating Gets a conversation going, keeps it going by defining problems, suggesting procedures, proposing tasks, and stimulating ideas.	*Encouraging* Being friendly, warm, and responsive to others.
Information/opinion seeking Draws out relevant information, opinions, suggestions, or concerns from the group.	*Approval/acceptance* Verbal or nonverbal approval of another member's input.
Information/opinion giving Shares relevant information, opinions, beliefs, suggestions, or concerns.	*Group sensitivity* Senses and expresses group feelings and moods; being aware of significant shifts in tone.
Clarifying/elaborating Clears up confusion, gives examples, points out alternatives, shares interpretations of what has been said.	*Harmonizing/compromising* Reduces tensions, works out disagreements, admits error, changes proposed course of action to help the group, looks for a middle ground.
Summarizing Pulls together what's been said, organizes related ideas, restates suggestions, offers conclusions for the group to accept or reject.	*Gate-keeper* Helps to keep communication channels open, helps others to participate, suppresses dominating speakers, encourages noncontributers.
Facilitating/terminating Moves the group toward decision or action checks for consensus, agreement or disagreement.	*Shares feelings* Shares personal feelings with the group, gets others to express their feelings.

to occur. Rather than merely highlighting occasions during the program in which the behaviors were expressed, the facilitator must probe deeper. If functional understanding is the goal, then the debrief questions must explore the function of these various roles in the past history of the team. Furthermore, the facilitator must seek to illuminate through debrief questions the potential impact of these task and maintenance roles in the team's future. By providing opportunities during the team challenge activities for individuals to practice new team roles and encouraging team members' commitment to utilize these behaviors on the job, the facilitator can provide a vehicle for change at a team level.

Should the facilitator set out to provoke organizational implementation by utilizing the distinction between task and maintenance behaviors during EBTD sessions, then debrief issues will examine the role of a diverse behavioral repertoire in addressing the specific business issues the team is wrestling with at work. The facilitator must help the team arrive at tangible and measurable action plans for integrating more of these team roles into the organizational culture. Perhaps the facilitator can help the team document the particular roles that each member will champion and monitor, while they tackle a specific work project awaiting them after their EBTD session.

Here are some examples of debrief questions that might be asked by facilitators related to task and maintenance issues for each of the three levels of programming identified by the Miller–Dixon EBTD model:

Awareness Building

How did you determine which role you were to play during the last activity? What happened in the afternoon session when nobody summarized the team's ideas before attempting to cross the river? What conditions were present during the program that allowed people to share both positive feelings and frustrations with their team mates?

Functional Understanding

What team task roles have been serving your team well thus far in the program, which are not being used as effectively on the job? During this last activity it seemed as though everyone bought into the goal of completion under 30 minutes: at work what have been the consequences of relying on your supervisors to set project deadlines for the team? Given the effectiveness of the gate-keeper role during the last stage of your expedition, describe three positive changes that could occur for your team, if the gate-keeper role was formally integrated into your weekly meetings?

Organizational Implementation

What steps will each team member take to ensure the behavior they have agreed to champion is utilized with greater frequency during the development of the new corporate strategy? How must the organization support you, if your department is to expand the team roles you are capable of accessing, and what are you going to do to sustain this support? What specific maintenance behaviors will you try to use on a routine basis between the end of this session and the next phase of your team's experiential training process? When and how do you intend to reflect on the impact that your new task behaviors are having on your team and the organization?

Facilitator as a Catalyst for Transformative Learning

Whether the team is in the throes of the storming stage of group development or is edging its way toward performing, one thing remains constant about the experiential facilitator's role. The facilitator provokes reflection during the debrief sessions. These discussions should follow all of the strategically designed learning opportunities during an experiential program. Although the structured team challenges allow for the team to act upon its own decisions, it is through the debrief process that the implicit knowledge of team dynamics becomes explicitly declared and thereby subject to transformation. Regardless of the team's development stage, the experiential facilitator must provide an environment of "emancipatory education" which at its best can foster what Mezirow (1990) termed as "critical self-reflection." While emancipatory education is the environment in which one facilitates transformative learning in others, the process for this type of learning is based on critical self-reflection. According to Mezirow, transformative learning requires acting on these insights (1990, p. 16).

Emancipatory education is an organized effort to facilitate "transformative learning" in others; more specifically, through an EBTD program a facilitator provides opportunities for the team to challenge their assumptions about teamwork and possibly change their behavior. Transformative learning is the vehicle by which organizational implementation is achieved, and critical self-reflection is the process by which transformative learning becomes possible. Below are several definitions taken from Mezirow's (1990) book titled *Fostering Critical Reflections in Adulthood*, which illustrate how EBTD facilitators can integrate adult education concepts into their experiential training programs and thereby provoke organizational renewal or transformation. The concepts behind emancipatory education can be linked to the facilitator's role for each level of intervention outlined by the Miller-Dixon EBTD model (1994).

Connecting Transformative Learning and EBTD Outcomes

In his chapter on how critical reflection triggers transformative learning, Jack Mezirow (1990, p. 14) declared that "perspective transformation may be individual, as in psychotherapy; group, as in Freire's (1970) learning circles . . . ; or collective, as in the . . . women's movement." In our discussion, we are particularly interested in how facilitators trigger transformative learning at a group or team level so that well-positioned teams can return to their organization and champion a renewal process. Consider the connections between the concepts offered by Mezirow's (1990, p. xvi) introduction of emancipatory education and those of Miller and Dixon's (1994) EBTD model:

Meaning Perspective

According to Mezirow (1990, p. 16) meaning perspectives are "The structure of assumptions that constitute a frame of reference for interpreting the meaning of an experience." By simply asking a team to brainstorm a list of "implicit truths" about the way teams work, a facilitator can obtain a baseline for this transformative process. For example, before starting an EBTD session in earnest, this tone-setting activity could lead to the discovery that the team holds a meaning perspective which includes a belief that all teams need designated leaders to perform well. This and other concepts behind the role of a team leader (i.e., they need to be the person with the most answers) could be subject to perspective transformation, should the debrief of an enlightening activity bring dissonance to the team's assumptions about leadership.

Reflection

Mezirow also states (1990) that reflection is the process of examining the justification for one's beliefs, primarily to guide action and to reassess the efficacy of the strategies and procedure used in problem solving" (p. 16). Here we have the foundation for an awareness building program. At this level of team learning, facilitators stay within the here-and-now of the EBTD session. During debriefs participants may discuss why they believe a certain team dynamic had manifested itself; however, the facilitator will not persistently challenge the team to make the link to their past performance in the workplace. Furthermore, the facilitator's invitation for commitment to changed behaviors will be limited to the context of the EBTD session, not extended into the work setting.

Critical Reflection

"Assessment of the validity of the presuppositions of one's meaning perspectives, and examination of their sources and consequences," (Mazirow, 1990, p. 16). At this level of team learning, the facilitator serves as a catalyst to the team's effort in reaching functional understanding. In short, their actions during EBTD activities are debriefed in connection to their past team behaviors in work situations (which are in part driven by their presupposition of teamwork). The debrief questions asked by the facilitator also challenge the group to consider future consequences anticipated by the team, if their current meaning perspectives remain unaltered.

Transformative Learning

"The process of learning through critical self-reflection, which results in the reformation of a meaning perspective to allow a more inclusive, discriminating, and integrative understanding of one's experience. Learning includes acting on these insights" (Mezirow, 1990, p. 16). Crucial to team learning on this level is that action takes place once a meaning perspective has been transformed. Second, note that the discovery process begins with the individual (self-reflection). The awareness generated on a personal level is shared and applied on a team level. "Personal experience can only be the necessary point of departure for gaining socially valid knowledge: it cannot itself constitute the whole universe of such knowledge" (Hart, 1990, p. 67).

The facilitator serves as a catalyst to organizational implementation by inviting team members to share their new insights into more discriminating, inclusive, and integrative behavioral options. Insights which illustrate the differences between various team roles are discriminating. Behavior which empowers other team members to perform to their potential are inclusive, while efforts to create synergy from the diverse talents in the team are integrative. The team is challenged by the facilitator to plan specific and measurable steps for utilizing these new behaviors within their organization in such a way that their actions improve the efficacy of their teamwork and transform their work environment.

Another author in Mezirow's book focused on the role of reflection in the workplace. A simple truth is found in Victoria Marsick's chapter on facilitating critically reflective learning, when she points out a consistent facilitation theme that holds true at all levels of team learning and at each stage of group development.

> In fact, the facilitator must be sensitive to issues the group may not even recognize, bringing them to people's attention and helping everyone make sense of them. In learning from experience, facilitators help people identify and reevaluate the frame of reference according to which they understand an experience. This is the heart of problem reformation, sometimes called reframing. (Marsick, 1990, p. 40)

Through this catalytic function of reframing, a facilitator provides the provocation for a team to move from one stage to the next in their developmental journey. However, for such transformative learning to occur at a team level, two crucial elements must be in place. One issue was addressed in the assertion above that action must follow the reformation of a meaning perspective. It is the role of the facilitator to assist team members in their effort to create a vehicle for acting on their insights after their training, as well as during their program.

The other great challenge facing a facilitator is in helping team members overcome what Mechthild Hart called "getting stuck in the personal" when they focus exclusively on the individual, rather than moving onto a collective analysis of the situation. Hart offered a caution which should particularly catch the attention of EBTD providers seeking to facilitate at the level of organizational implementation. Hart (1990) wrote that "the real danger therefore *does* not reside in the topic itself, but in the group members' inability or unwillingness to see an experience or a problem as testimony for a general state of affairs rather than as an individual problem calling for individual solutions" (p. 54).

Let us now look at some group development issues that experiential facilitators must be sensitive to as they provoke dissonance-producing insights and thereby invite participants to reframe their meaning perspectives so that an organizational transformation is possible. Provided the team has a realm of influence in the organization that allows transformed team members to lead by example, and the experiential learning process has nurtured the behaviors necessary to alter how the transformed team approaches organizational problems, then a significant organizational shift is possible without rolling out an experiential intervention across the entire organization. In short, not every employee needs to participate in a similar program for organizational renewal to occur.

EBTD LITERATURE REVIEW AND GROUP DEVELOPMENT

According to Priest, Attarian, and Schubert (1993, p. 13), research an EBTD outcomes can be clustered into three general categories: "personal development of the individual, group development, and cultural development of the organization." These researchers summarized key findings from the few empirical studies on the efficacy of EBTD sessions. For the purpose of this chapter, rather than exploring empirical evidence in detail, testimonial and anecdotal accounts related to team or group issues will be examined.

Evaluating gains from an EBTD program on a group level, research by Baldwin, Wagner, and Rolan (1991) indicated the training had a moderate impact on group awareness and effectiveness. Furthermore, the study by Bronson et al. (1992), which included a control group, demonstrated that the experimental group had significantly improved on measures of teamwork such as group goals, genuine concern, effective listening, decision making, respect for diversity, high standards, recognition of ideas, and encouragement for feedback.

An EBTD literature review will be organized according to the five stages of group development offered by Tuckman and Jensen's (1977) model. The focus of the literature review will be to program issues for the newly formed team which is often an outcome of a downsizing or reengineering process. Thus an emphasis will be placed on the key stage for a new team—the forming stage. In a changing organizational setting, the creation of a new team for specific projects or following a reorganization can be supported by using an experiential process to accelerate the work group's development through the stages outlined by Tuckman and Jensen (1977): forming, storming, norming, performing, and finally adjourning stages.

Literature Featuring the Forming Stage

Veron Foester, co-owner of a 21-store Canadian Tire franchise in the Vancouver area, intended to have the 60 store managers and assistants he had participating in a rock climbing session develop more self-confidence and therefore a greater willingness to accept risks (Boyes, 1990). Boyes noted that "the development of a greater sense of teamwork was an unexpected benefit of the exercise." The very fact that these participants gathered and shared an adventure-based learning experience within the same organizational context began the team formation process. In respect to the intentional use of an EBTD session to accelerate the group forming process, Herman Maynard, a sales group manager with Du Pont and a self-declared "adventure training veteran," explained "What you are doing when you participate in one of these programs is developing a bonding in three or four days that could take three or four years to occur in the workplace, given the low frequency of contact and natural barriers to openness and trust that occur in the business environment" (Gall, 1987, p. 56).

Richard Broderick, former assistant editor for *Training* magazine, wrote an article about his 4 days at Pecos River Learning Center in New Mexico with a group of managers and executives from R. A. Mueller, a company located in Cincinnati. Broderick offers a glimpse at what could loosely be interpreted as a program for a newly formed team, in that he joined a team as a "visitor" for an EBTD session which probably altered the group dynamics. According to Broderick (1989, p. 82), Larry Wilson, the founder of the Pecos River experience, informed him and his fellow group members that the program helps "participants lower some of their defense mechanisms, fears, insecurities, and self-delusions that hinder growth and short-circuit the ability to connect with other people. The high drama and simulated crises of the ropes course forge a powerful sense of group solidarity, even among people who start out as strangers."

While recounting his perspective of a portion of the program, Broderick (1989, p. 82) indirectly provided an interesting example of the stress or hardship which leads to the "shared adversity" that has been identified as a primary contributor to the success of many wilderness based programs. Broderick talks about the bonding that occurs for the group he participates with, the group identifying themselves as "the chimps."

> Like the group hugs we were also instructed to perform, the cheer was supposed to do two things; strengthen our *esprit de corps* while lowering

our fear of looking ridiculous by making everyone in the program engage in mildly ridiculous behavior. Instead of loosening me up and engendering a genuine sense of playfulness and spontaneity, however, the group cheers, hugs and silly games more often felt painfully unspontaneous.... After a while, as our mutual respect grew, many of the Chimps executed the team cheers and team hugs with the self-mocking spirit of people bound together by a shared crisis—in this case, the ropes course.

Galagan (1987, p. 46) also quoted Larry Wilson in an article about his own personal experience in the Leadership Experiential Adventure Program (LEAP) at Pecos. Referring to a model of the growth process developed by George Land, the author of *Growth or Die,* Wilson stated:

In the biology model of growth, there are three phases. Phases I is formative. It's the beginning. It's a period of trial and error. If you're starting a new company, this is the entrepreneurial period. If you are starting a relationship, this is when you look for ways to connect. You're looking for roles. The goal of Phase I is to get to a replicable process. (Wilson, 1989, p. 15)

Although Galagan's experience was one which began in a group of strangers, the notion put forward by Wilson speaks to the need of all new work teams during the forming stage. During this stage, the team is in a struggle to find roles and a replicable problem-solving process which will serve them as they evolve into a storming process.

During experiential training programs, according to Honey and Lobley (1986), teams move through a sequential progression of five distinct levels of awareness. These authors claimed the shock of failure during certain activities inevitably pushes a team upward in its awareness-building process. Perhaps Honey and Lobley's model offers an appropriate conceptual representation of the sequential development of awareness characteristic of new teams in the forming process. Their model is outlined below.

Levels of Group Awareness

If a new team is not ready to deal with conflicting perspectives inherent to the storming stage, they may still be able to develop an awareness of the progressively more challenging issues proposed by Honey and Lobley's model. During the forming stage the team may move from one level of awareness to the next, yet remain in their conflict free "honeymoon" state. However, the high performance which becomes possible once norms are created from the fallout of the storming state will not be achieved without explicitly addressing conflict at each of these levels of awareness.

In 1984 Roger Lobley of ICI's Petrochemical and Plastic Division invited Peter Honey, who had authored a book on learning styles, to help develop for ICI an outdoor training program with the Eskdale Outward Bound School in Cumbria. Based upon their experience with this program, Honey and Lobley (1986) wrote an article which details the program's seven activities and subsequent "learning reviews," as well as a group awareness model akin to Maslow's hierarchy of needs. In their model, the level of awareness evolves as the group works together, beginning with an understanding of the task requirements at the lowest level to emotional awareness being the fifth level at the apex.

The model predicts that a newly formed group will focus most of their attention upon the task at hand, ignoring process issues. With the participants of the ICI program, this is exactly what Honey and Lobley (1986, p. 9) found to happen: "it is all task and no process and the task achievement suffers the consequence. The shock of failure inevitably pushes the group up the hierarchy to level 2 where they see the need to have some sort of process for agreeing on objectives, making sound plans and managing time."

Literature Featuring the Storming Stage

Perhaps Janet Long's experience as a participant in a Corporate Development Program offered by Colorado Outward Bound provides an example of the storming process brought about during an experiential training program. Long (1984, p. 64) declared that "Group cohesion had dissipated rapidly. Lured into overconfidence by our success in previous exercises, we had neglected most of the principles of effective group process."

Norman Crawford wrote of an outdoor management development program in which participants were students in a full-time personnel management and administration program who had finished placements with a variety of organizations. In an attempt to evaluate the effectiveness of the program, Crawford sought reflective statements from the participants 6 weeks after the course. Several of these comments pointed to various group processes which can develop during experiential training sessions even when the group does not represent an intact work team with a long history together.

One participant was cited by Crawford (1988, p. 18) as saying, "During the outdoor course, my team would not let me ignore their views. This had acted as a strong and frequent stimulus to change my actions and behaviors." While another person stated, "I lost various opportunities along the way because I was overinfluenced at certain times by my own negative attitudes and at other times by those of others.... By remaining largely passive I didn't really derive any benefit from the activities."

In short, Crawford's example demonstrates the powerful influence that others in the group can have as a catalyst toward changing the behavior and opinions of group members. However, if an avoidance of conflict persists during an EBTD session, then the group will not get past the honeymoon stage. This storming process is necessary to derive benefit greater than "getting to know one another a little better."

Literature Featuring the Norming Stage

In an article on outdoor training by Wagner, Baldwin, and Roland (1991, p. 16) Nelson Farris, a vice-president at Nike Corporate, was quoted as saying

> Trust is an important issue to address in experiential programs, though it is seldom the main goal. Facilitators frequently use trust falls, trust walks, and other activities to help participants place trust issues on the table for discussion. Such issues can be a delicate topic; the experiential activities help to create a level of comfort that may encourage participants to talk about trust. (p. 54)

A key challenge for the facilitator during the norming stage is to guide the team in establishing norms for a trusting environment at work. If seeking more than awareness level learning, the crux during debrief conversations is to get to a level that is more applicable than the team behaviors associated with catching a colleague as he or she falls from a table into the team's outstretched arms.

From Sewell's (1990) article, "Outside the Indoor Medium," we get the sense that the experiential training session can allow groups to formulate some standards for working together that may be dramatically different in comparison to the way they have problem solved in the workplace.

Groups accepted that all individuals had something of value to contribute. They recognised that they performed better if they planned and communicated effectively. A realization dawned that the "leader" need not be an autocrat in every situation neither should the leader be expected to always have the correct answer. (Sewell, 1990, p. 8)

As a new team experiments with alternative approaches to problem solving, they are able to learn what are effective team behaviors from both their successes, as well as their setbacks. Based on these insights, teams are able to formulate norms for operating back at work, as well as during their EBTD session.

Literature Featuring the Performing Stage

In an article written by Boyes (1990) we find indication that groups working together for as little as a month can achieve a greater degree of team performance even from a brief EBTD session. Boyes (1990, p. 7) quoted Sheila Legon, an HRD consultant with the Canadian Imperial Bank of Commerce. Legon had developed a one-day outdoor session with the Canadian Outward Bound Wilderness School, as part of a month-long training initiative for employees in the newly created role of district manager. Legon explained that the position had been changed to place much more emphasis on the role of leading a team within the district and that the program facilitated growth in this direction.

> Much effort was on getting the district managers away from the Lone Ranger mentality, while at the same time getting them to work together more effectively instead of competing for results. They get plenty of surprises around things like who contributes most or who really steps in and leads, when a person might not have demonstrated those back in the work setting. They get a better idea of the whole potential of other people and how their own behavior detracts or adds to the fulfilment of a specific task or goal.

Sewell's (1990) account of learning transferred from an EBTD program to a work setting represents a group so successful in developing to the performing stage that organizational implementation was the training outcome. The participants were brought together because they fulfilled similar roles in their organization, versus working together as a team on a regular basis. Thus the program that Sewell writes of is not dissimilar to a program for a newly formed functional team, in that these participants gathered for the purpose of creating and implementing special projects back at work but had a brief history together.

> In both individual and group action plans two projects were decided upon. Time was spent evaluating the practicalities of implementing these projects and putting a realistic time limit on them. Monitoring techniques, which included a "report back" session, were established to measure progress toward the desired result.... In the case of the Brewers the new plant is in production and meeting targets. Job demarcation is much less apparent within that one section of the brewery. Supervisors meet regularly to discuss and circumvent each others' problems, which was one of their declared action plans. (1990, p. 8)

Literature Featuring the Adjourning Stage

Of course, an exploration of the adjourning stage for the newly formed team does not fit into the premise of this chapter that team based programming serves to help work teams which have a life beyond the EBTD session. Those occasions during which an EBTD facilitator does help a group resolve the issues of the forming stage right through to the adjourning stage would best be described as open enrollment. Even if the random collection of participants come from the same organization, unless the participants have membership in a group with some shared purpose back at work then it is not team based EBTD. However, there is a common dilemma highlighted by one writer when it comes to facilitating an EBTD session with a team approaching the adjourning stage.

In an article by Gall (1987, p. 56) the assertion was made that a common problem with transfer arises when the work teams that have participated in a program together are later split up at work. Gall offers anecdotal support for this notion when she quotes Codex Corporation's Lynn Feuling, whose sales group experienced reorganization after an experiential program. "I report to different people now and those of us who went on the course work together less and less as an intact group. So, typically, we are interacting with people who don't understand the experience and don't know how to relate to metaphors we might want to use." There is a special challenge for EBTD facilitators whose clients will be returning to a work setting in which colleagues do not share the metaphor of a common training session. The facilitator must approach such a learning opportunity as one for nurturing team skills within individuals rather than team building per se. But the experiential trainee as an individual is not the focus of this chapter and is unlikely to contribute to an organized effort to nurture an organizational renewal.

Conclusion

Organizational transformation is only one of three levels of learning that these action-based, experiential programs can facilitate. To use experiential training to provoke organizational renewal in a changing environment, the transformation must begin with an awareness building process on an individual level. Such personal learning should produce a set of explicit action plans on how each team member intends to apply effective team behaviors during their problem solving process at work. By using an experiential learning approach in which the actions of program participants are discussed in a reflective debrief process, these programs invite the reformation of each participant's perspective to allow a more inclusive, discriminating, and integrative understanding of one's experience in connection to the changes occurring within their organization.

Team learning requires supporting colleagues in acting on these insights within the workplace. A significant organizational renewal is possible without rolling out an experiential intervention across the entire organization, provided the participating team or teams have a realm of influence in the organization that allows transformed team members to lead by example, and if the experiential learning process has nurtured the behaviors necessary to alter how the transformed teams approach organizational problems.

REFERENCES

Baldwin, T. T., Wagner, R. J., & Rolan, C. C. (1991). Effects of outdoor challenge training on group and individual outcomes. Indiana University, School of Management: Bloomington. (Unpublished manuscript)

Boyes, S. (1990, September). Adventure training: Does it build teamwork or super-jock execs? *Human Resource Reporter*, 6–8.

Broderick, R. (1989, October). Learning the ropes, *Training*, 78–86.

Bronson, J., Gibson, S., Kichar, R., & Priest, S. (1992). Evaluation of team development in a corporate adventure training program. *Journal of Experiential Education, 15*(2), 50–54.

Buller, P. F., Cragun, J. R., & McEnvoy, G. M. (1991, March). Getting the most out of outdoor training. *Training and Development Journal,* 58–61.

Crawford, N. (1988). Outdoor management development: A practical evaluation. *JEIT, 12*(8), 17–20.

Freire, P. (1970). *Pedagogy of the oppressed.* New York: Herter & Herter.

Galagan, P. (1987). Between two trapezes. *Training and Development Journal, 41*(3), 40–50.

Gall, A. L. (1987). You can take the manager out of the woods, but. . . . *Training and Development Journal, 41*(3), 54–59.

Hart, M. U. (1990). Liberation through consciousness raising. In J. Mezirow (Ed.), *Fostering critical reflection in adulthood: A guide to transformative and emancipatory learning* (pp. 47–73). San Francisco: Jossey-Bass.

Honey, P., & Lobley, R. (1986, November/December). Learning from outdoor activities: Getting the right balance. *ICT,* 7–12.

Long, J. W. (1984). The wilderness lab. *Training and Development Journal, 38*(5), 58–69.

Marsick, V. (1990). Action learning and reflection in the workplace. In J. Mezirow (Ed.), *Fostering critical reflection in adulthood: A guide to transformative and emancipatory learning* (pp. 23–46). San Francisco: Jossey-Bass.

Mezirow, J. (Ed.). (1990). *Fostering critical reflection in adulthood: A guide to transformative and emancipatory learning.* San Francisco: Jossey-Bass.

Miller, D., & Dixon, T. (1994). Toward a conceptual model for EBTD program outcomes [Summary]. *Proceedings of the 21st Annual International Conference of the Association for Experiential Education* (pp. 123–126). Boulder, CO: Association for Experiential Education.

Parsons, T. (1951). *The Social System.* Glencoe, IL: Free Press.

Priest, S., Attarian, A., & Schubert, S. (1993). Conduction research in experience-based training and development: Pass keys to locked doors. *Journal of Experiential Education, 16*(2), 11–19.

Sewell, C. (1990, August). Outside the indoor medium. *Training Personnel,* 6–8.

Thompson, B. L. (1991, May). Training in the great outdoors. *Training,* 46–52.

Tuckman, B. W., & Jensen, M. A. C. (1977). Stages of small-group development revisited. *Group & Organization Studies, 2*(4), 419–427.

Wagner, R. J., Baldwin, T. T., & Roland, C. C. (1991). Outdoor training: Revolution or fad? *Training and Development Journal, 45*(3), 51–55.

Williams, M. (1990, July). Making the most of the outdoors. *Transition,* 14–19.

15.

Organizational Renewal: Outcome Management—The Other Side of Process Management

JOHN F. C. McLACHLAN, Ph.D.

Is the organization to which you consult like a ship drifting at sea, sometimes in a fog, a ship that has neither compass nor rudder, is tossed by the waves, and moves about at random? Process improvement is like putting on a rudder. The ship can be steered. Outcome management is adding a compass. The ship is steered to a known and preferred destination.

Rheumatologist James Reinertsen used this illustration in October 1990 when he spoke about the balanced approach to quality management attempted at Park Nicolett, a group of 300 physicians in Minnesota on the cutting edge of quality health care.

Whether your client is a hospital or a manufacturer, you are likely to have been exposed to the principles of quality management. They are an important thrust of the 1980s and 1990s, forcing us all to examine ways in which the quality of work can be improved on a continuous basis. Organizations have examined the way they do things, listened to their internal and external customers, built teams of empowered employees, trained managers to be coaches, worked at recognizing contributions of every member of their staff, rewarded initiative, reorganized their work, examined their roles, coped with change, and discussed strategic quality. At the best of times, the ship has a rudder.

Does it have a compass, a method to ensure it stays on course? This chapter presents an approach for managing a business in real time through tracking the attainment of important organizational goals. The business in question is health care in the broadest sense and includes hospitals and clinics although there is also application to private practitioners.

In most organizations, the outcomes to be managed are apt to be the key quality indicators. Outcomes differ from quality management approaches in that they are installed; they are not a one-time collection of information or a single evaluation study. They represent the ongoing vital signs of the organization. They chart the organization's health as if it were connected to a continuous electrocardiogram.

There are different levels at which outcome measures can be collected. They can be derived from ongoing consumer satisfaction surveys for the entire organization. They can reflect signs of clinical improvement in patients of a particular type on a particular unit.

Wherever they are collected, the purpose is to provide a compass to determine how close a unit, division, or organization is to approaching its goal. The data show what is happening compared to what is expected. When results fall below the mark, they signal the need to reexamine the processes used. When they are high, they offer a basis for confidence in what one does and the opportunity to promote one's effectiveness.

A number of factors indicate that the time is right to consider use of outcome management in a health care facility. Outcome management is receiving increased attention on both sides of the Canada/U.S. border. The Canadian Council of Health Facilities Accreditation is placing increased emphasis on measurement in quality management for the accreditation of facilities. In the United States, Donald Berwick (1988) installed a system to integrate computerized medical records with quality-improvement techniques in the Harvard Community Health Plan. The Shattuck Lecture to the Massachusetts Medical Society was devoted to the topic by Paul Elwood (1988) who also founded InterStudy, an organization to support the development of outcome management programs across North America.

At this point it should be acknowledged that outcome management is not the same as research using randomized controlled trials. It does not employ the same scientific rigor and is not as selective in admitting subjects for study. It is not a one-time evaluation study; it aims to provide ongoing information on treatment results and to be an intrinsic part of the clinical practice. Outcome management bridges the gap between scientific trials and anecdotal recall by providing a better knowledge base for clinicians (Wetzler and Elwood, 1991). Also, the clinicians own and use the data more than they do in a study conducted by others.

THE PREPARATION PHASE

As with most types of organizational change, outcome management should be supported by the people at the top. In a hospital, without question this means the chief executive officer and the chief of medical staff. With the interest and commitment of the key organizational players, the initial planning can be accomplished. They will play pivotal roles in obtaining the buy-in of senior management, the board of directors, the physicians, and the other health care professionals and supporting staff. The contributions of senior administrators will also be essential in steering the development of outcome management to keep it focused on desired objectives.

In the initial planning phase, there should be one individual designated to drive the process. Such a person should have a measurement background in one of the social or health sciences, know how to define data operationally, have experience in writing questionnaire items, understand statistical analysis, be knowledgeable in an area of research, be familiar with database design and report generation, and have interpersonal negotiating skills. Failing this, an external consultant with these skills should be engaged to provide guidance to the designated outcome management driver. The driver or director should be able to devote at least half of his or her time to the position and at some stage may require an assistant.

An early task of the director (with the help of senior medical and administrative chiefs) is to draw up a list of interested parties and include them in the decision-making process. Such individuals will need to know how they will benefit from their efforts to support outcome management. Health care practitioners may, for example, expect information on clinical efficacy and access to data for publishing or presenting papers at professional meetings. Administrators may expect the development of a tool for managing the effects of health care and to be able to promote their facility's attention to results.

THE IMPLEMENTATION APPROACH

One method of implementing outcome management is to select one or more areas for a pilot project. The clinical areas may be selected on the basis of a unit with known problems or it may be just the opposite—focusing on a group with high morale and an interest in monitoring quality.

Another approach is to require each department to develop an outcome management project to collect data for at least one procedure, diagnosis, or case-mix group.

Both approaches require acceptance, willingness, and even enthusiasm on the part of the clinical teams involved. Considerable time and effort in individual and group meetings may be required to achieve the necessary acceptance. The director of outcome management will need to devote sufficient time to this process to achieve and consolidate the buy-in. He or she will then act as a regular resource as the projects are planned and implemented.

The approach used will determine budget requirements. Costs themselves may depend on the elegance of the data collection system designed. An external grant or internal budget should be developed for an outcome management cost center. The anticipated costs include equipment, software development, data entry personnel, statistical analysis time, consultants, travel and training along with the usual costs of maintaining an office.

The equipment and software needs will depend on the current state of information technology in the health care facility and the approach taken. If outcome management is implemented widely throughout the organization then additions to the admission procedures can be considered, especially if there are common needs for demographic data which are not currently acquired. If additional storage is needed in the current information system, purchase of a hard disk for the facility computer may gain favorable attention from the information technology director. Decisions will need to be made concerning whether to add clinical information to the existing computer system or take an alternative route such as using dedicated personal computers. In either case, the offer of funding for such purposes may change a lukewarm response on the part of a health care team into one that is supportive and cooperative.

LOCAL OR FACILITYWIDE COMPUTERS

The decision to use personal computers supported by their users (or the outcome management staff) versus the facility's computer and information specialists (or some combination) requires examination and dialogue. The arguments for central computer usage revolve around control of data and computing by the data professionals as well as with central access to information and backup, and avoiding reinvention of the wheel. The arguments for use of personal computers include immediate development and testing of software (databases or spreadsheets) and, therefore, local control and adaptation of the process.

In the early phases of an outcome management project, there is the need for frequent change of data requirements. Despite careful planning, when data collection takes place changes are inevitable. For this reason, plans for use of optical scanning should be put on hold until one is certain of the data set. (Once a data collection form is "frozen" enough and the artwork prepared, it is expensive to modify. Although software for this purpose is becoming increasingly reasonable in cost, it is not trivial to modify a questionnaire and its computerized database once it has been put into use.) In many cases a compromise solution will work best with capture of data by personal computer, uploading and downloading links ultimately established with the facility computer, and data analysis conducted either locally or centrally. Definition of the database which will be used on the facility computer may take several iterations before it is finalized. It may be better to experiment with it locally for a period of time before it, too, becomes immutable.

FOLLOW-UP STRATEGIES

Initial and follow-up data are required. Ideally, depending on the condition, it would be valuable to have follow-up data at discharge and 6, 12, 24, and 36 months postdischarge. A compromise is to collect data on admission and discharge and 6 or 12 months later. (For a condition with seasonal variation, such as asthma, 12 rather than 6 months should be used.) From the beginning, it is important to plan how this data will be collected and who will do it. This is a major cost of outcome management. It may be done by telephone, mail-in, or one-on-one personal interview. The latter is best for compliance but most expensive. One day for interviews to be conducted is by scheduling a 6-month clinical checkup, collecting the outcome status at that time, and offering feedback with recommendations to the patient. For those who do not return for the session, a combination of mail and telephone interviewing may be used. In this way, follow-up visits can become part of the ongoing cost of the department and an expected form of treatment. However, outcome data limited to only those who return result in biased information, and concerted efforts need to be made to determine the status of those who do not come back.

Is every patient involved in an outcome project? If care is defined as ongoing and linked to follow-up, the clinical team may decide that all patients of a designated condition or diagnosis will participate. They may, however, limit participation to something like every 10th patient of the condition monitored. This may apply only to follow-up or to the entire data set used for outcome monitoring. However, as clinical support systems are built upon admission information, the team may wish to involve all patients of a given type in admission (and discharge) measurements but only every nth patient in the follow-up.

The information acquired at follow-up will likely be a subset of information gathered at admission or during treatment. It will include some indication of clinical status and a general measure of functional status or well-being. The former will be coded into some form of outcome status. For cardiac patients, for example, a traditional outcome of dead or alive can take the living status and separate out levels of improvement. This could take the form of a scale with three or more points. One relatively simple scale would have the levels of (1) deceased due to cardiac reasons; (2) complicated recovery; and (3) uncomplicated recovery.

REQUIRED INFORMATION

In addition to follow-up status, there are six general categories of data acquired in an outcome management system—clinical, course, economic, demographic, quality of life, and progress during treatment. The degree of effort necessary in obtaining data of this type depends on how advanced a particular health care facility is in the direction of computerization of clinical records. Considerably more efforts are called for if clinical information is not computerized. If this has already been accomplished then additional data requirements for outcome management can be identified and the emphasis placed on following up patients relatively early in the process.

CLINICAL INFORMATION

The clinical data rest upon known risk factors or indicators of severity. Risk factors for developing myocardial infarction (MI), for example, are not necessarily the same as those which will predict the outcome of treatment for MI. Usually the severity of a condition is more likely to predict outcome, suggest treatment alternatives, and offer more in the way of information to support clinical decision making. Severity corrections of outcome data are particularly important since clinicians do not want to overreact to reports of low outcomes in a group of severely ill patients.

Those who already have a system which acquires a minimal data set relevant to a specific condition are well on the way to defining the required outcome management data. Others may have been looking for just such data and be ready to quantify it for clinical use. Practice standards with respect to different conditions are becoming more prevalent and represent an excellent starting place. Outcome data sets can also be developed by examining various published follow-up studies.

There is also an organization which directs its energies to support outcome management. At InterStudy, instruments have been developed to capture the essence of various clinical conditions. These are called Technology of Patient Experience (TyPE) questionnaires. The outcome management aspect of InterStudy is now handled by the Health Outcomes Institute in Bloomington, Minnesota. There are also a number of sources for clinical data sets similar to the TyPE instruments. It is hoped that as more organizations use standard data collection instruments that comparisons can be made across facilities and normative standards developed. In practical application of any data set, local clinicians are apt to want to modify it. Wherever possible, this should be in the form of adding to it, rather than changing it, so that external comparisons can be made on the core information.

A specific condition may be more severe when complicated by the presence of certain other diseases. Thus for any condition studied, it is important to identify which comorbidities will be documented. In some cases these are identified on the TyPE instrument.

Admission laboratory findings are often used to identify the severity of a condition. In the APACHE systems (Wong & Knaus, 1991), biochemical data make significant contributions to the estimates of severity and longevity.

Behavioral data such as use of alcohol and tobacco may also be of value to collect. Smokers, for example, have been found to be noncompliant with a number of medical procedures.

COURSE INDICATORS

The health care team may wish to log change in clinical status during treatment in a way that will assist them to make sense of outcome data. For example, on a coronary care unit various complications in the course of a patient's treatment may develop. Such complications should be anticipated and recorded in an outcome management system.

Plans should also be made to record the instances in which treatment departs from the norm, or in which there are different treatments of choice. These can help in understanding how well practice guidelines have been followed. In more elegant outcome management systems, complete care maps will be considered and the achieved milestones recorded. In simpler projects, normal versus special (or additional) treatment may be all that is documented.

ECONOMIC INFORMATION

Information which can be used to examine costs and cost savings is often collected to demonstrate the impact of treatment changes on costs to the system. Utilization of health services is commonly recorded. Previous hospitalizations, emergency room visits, use of home care, and office consultations in a given period (such as the year before admission) are useful to gather at intake and follow-up. Other economic losses may be included such as absences from work or school or other variables which are a direct or indirect cost to society or the patient. On discharge, length of stay is an important treatment variable with potential for direct management by the treatment team.

DEMOGRAPHIC DATA

In a research hospital, the admission procedures may do a careful job of documenting demographic characteristics. In other facilities, the routinely gathered information may not be what is needed. Demographics can be useful in describing the patients worked with, comparing them with others, and examining whether outcomes vary for individuals of different backgrounds. Typical demographic variables include marital status, education, employment status, usual occupation, the previous year's total family income before taxes, number of dependents, ethnic origin, age and sex.

QUALITY OF LIFE

In outcome management studies, a general measure of well-being is commonly administered on admission and follow-up. There is considerable interest in how health care treatment for a specific condition may have spin-off to affect well-being. Clinical management of particular patients may also be modified when it is known that they are low or high in areas of well-being.

There are several quality of life measures. These include the Quality of Well Being Scale, the Sickness Impact Profile, the Duke Health Profile, the Dartmouth Primary Care Cooperative Information Project Scale, and the SF-36 Health Status Questionnaire. These five instruments appear frequently in the health care research literature and a convenient summary of them is available (Kraus, 1991).

At Peel Memorial Hospital, the SF-36 Health Status Questionnaire (SF-36) was selected. The SF-36 is a short form, 36-item summary of questions used in the medical outcome study (Stewart et al., 1989; Wells et al., 1989) developed by John Ware (Stewart, Haynes, & Ware, 1988; Ware, Snow, Kosinski, & Gandek, 1993) with support from the Rand Corporation. The questionnaire is scored from a variety of short scales which reflect functional status—Physical Functioning, Social Functioning, Role Limitations Attributed to Physical Problems, and Role Limitations Attributed to Emotional Problems. There are also three brief scales which evaluate well-being—Mental Health, Energy, and Pain. Finally, there is an indicator of change in health which is derived from a single question. The eight scales are reasonably reliable and valid despite their brevity. They are only slightly less reliable than the longer counterparts used in the medical outcome study. The 36 items can be presented on two sides of a single page, or by computer, and take a patient about 10 minutes to complete. (The SF-36 is available through the Medical Outcomes Trust, PO Box 1917, Boston, MA 02205-8516. A software version is available from CogniSyst Inc., 3937 Nottaway Road, Durham, NC 27707.)

CONSUMER SATISFACTION AND PROGRESS

The patient's report of satisfaction with treatment and rating of progress should be measured at discharge and/or follow-up. Progress during treatment should also be rated by the health care professional discharging the patient. Progress ratings by patients and therapists in psychotherapy have been found to constitute different factors (McLachlan, 1972) and to relate differently to outcome (McLachlan, 1974). This is likely to be the case in other types of treatment since patients often view their treatment and recovery differently from health care professionals. Any system of managing results should attend to the patient's perception.

IMPLEMENTATION CONSIDERATIONS

It should be clear that outcome management relies on regular measurement of outcomes and other information relevant to an evaluation of outcomes. This well-defined and carefully gathered information constitutes what perhaps the normal hospital record should contain. It is, therefore, particularly timely to design data requirements for outcome management at a time when a new or revised hospital data system is considered. Then costs can be built in to the hospital records and computer systems and duplication avoided.

In other instances, it may be possible to redesign data collected by a unit to serve goals of clinical care as well as outcome management (although ideally these should be seen as one and the same). For example, the nursing history or physician's examination on admission may include some outcome management data and be integrated into the process. The revised recording forms are likely to gain from being more operational in nature, with data which is not currently computerized entered into the system.

MANAGING OUTCOMES

The data developed from the measurement of information related to outcomes are for the purpose of managing patient care. To facilitate this a number of reports are helpful.

First, there are clinical reports such as the printout on the patient's functional status derived from the SF-36, the TyPE instruments, or the initial history. When a TyPE questionnaire and nursing notes are combined into a structured interview, regular clinical reports can be generated by the computer. These can be used to provide a decision-support system. Such a support system can be more useful as outcome data are analyzed with reference to the predictors and programmed into the results. At Duke University, for example, there is a carefully defined and detailed data set on cardiac patients which is used for ongoing research and study. At Peel Memorial Hospital, it was found that patients with MI who had better outcomes after treatment experienced positive change on four SF-36 scales of well-being. Outcome status for the MI patients was predicted by the presence of cardiomegaly, congestive heart failure, age, and number of prior hospitalizations for cardiac reasons. Although other predictors of outcome were found, these four contained the majority of the variance and formed factors in a multiple linear regression prediction of outcome which could be used for estimates of clinical severity (McLachlan et al., 1994). Estimates such as these can be calculated by the computer routinely on admission.

A second type of computer output is descriptive—a regular report on the demographics and incidence of patient conditions on a given unit can provide ongoing snapshots of changing patient needs.

Once follow-up has begun, a third type of report can be made available, one which is the heart and soul of outcome management. This report presents how well patients fared after their treatment. The outcome of patients for the current month can be compared with those of the previous month (or the same month a year ago). Analysis of outcome data can be presented for the current month (and year to date) by length of stay, type and amount of treatment, initial severity of condition, provider or provider type, demographics and other factors of interest. The physician may receive a report for only his or her patients while the department may receive a printout for all the patients treated. This is where trends can be detected and clinicians can view the results of their efforts. (Some examples of reports are found in McLachlan, 1992.)

Findings and action on findings should be discussed by the clinical team. The focus should be on measuring the system, not individual practitioners. A supportive, not a threatening, context is required. The team should engage in hypothesis testing, developing "What if?" scenarios. Planning is necessary for this process and training may be required in how to communicate frankly about sensitive issues. Of course, the process works best if the team members are imbued with a desire for continuous quality improvement. This is the primary purpose of an outcome management program—to help clinicians improve the effectiveness of their care.

Since physicians and other health care professionals are the major beneficiaries of outcome management, they should be actively involved in the planning process and anticipate what the final printouts will portray. The development of outcome management is an iterative process and frequent feedback of results should be provided, starting with simpler information and building toward the optimal. As the clinicians working with the system use and modify it, their confidence in it (and, therefore, their commitment) will increase and they will be more inclined to reflect on ways to enhance treatment.

As mentioned previously, some of the clinicians involved in outcome management will be curious enough to request specific analyses and share interesting findings with their colleagues at conferences.

OUTCOME AND QUALITY MANAGEMENT

Both a rudder and a compass are necessary to steer a ship. Outcome and quality management processes should work together to improve an organization. Wherever possible, quality improvement initiatives should be linked closely to outcomes management. Explaining the variation in outcome requires an examination of the process of achieving it. Improved outcomes result from improved processes.

REFERENCES

Berwick, D. M. (1988). Toward an applied technology for quality measurement in health care. *Medical Decision Making, 8*(4), 253–258.

Elwood, P. M. (1988). Shattuck lecture—Outcomes management: A technology of patient experience. *New England Journal of Medicine, 26,* 724–735.

Kraus, N. (1991). General health status measures. *The InterStudy Quality Edge, 1*(1), 5–39.

McLachlan, J. F. C. (1972). Benefit from group therapy as a function of patient-therapist match on conceptual level. *Psychotherapy: Theory, research and practice, 9,* 317–323.

McLachlan, J. F. C. (1974). Therapy strategies, personality orientation and recovery from alcoholism. *Canadian Psychiatric Association Journal, 19,* 25–30.

McLachlan, J. F. C. (1992). Outcome management in a community hospital. *Canadian Journal of Quality in Health Care, 9*(3), 11–15.

McLachlan, J. F. C., Borts, D., Armitage, D. P., Hill, L., Joza, P., Hansen, D., Petrevan, S., & Purdy, N. (1994). *Outcomes of Community Hospital Treatment for Acute Myocardial Infarction.* Peel Memorial Hospital, Brampton, Ontario. (Unpublished manuscript).

Stewart, A. L., Greenfield, S., Hays, R. D., Wells, K., Rogers, W. H., Berry, S. D., McGlynn, E. A., & Ware, J. E. (1989). Functional status and well-being of patients with chronic conditions: Results from the medical outcomes study. *Journal of the American Medical Association, 262*(7), 907–913.

Stewart, A. L., Haynes, R. D., & Ware, J. E. (1988). The MOS short form general health survey: Reliability and validity in a patient population. *Medical Care, 26,* 724–735.

Ware, J. E., Snow, K. K., Kosinski, M., & Gandek, B. (1993). *SF-36 Health Survey Manual and Interpretive Guide.* Boston: Health Institute, New England Medical Center.

Wells, K. B., Stewart, A., Hays, R., Burnam, M. A., Rogers, W., Daniels, M., Berry, S., Greenfield, S., & Ware, J. (1989). The functioning and well-being of depressed patients: Results from the medical outcomes study. *Journal of the American Medical Association. 262*(7), 914–919.

Wetzler, H. P., & Elwood, P. M. (1991). Successful outcomes management. *Frontiers of Health Services Management. 8*(2), 58–61.

Wong, D. T., & Knaus, W. A. (1991). Predicting outcome in critical care: The current status of the APACHE prognostic scoring system. *Canadian Journal of Anaesthesiology. 38*(3), 374–383.

Name Index

Abrahms, E., 160
Abrams, M., 157, 160, 169
Aburdene, P., 79
Adler, S., 15, 133
Ainslie, G., 64–65
Aitken, M., 55
Alarcon, G., 142
Allen, B. A., 38
Alpert, N. M., 175
Andersen, C. M., 117
Anderson, L., 221
Antonovsky, A., 227
Appelbaum, S. H., 118
Arachtingi, B. M., 142
Aranya, N., 23
Armenakis, A. A., 209
Armitage, D. P., 271
Aronson, E., 102, 106, 108, 110, 113, 118, 119
Atkinson, J. H., 142
Attarian, A., 252
Aurelius, M., 178

Baba, V. V., 130
Backer, T. E., 199, 204, 205–206, 207, 208, 209, 210, 212, 214
Baer, L., 175
Baldwin, T. T., 240, 252, 256
Bandura, A., 227
Baral, J., 55
Barber, A. E., 84
Barbor, T. F., 35
Barling, J., 81, 82, 92, 93
Bar-On, R., 39

Barsade, S. G., 7
Bartelt, D. W., 220
Bartol, K. M., 24
Battista, R. N., 35
Beardslee, W. R., 230
Beatty, W., 14
Beck, A. T., 107
Becker, I., 189
Belohlav, J. A., 133
Ben-Avi, I., 132
Bentson, C., 14
Berkman, L. F., 36–37
Berry, S. D., 141, 269
Berwick, D. M., 262
Best, K. M., 220
Birati, A., 14
Bishop, F. M., 4
Blum, M., 104, 105
Bobko, P., 28
Bodnar, J. C., 166
Boeren, R. G. B., 142–143
Bogardis, J., 193
Bogduk, N., 139, 140, 147
Boice, R., 64, 65
Bonica, J. J., 142
Borts, D., 271
Bossio, L. M., 227
Bowers, K. S., 160
Boyd, J. H., 134
Boyes, S., 253, 257
Brakke, M. L., 35
Bray, D. W., 14
Breaugh, J. A., 133
Breiter, H. C. R., 175

Breslow, L., 36–37
Bridges, W., 209
Briordy, R., 55
Broderick, R., 253–254
Bronson, J., 241, 252
Brooke, P. P., 128
Brush, C. C., 89
Buller, P. F., 241
Burden, D. S., 92
Burka, J. B., 58, 61, 71–72
Burke, S., 134
Burke, W. W., 211–212
Burnam, M. A., 141
Burns, D. D., 189
Buunk, B., 128
Byham, W. C., 14
Byrne, B. M., 105

Campbell, J., 210
Cangemi, J. P., 24, 25, 26
Carayon, P., 103
Carrell, M. R., 128
Carter, G. W., 12
Cartwright, S., 87
Carver, C. S., 227
Cascio, W. F., 203
Casten, R. J., 142, 146–147
Caudill, M. A., 142
Chabot, A., 55
Chapman, C. F., 140
Cheloha, R. S., 133
Cherniss, C., 102, 105, 108, 110–111
Cleveland, J. N., 14, 28
Coberly, S., 87, 94
Colella, A., 28
Colligan, R. C., 229
Comstock, G. W., 160
Conner, D. R., 208
Connerley, M. L., 15
Conze, E., 178
Cook, F., 36
Cook, M., 118

Cooper, C. L., 87
Cordery, J. L., 133
Cordes, C. L., 104, 105
Corey, D. M., 103
Costa, P. T., 56, 229
Covey, S. R., 57–58, 191
Covin, T. J., 89
Cragun, J. R., 241
Crain, J., 80
Crawford, N., 255–256
Crawford, T., 163
Cronin, M. P., 97
Cronshaw, S. F., 12
Crouter, A. C., 82, 93, 94
Crump, C. E., 103
Cutler, S., 35

Dahan, M., 14
Daniels, M., 141
Dass, P., 96
Davenport, T., 212–213
Davies, J. W., 36
Davis, K. S., 27
Davis, S., 106
Dawis, R. V., 24–25
DeFriese, G. H., 35
DeGood, D. E., 140–141
DeMarr, B., 96
DeVore Jognson, D., 142
DiClemente, C. C., 13, 179–180
DiGiuseppe, R., 31
DiMattia, D. J., 31, 189
Dittrich, J. E., 128
Dixon, T., 200–201, 243–245, 249
Doan, B., 142
Dougherty, T. W., 104, 105
Drucker, P. F., 206, 207, 215
Dryden, W., 30, 160, 169
Dugoni, B. L., 28
Dunham, R. B., 84
Dunnette, M. D., 12

Elder, V. T., 104

Name Index

Elliot, G. R., 36
Ellis, A., 4, 24, 29–30, 61, 62–63, 65, 73, 107, 109, 133–134, 139, 147, 151, 157, 159, 160–161, 163, 164, 166, 169, 174, 175, 178, 188, 189, 195, 228, 230
Elwood, P. M., 262
Emlen, A. C., 82
Engel, G. V., 24
Epictetus, 160, 178
Esterling, B. A., 166
Eysenck, H. J., 56

Fabiano, E., 38
Farr, J. L., 133
Farrell, J. M., 188
Farris, N., 256
Fassel, D., 103
Feldman, C. D., 101
Feltham, R., 14
Fernandez, J. P., 82
Ferrari, J. R., 55, 56–57, 61, 68
Ferrell, D. K., 1–2
Feuling, L., 258
Feymoyer, J., 141
Fierman, J., 83
Filipczak, B., 105, 108
Finneran, M., 113
Firth, H., 105
Fischman, A. J., 175
Fisher, A. B., 208, 213
Flett, G. L., 73
Foerge, W. H., 36
Foester, V., 253
Fordyce, W. E., 142
France, R., 141
Frankel, M. L., 2–3, 88, 92
Frayne, C. A., 133
Frederick, C. J., 229–230
Freedman, S. M., 104
Freire, P., 249
French, J. R. P., 160

Freudenberger, H., 102, 105, 107
Friedman, D. E., 79, 81, 82, 85, 87, 96

Gaiennie, L. R., 14
Galagan, P., 254
Galinsky, E., 79, 81, 82, 83, 85, 87, 96
Gall, A. L., 253, 258
Gallagher, R. M., 141
Gallup, J., 2
Gambill, D., 213
Gandek, B., 269
Garand, J. C., 80, 84
Garfield, C., 210
Garfin, S. R., 142
Garmenzy, P., 220
Gaugler, B. B., 14
Gebhardt, D. L., 103
Genasci, L., 81
George, J. M., 133
Geurts, S., 128
Gibson, S., 241, 252
Gier, J. A., 12
Glaser, R., 166
Glogow, E., 107, 113
Goff, S. J., 82, 93
Golan, J., 133
Goldberg, L., 160
Goldman, L., 36
Goleman, D., 187
Goodwin, W. R., 119
Gordon, E. W., 220
Gordon, J., 4
Grant, I., 142
Green, M., 132
Greenfield, S., 141, 269
Grensing, L., 105
Guion, R. M., 131
Guzzo, R. A., 89

Hackett, R. D., 131, 132
Hackman, J. R., 27, 133
Hackman, R. J., 94

Hagglund, K., 142
Haines, A. P., 35
Haley, W. E., 141, 142
Hall, D. T., 84, 92, 133
Hamburg, D. A., 36
Hammer, M., 212, 213
Hammer, T. H., 129–130, 133
Hand, S., 85
Handy, C., 159
Hansen, D., 271
Harper, R. A., 189, 228
Harris, S. G., 209
Hart, M. U., 241, 250, 251
Haugh, L. D., 141
Hayes, N. J., 28
Haynes, R. D., 269
Hays, R. D., 141, 269
Hendler, N., 142
Hendricks, C., 13
Herbiniak, L. G., 133
Hernstein, R. J., 65
Hester, R., 193
Hewitt, P. L., 73
Hill, D., 55
Hill, L., 271
Hill, M., 55
Hoffman, L. W., 93
Hogan, J. J., 113
Holmes, T. H., 159
Honey, P., 254–255
Hughes, D., 81, 82, 87
Hunsaker, J. S., 118
Hunt, G. G., 87, 94
Hunt, J. W., 108, 113
Hurrell, Jr. J. J., 103

Idelson, R. K., 37
Ilgen, D. R., 28, 129
Ironson, G., 87
Ivancevich, J. M., 104, 133

Jackson, S. E., 105

Jamison, R. L., 82, 93
Jenike, M. A., 175
Jenner, L., 85, 87, 88, 96
Jensen, M. A. C., 252
Johns, G., 127–128
Johnson, J., 55, 56–57
Johnson, J. L., 61, 68
Joseph, J. M., 227–228
Joyce, L. W., 14
Joza, P., 271
Jud, B., 101

Kahn, R. L., 158
Kaley, W., 142
Kanter, R. M., 81–82, 92, 94
Katz, I. R., 142, 146–147
Katzell, R. A., 103–104, 106, 111
Keefe, F. J., 141
Keijsers, G. J., 103
Keita, G. P., 103
Kellner, R., 140
Kelly, P., 160
Kennedy, P., 204–205
Kets de Vries, M. F. R., 187–188
Kichar, R., 241, 252
Kiecolt-Glaser, J. K., 166
Kiel, L. D., 214
Kiernan, B., 140–141
Killinger, B., 110
Kirby, P., 31
Kirchmeyer, C., 84, 92, 94–95, 97
Klapow, J. C., 142
Klarreich, S. H., 31, 158, 199–200
Kleban, M. H., 142, 146–147
Klein, B. W., 126
Klimoski, R. J., 28
Knaus, W., 1, 3, 49
Knaus, W. A., 267
Knaus, W. J., 13, 14, 15, 18, 61, 133–134
Kobasa, S. C., 226–227
Kole-Snijders, A. M. J., 142–143

Kopec, A. M., 1-2
Kopecky, G., 189
Koren, P., 82
Kosinski, M., 269
Kossek, E. E., 96
Kotter, J., 205
Kottke, T. E., 35
Kozak, R. E., 26
Kraus, N., 269
Kuhnert, K. W., 101
Kush, K. S., 88, 91

La Forge, J., 157
Lachman, R., 23
Lalonde, M., 36
Land, G., 254
Landau, J., 129-130, 133
Landsbergis, P. A., 113
Landy, F. J., 110
Lang, J. M., 113
Latham, G. P., 129, 133
Launier, R., 160
Lawler, E. E., 128, 133
Lawler, E. E. III, 27
Lawton, M. P., 142, 146-147
Lay, C. H., 61, 64
Lazarus, R. S., 160
Leana, C. R., 101
Lee, R. T., 105
Leiter, M. P., 105
Leo, G. I., 193
Levant, R. F., 189
Levine, S., 37
Lewin, K., 208
Lichtenberg, J. W., 142
Lichtenfels, P. A., 12
Lobley, R., 254-255
Loeser, J., 140
Lofquist, L. H., 24-25
Long, J. W., 239, 255
Lowman, R. L., 101, 110, 111
Luciano, L., 83

Maccoby, M., 24, 114
MacIntosh, M. C., 38
Magni, G., 141
Malinchoe, M., 229
Manzo, P. A., 175
Marcus, N. J., 142
Markels, A., 191
Marshall, J., 208
Marsick, V., 251
Maslach, C., 102, 105, 107
Maslow, A., 25-26
Masten, A. S., 220
Matteson, M. T., 104
Maukisch, H., 14
Maultsby, M. C., Jr., 182, 192
Maurer, S. D., 12
Mawhinney, T. C., 104
Maxmen, J. S., 140
Maynard, H., 253
Mazur, J. E., 65
McCann, C., 36
McCarthy, E., 96
McClellan, E. L., 132
McCord, J., 220-221
McCown, W. G., 55, 56-57, 61, 68
McCrae, R. R., 56
McDaniel, M. A., 12
McDermid, C. D., 26
McEvoy, G. M., 14, 241
McGinnis, J. M., 36
McGlynn, E. A., 269
McGrath, J. E., 160
McGregor, D., 24
McLachlan, J. F. C., 201, 270, 271
McShane, S. L., 131
Meier, S., 106
Meir, E. I., 14
Melamed, S., 132
Mennen, S., 189
Merskey, H., 147
Merskey, S., 139, 140
Mezirow, J., 248-251
Michaels, B., 96

Middlestadt, S. E., 12
Miguel, E. C., 175
Milhous, R., 141
Miller, D., 243–245, 249
Miller, W. R., 179
Millson, W. A., 38
Minuchin, S., 82
Miranda, D. R., 103
Mirvis, P. H., 212
Mitchell, D. W., 24, 25
Monroe, P. A., 80, 84
Montaque, J., 108, 113
Moretti, C., 175
Morris, G. B., 3–4, 28–29, 139
Morrison, J., 140
Moses, J. L., 14
Mossholder, K. W., 209
Motowidlo, S. J., 12
Mount, M. K., 82, 93
Mueller, W. S., 133
Murphy, K., 28
Murphy, L. R., 103

Nadler, D. M., 212
Naisbitt, J., 79
Nardi, T. J., 107, 109–110
Nelson, G. L., 89
Nelson, K. L., 83
Newman, J. E., 128, 133
Newstrom, J. W., 84
Nicholson, N., 127–128
Nolen-Hoeksema, S., 229
Noonan, K. A., 89
Norcross, J. C., 13, 179–180
Norman, G., 230
Nowack, K. M., 104, 105

O'Connell, S. E., 10
Odon, C. R., 10
Offord, K. P., 229
O'Hara, K., 205–206, 208
Oldham, G. R., 94

Orr, E., 227
Orthner, D. K., 93, 97
O'Toole, J., 212

Palmer, W. H., 38
Parmelee, P. A., 142, 146–147
Parron, D. L., 36
Parsons, T., 245
Patchen, M., 128
Patterson, T. L., 142
Peak, M. H., 88
Perlow, L. A., 91
Peters, H., 239–240
Peters, T., 207
Peterson, C., 227
Petrevan, S., 271
Petzel, T., 55
Phillips, H. C., 142
Phillips, J. S., 104
Pierce, J. L., 84
Pines, A., 102, 106, 108, 110, 113, 118, 119
Piotrkowski, C. S., 81
Pittman, J. F., 93, 97
Polance, C., 104, 119
Poland, T. D., 27
Pond, S. B., 14
Popp, P. O., 133
Porporino, F. J., 38
Porras, J. I., 212
Porter, L. W., 27, 128, 132
Porterfield, J. M., 199, 204, 208, 209, 214
Potter, B., 118, 119
Premack, S. C., 27
Priest, S., 241, 252
Prochaska, J. O., 13, 179–180
Purdy, N., 271
Pursell, E. D., 12, 129

Quinn, R. P., 158

Rabinowitz, S., 133

Rachman, S. J., 227
Rahe, R. H., 159
Rauch, S. L., 175
Raudsepp, E., 119
Rauk, V., 141
Regan, M., 96
Reinertsen, J., 261
Reveille, J., 142
Rhee, J., 101
Rhodes, S. R., 126, 127, 128, 129
Richardson, L. D., 231
Richman, D. R., 3, 23, 24, 30, 107, 108, 109–110, 118
Richter, J., 84–85, 92
Rieger, D. A., 134
Rigsby, L. C., 220
Ritchie, R. J., 14
Roach, B. L., 101, 107
Roach, D., 132, 133
Robb, H. B., 2, 174
Roberts, R., 56
Robertson, P. J., 212
Robinson, D., 38
Roemer, M. I., 36
Rogers, W., 141, 269
Rohman, M., 37
Roland, C. C., 240, 252, 256
Rollnick, S., 179
Romano, J. L., 117
Romano, J. M., 141, 142
Rose, F., 210
Rosenbaum, M., 228
Rosenthal, D. B., 14
Rosenthal, R. A., 158
Roskies, E., 157
Rossi, E. L., 234
Roteman, M. R., 133
Rothblum, E. D., 55
Rottenberg, L., 230
Rowland, A., 177
Russell, D. W., 117
Rynes, S. L., 15

Saal, F. E., 133
Saltzman, A., 80, 81, 91
Sanchez-Craig, M., 38
Sapiro, 56
Sauter, S. L., 103
Savage, C. R., 175
Savery, L. K., 108
Sayles, L. R., 26
Schaufeli, W. B., 103, 107, 128
Scheier, M. F., 227
Schein, E. M., 24
Schiska, A., 118
Schmidt, F. L., 12
Schoewenburg, H. C., 61, 64
Schonfeld, I. S., 101, 106
Schroeder, D. H., 229
Schubert, S., 252
Schulman, P., 229
Scott, K. D., 131, 132
Scott, W. G., 26
Seligman, M. E. P., 229
Semenciw, M. R., 36
Senge, P. M., 29, 104, 110
Sewell, C., 256–258
Seyle, H., 166
Seyler, D. L., 80, 84
Shalowitz, D., 113, 117
Shamir, B., 89
Shaw, G. B., 211
Shaw, I. A., 188
Shaw, R. A., 212
Sherman, S., 209
Shipley, W. C., 55
Shutty, M. S., 141
Skelly, J., 141
Skinner, B. F., 65
Skinner, H. A., 2, 36, 37, 38
Skinner, K., 117
Skinner, W., 193
Sladek, C., 97
Slater, M. A., 142
Smith, F. J., 133
Smith, L. M., 133

Smulders, P. G., 130
Snoek, J. D., 158
Snow, K. K., 269
Sobell, L. C., 193
Sobell, M. B., 193
Solomon, C. M., 80, 83–84
Solomon, L. J., 55
Somers, M. J., 132
Song, L. D., 220
Sperling, J., 110
Stallworth, H. F., 101, 105
Stanton, J., 212, 213
Steers, R. M., 27, 126, 127, 128, 129, 132
Stein, P. J., 83
Stein, S. J., 2
Stellman, J. M., 106, 113
Steward, A., 141
Stewart, A. L., 269
Stewart, T. A., 102
Stewart, T. H., 205, 209
Stockman, 200
Straw, B. M., 7
Stroh, L. K., 88, 91
Suz, J., 132

Taylor, G. S., 131
Taylor, J. O., 37
Taylor, R. D., 221
Terpstra, D. E., 7
Thayer, P. W., 14
Thomas, R. M., 73
Thompson, B. L., 241
Thompson, D. E., 103–104
Thornton, G. C., 14
Thornton, K. M., 229
Thornton, N., 229
Tippins, N., 12
Toffler, A., 159
Toomey, E. L., 118
Towery, T. L., 105
Tuckman, B. W., 252

Turner, J. A., 141, 142
Tziner, A., 12, 14

Umiker, W., 105
Unden, A., 133
Urban, B., 141

Vaill, P., 206
Vallen, G. K., 104
Van Alphen, T., 85, 87
van Eek, H., 142–143
Van Ness, R., 71
Vance, R. J., 101
Vash, C. L., 206
Vasudevan, S. V., 142
Vega, G., 189
Vlaeyen, J. W. S., 142–143
Von Baeyer, C., 142
Voydanoff, P., 81
Vroom, V., 128

Wadden, N., 142
Wagenaar, J., 157
Wagner, R. J., 240, 252, 256
Waldrep, M., 214
Wallace, P. G., 35
Walton, E., 212
Wanous, J. P., 27
Ward, B., 83
Ward, N. G., 140
Ware, J., 141
Ware, J. E., 269
Waters, L. K., 132, 133
Watson, C. J., 133
Wechsler, H., 37
Weekes, J. R., 38
Weekley, J. A., 12
Weickgenant, A. L., 142
Weisberg, J., 101
Wells, K. B., 141, 269
Werner, E. E., 227, 230
Westman, M., 227

Wetzler, H. P., 262
Whetzel, D. L., 12
Whiteley, J. M., 160–161
Wiener, L., 80, 81, 91
Wiesner, W. H., 12
Wigle, D. T., 36
Williams, D. A., 141
Williams, M., 239–240
Williams, R. A., 141
Wilson, L., 253–254
Wolf, G. D., 103
Wolfe, D. M., 158

Wong, D. T., 267
Wright, P. M., 12

Xia, F., 101

Young, H., 174
Yuen, L. M., 58, 61, 71–72

Zaxacki, R A., 85
Zedeck, S., 12, 81–82, 92
Zimmerman, M. A., 230

Subject Index

ABCDE framework, 162–164
Absence behaviors, 127
Absence cultures, 127–128
Absenteeism
  attitudes and, 129–131
  causes of, 127
  cognitions and, 133–135
  cognitive perspective on, 125–135
  contradictory empirical studies of, 131–133
  costs of, 2, 3, 85–87, 125–126
  frequency and duration measures of, 130–131
  models for study of, 126–128
  patterns of, 126
  social view of, 127–128
  voluntary and involuntary, 129–130
  work-family programs and, 94
Absolutist evaluations, 30
Acceptance, 63–64
Action
  blocks against, 72–75
  timetables of, for resiliency, 235
Action based experiential programs, 200–201
Action-reflection cycle, 240
Adaptation, successful, 220–221
Advisors, 235
Affect, chronic pain-related, 145–147
Alcohol use
  absenteeism and, 134
  reducing, 192–193
Alcoholics Anonymous, weekend retreats, 194

Alexithymia, 188
Always and never thinking, 162–163
Anger, pain-related, 145–146
Anxiety
  with chronic pain, 141–142, 145–146
  neurotic, 134–135
  procrastination and, 56–57
APACHE systems, 267
Assessment center approach
  developing program of, 17–19
  establishing direction for, 16–17
  evaluation in, 5–6
  irregularities of, 15
  in selection for growing companies, 13–15
Assessment center systems
  consulting opportunities in, 49–50
  costs of, 10–11
  profitability of, 10
Assessment issues, 11–13
AT&T, downsizing of, 203–204
Attendance motivation, 127
Attitudes
  absenteeism and, 129–131
  differences in, 1–2
  resiliency and, 224
Attitudinal differentiation, 23–32
Awareness building, 244
  in Miller-Dixon EBTD model, 247
  process of, 240–241
Awfulizing, 30, 161, 162, 165–166
  blocking planning, 68–70

Balance, 211

285

Beauty, inspiration of, 195
Behavior
  developmental factors in, 186
  evolutionary factors in, 184
  historical factors in, 185
Behavioral data, 267
Behavioral techniques, 4, 173
  for wellness in workplace, 189–193
  workplace stress, 169
Belief systems
  analysis of, 23–32
  identifying in workplace, 27–29
  incongruity of, 29–31
  irrational, 30–31
  in job burnout, 107
  of organization vs. individual, 1–2
Beliefs
  emotional and behavioral consequences of, 163–164
  in general adaptive syndrome, 166
  incongruent, 23–32
  irrational, 168–169, 183–184
  regulation of, 228
  in stress, 162–163, 167–169
  wellness and, 177–178
Bingeing, 64–66
Biofeedback, workplace stress, 169
Biographical forms, 17
Biology issues, 36
Biopsychosocial approach, 142–154
Blame, 140–141, 149
Boosters, 235
Boss, relationship with, 158
Boundaryless organization, 210
Brain, functioning of, 181–182
Breathing, deep diaphragmatic, 190
Breathing exercises, 182
Buddhist beliefs, 178–179
Burnout
  cognitive components of, 105, 106–107
  depression and, 106
  individual factors in, 103–104
  job market and, 102
  prevention of, 119–120
  stress and, 105–106
  three-factor model of, 105
  workplace factors in, 103
Burnout beliefs, 3, 108–118
Busyness and bingeing phenomenon, 64–65
  overcoming, 65–66

Candidate selection consulting, 8–9
Career counseling, 2
  in community, 53
Career development, xvi–xvii
  to prevent job burnout, 117–118
Career skill sets, improvement of, xvii
Challenge, in job burnout, 109, 114–115
Change. *See also* Organizational change
  avoidance of, 115–116
  awareness of, 240–241
  changing nature of, 199, 207
  human side of, 211–212, 214
  increasing amount of, 207
  increasing pace of, 207
  increasing rate of, xv
  interventions for, 204–205
  meaning of, 206–207
  organizational renewal with, 199–201
  planned, 206
  readiness for, 209
  resiliency to, 219–237
  resistance to, 208, 212
  responding to, 208–211
  strategic thinking about, 204
  understanding, 209
  why it hurts, 207–208
  in workplace, 203–215
Change expert, 204
Change management programs,

failure of, 219–220
Chaos, 214
Chemicals, effects of, 175–176
Child abuse, increase in, xi
Child care
    absenteeism related to, 85–87
    on-site centers for, 81
ChildFree Network, 87
Chronic pain
    achieving identity with, 151–152
    affect dimension of, 145–147
    complex, 140
    definitions of, 140
    increase in, 3
    management of, 3–4
    measuring success of managing, 152–153
    PATHWAY for dealing with, 139–154
    persistent, 140
    prevalence of, 139
    psychological correlates of, 140–142
    unspecified, 140
    work and, 150–151
Chronic pain syndromes, 140
Clinical data, 267
Coaching, xiii
Cognitions
    absenteeism and, 133–135
    in job burnout, 105, 106–107
Cognitions-beliefs, regulation of, 228
Cognitive approaches
    to wellness in workplace, 178–186
    workplace stress, 169
Cognitive career counseling, 118
Cognitive control, 119–120
Cognitive resiliency skills, 233
Cognitive techniques, 4, 173
Cognitive-behavioral approach
    to chronic pain management, 142–143
    for job burnout prevention, 109–110

Comforts, in job burnout, 110, 115–116
Commitment
    attitudinal and behavioral, 111
    in job burnout, 109, 110–111
Community career counseling, 53
Company
    consulting relationship with, 47–48
    professional understanding of, 45–47
Company tours, candidates' responses during, 18
Compass setting, 57–66
Competence
    beliefs about, in job burnout, 109, 111–113
    evaluation of, 112
    rewards and, 112–113
Competition, recruitment, 11–13
Complexity sciences, 214–215
Computer databases, consulting, 44
Computerized Lifestyle Assessment (CLA), 2
    benefits of, 37–40
    content areas of, 38–39
    need for, 35–36
    problem in, 35–37
Computers
    in outcome management, 264–265
    output from, 270
Confidants, 235
Consciousness, evolution of, 184
Consultant-relationship attributes, 48
Consultants, 43
    basics of good relationship for, 47–48
    getting through gate, 44–47
    opportunities for, in growth companies, 48–54
    roles of, 16–17
Consulting, xiii
Consumer satisfaction, 270
Contract work, xv–xvi

Contract workers, 222–223
Control
  internal locus of, 226–227
  in job burnout, 109, 113–114
Conversation, task-oriented, 229–230
Core belief systems, 107
Corporate adventure training, 240
Corporate belief system analysis, 23–32
Corporate structure, resiliency in, 221–226
Corporations
  characteristics of, 24–26
  definition of, 26
Counseling, xiii
Course indicators, 268
Critical self-reflection, 248–249, 250
  facilitation of, 251
Cross-transfer programs, 2
  consulting opportunities in, 50–51
Cross-validation strategies, 17

Damnation, 162
Dartmouth Primary Care Cooperative Information Project Scale, 269
Death, factors contributing to, 36
Debriefing questions, 245–247
Decision latitude, low, 113
Deep diaphragmatic breathing, 190
Demandingness, 30
  antidote to, 63–64
  with chronic pain, 147–149
  shoulds of, 62–63, 67–68
  in stress, 164–165
Demographic data, 268–269
Depression
  absenteeism and, 134
  burnout with, 106
  with chronic pain, 141–142
Desensitization techniques, 181
Developmental stages, thinking and, 186

Discomfort disturbance, 166
Disease prevention, 35
Downsizing, 200
  effects of, xi, 203–204
  resiliency to, 225
Drugs
  absenteeism and, 134
  effects of, 175–176
DUD tasks, 71
Duke Health Profile, 269
Dysfunctional corporate culture, 205

Early retirement
  burnout and, 104
  packages for, xvi
Economic data, 268
Educational programs, for belief system congruity, 31–32
Ego disturbance, 166
Emancipatory education, 248–249
Emotional disturbance, 165–166
Emotional intelligence, 39
Emotional support, 231
Emotions
  awareness of, 186–187
  choosing, 189
  evaluation of, 187
  naming, 188–189
  taking responsibility for, 186–189
Emotive techniques, 4, 173
  for wellness in workplace, 186–189
  workplace stress, 169
Empirically valid assessment methods, 8
Employee assistance programs (EAPs), 31, 103
Employee conferences
  with consultant, 52
  programs, 2
Employee involvement groups, 213–214
Employee-employer conflicts, 23–24

Subject Index

analysis of, 24–32
resolving, 24
Employees
belief systems of, 24–26
burnout in, 103–104
health promotion of, 1–4
life-style assessment and morale of, 39
life-style issues for, 2
resistance to change of, 205, 208
Entitlement attitude, 222
Environment, 36
changing, 199–200
Environmental stressors, 159–160
Eupsychian Management (Maslow), 25–26
Evocative techniques, 187–188
Excuses, not to take action, 74–75
Experience-based training and development (EBTD), 242
facilitator's role in, 245–249
literature review of, 252–259
team learning levels in, 242–252
transformative learning and outcomes of, 249–252
Experiential learning, xiii
Experiential training program
for organizational transformation, 239–259
renewal benefits in, 240–242
team learning levels in, 242–252
Explanatory style-perceptions, 229
in resiliency, 233

Facilitator
in promoting EBTD team development, 245–248
as transformative learning catalyst, 248–249
Family. *See also* Work-family conflicts; Work-family connections; Work-family programs

absenteeism and obligations to, 134
change in, xi–xii
dual career, xi
in job satisfaction, 92–93
negative impact of, on work, 82–83
positive spillover to work of, 92–93, 94–95
stressors from, 159
Family friendly programs, 2–3
Family friendly workplace, 81–85
barriers to, 85–91
changes toward, 91–98
need for, 79–81
Family leave, 81, 83
Family-responsive benefits, 83–84
Family-responsive interventions
in antagonistic culture, 89, 91
barriers to, 85–87
employee-focused versus organizationally focused, 84–86
inappropriate, 89
low need for, 88
negative effects of, 88
obstacles to adoption of, 88–89
obstacles to use of, 89–91
outmoded attitudes toward work and, 90–91
perceived cost of, 88–89
poor marketing of, 90
poor quality control of, 89–90
Family-work balance, xvii
Fasting, 194
Flextime, 83
meta-analysis of, 84
Focus, lack of, 56–57
Follow-up strategies, 265–266
Fostering Critical Reflections in Adulthood (Mezirow), 248–249
Frustration tolerance, low, 30, 115–116, 162
with chronic pain, 148–149
disputing, 168

Functional understanding, 244
  in Miller-Dixon EBTD model, 247

Gate-keeper role, 246, 247
General adaptive syndrome, 166
Geographical mobility, 158
Globalization, resiliency in, 221–223
Goal setting, 57
  helping individuals with, 57–60
Goals
  incongruity of, 1–2, 23–32
  job satisfaction and, 28
Group awareness, levels of, 254–255
Group development
  adjourning stage of, 258–259
  EBTD literature review and, 252–259
  forming stage of, 253–256
  issues of, 251–252
  norming stage of, 256–257
  performing stage of, 257–258
  stages of, 252
  storming stage of, 254–255
Group development theory, 200–201
Group Task and maintenance behaviors, 245–248
Growth companies
  consulting opportunities in, 48–54
  evaluating personnel for, 1, 5–19
  people's role in success of, 2
Guilt
  with chronic pain, 145
  in stress, 163

Hardiness, 226–227
Hassles, avoidance of, 68
Health
  absenteeism and, 128
  determinants of, 36
  promotion of, 35
  workplace stressors and, xvii
Health benefits, increased
  expenditures in, 2
Health care
  as determinant of health, 36
  escalating costs of, xii
  restructuring of, xii
Health insurance, historic background of, 177
Health risk behaviors, 35–36
Health risk factors, 36–37
Hookey players, 134
Hoover Company Profiles, 44
Human resource assessment, 11–13
Human resource selection
  cost factors of, 9–11
  in growing companies, 13–15
  strategies for growth companies, 7–19
Human services systems, profitability of, 10
Hypnosis, 181

Impulsiveness, 56–57
In-basket problem simulations, 18
Incompetent job behaviors, 111–112
Individual responsibility, 176
Information-skill development interventions, 204–205
In-house promotion system, 13
Innovation production, 206–207
Interconnectedness, 210
Interpersonal conflict, 158
InterStudy, 262
  instruments used by, 267
Interview
  methods of, 7
  standardized, 17
Interview systems
  inconsistency of, 12
  limitations of, 12–13
Irrational beliefs, 163
  disputing, 168–169
Irrational thinking styles, 30–31

Irrationality, 157, 162

Jaguar of North America,
    reorganization of, 213–214
Job burnout
    burnout beliefs and, 108–118
    cognitive components of, 106–107
    complexity of, 101
    definition of, 104–106
    prevention of, 119–120
    unrealistic expectations and, 107–108
Job burnout syndrome, 3
Job dissatisfaction, 158
Job involvement, 3, 127, 131–133
Job market, 102
Job performance, 111–112
Job preview, 15
    realistic, 27–28
Job relevant evaluation dimensions, 14–15
Job satisfaction
    absenteeism and, 3, 127, 131–133
    burnout and, 103–104
    family life and, 92–93
    goals and expectations in, 28
Jobs
    adjustment to change in, xvi
    changing nature of, xv–xvi

Knee-jerk thinking, deconditioning of, 181

Layoffs, 223
    burnout and, 104
Leadership Experiential Adventure Program (LEAP), 254
Learned helplessness, 113–114
Life-style, 2
    balancing to prevent job burnout, 118–119
    computerized assessment of, 35–40
    importance of, 36
    in premature death risk, 36–37
Life-style balance sheet, 37
Loss-fear-anxiety cycle, 208

Maladaption, 28–29
Managing in a Time of Great Change (Drucker), 215
Market research, 2, 54
Maternity leave, 83, 84
Meaning perspectives, 249
Meaningful relationship building, 234
Mental frameworks, creating resiliency or vulnerability, 233
Mental health day absenteeism, 135
Mental health interventions, 2
    by consultant, 51–52
Mental health professionals, 176–178
Mentors, 235
Mergers, resiliency during, 223–224
Miller-Dixon EBTD model
    Levels of Intervention, 243–245
    programming levels of, 247–248
Mind expanders, 175–176
Mindful behavior, 227–228
Mistakes, willingness to make, 225–226
Moderation, 195
Morale, 224–225
Motivation, burnout and, 104
Mourning process, 145–146
Must's, 62–63
    disputing, 168
    in stress, 164–165

Needs, hierarchy of, 26
Negative emotions, 163–164

Objective prescreening strategies, 17
Occupational stressors, 158–159
Open environment, 48
Optimism, resiliency and, 227
Optimistic explanatory style, 229

Options, diversity of, 185
"Organization man" mentality, 188
Organizational change
  belief systems in, 32
  individual consequences of, 205–206
  issues of, xi
  resiliency in, 219–237
Organizational goals
  incongruent, 1–2, 23–32
  job satisfaction and, 28
Organizational health promotion, 1–4
Organizational health psychology
  channels of help from, xiii
  future for, xv–xvii
  need for, xii–xiii
Organizational implementation
  level programming, 244–245
  in Miller-Dixon EBTD model, 248
Organizational psychologists
  benefits of, 8–9
  in company growth, 9
  training and knowledge of, 8
  in wellness, 37–40
Organizational renewal
  outcome management in, 261–272
  programs for, 199–201
Organizational transformation
  application of change interventions to, 211–214
  experiential training for, 239–259
  reasons for failure of, 205–206
Organizational-individual goal incongruities, 1–2
Organizations
  assumptions about employees, 25–26
  belief systems of, 25–26
Outcome management, 201, 261–262, 270–272
  clinical information for, 267
  consumer satisfaction and progress in, 270
  course indicators in, 268
  demographic data in, 268–269
  economic information in, 268
  follow-up strategies in, 265–266
  implementation approach in, 263–264
  implementation considerations in, 270
  local or facilitywide computers in, 264–265
  preparation phase of, 263
  quality management and, 272
  quality of life and, 269
  required information for, 266
Outdoor experiential training, 241, 255
Outplacement services, 2, 53
Overemoters, 187

Pain. *See also* Chronic pain
  achieving identity with, 151–152
  affect dimension of, 145–147
  biopsychosocial management of, 139, 142–154
  health dimension of, 149–150
  physical dimension of, 144–145
  thinking about, 147–149
  work and, 150–151
Paradigm shift, 207
Parental abuse, increase in, xi–xii
Participative design, 200
Partnership, work-family, 95, 97
Part-time work option, 83
PATHWAY model
  for chronic pain management, 142–154
  components of, 144–153
Pensions, historic background of, 177
Performance evaluation, 28
Performance expectations
  corporate belief systems and, 23–32
  of organization vs. individual, 1–2

Performance standards, self-generated high, 73–74
Person rating, 70–71
Personality factors, 56–57
Personality profile, 12
Personnel evaluation, for growth companies, 1, 5–19
Personnel selection technology, 7–19
Pessimistic explanatory style, 229
Physical resiliency skills, 234
Planning, 66–67
  awfulizing that blocks, 68–70
  to make work easier, 71–72
  person rating and, 70–71
  for resiliency, 235
  of rewards, 72
  should's that block, 67–68
  for unplanned, 72
  worst things first, 71
Poor hires, cost of, 10
Prediction, should of, 67
Pregnancy, benefits for, 84
Premature death, factors in, 36
Preparing for the Twenty-First Century (Kennedy), 204–205
Prescreening
  payback factors of, 10
  strategies for, 1
Prescreening personnel assessment, 2
Prescreening selection programs, validity and reliability of, 11–13
Prioritizing, 57, 191
Problem drinkers, 193
Problem-solving dialog, 50–51
Problem-solving process, group, 254
Procrastination
  goal setting to overcome, 57–60
  incidence of, 55–56
  overcoming problem of, 2
  personality factors in, 56–57
  versus prioritizing, 55
  reducing, 55–75
Procrastinators, chronic, 2

Productivity
  interventions to promote, 1–4
  personnel selection approach and, 10
Promotion from within, 13
Psychological competence, internal locus of, 226–227
Psychological consultant. *See* Consultant
Psychological momentum, 191–192
Psychological stress, 141
Psychometric inventories, 18

Quality indicators, 262
Quality management, 272
  measurement in, 262
Quality of life, measures of, 269
Quality of Well Being Scale, 269

Rational belief, 163
Rational-emotive behavior therapy, 4, 29, 157
  ABCDE framework in, 162–164
  basis of, 174–175
  for belief system incongruity, 29–32
  for chronic pain management, 147–149
  focus on moderation and balance in, 195
  irrationality in, 162
  for job burnout, 109
  in mastering stress and emotional disturbance, 165–169
  overview of, 159–161
  person rating and, 70
  rationality in, 161–162
  techniques used in, 173
  three major musts in, 164–165
Rationality, 161–162
Real-life problem-solving conditions, 18
REBT. *See* Rational-emotive behavior therapy

Recruiting programs
  competitive issues of, 11–13
  consulting opportunities in, 49–50
Reengineering, 200
  failure of, 212–213
Reference checks, 7
Reflection
  process of, 249–250
  in workplace, 251
Relaxation techniques
  before active work, 74
  progressive muscle, 181, 190–191
  workplace stress, 169
Resentment, 134
Resiliency, 219–237
  biological underpinnings of, 232
  core components of, 226–231
  in corporate landscape, 221–226
  definitions of, 220–221
  mental frameworks creating, 233
  personal experiences of, 232
  versus vulnerability, 232
  workplace barriers to, 232–233
Resiliency interview schedule, 236–237
Resiliency network, 235
Resiliency skills training, 231–235
Resiliency symbols, 235
Resiliency trends, 231
Respite care benefits, 81
Restricted psychological measures, 8
Resume review, 7
Rewards
  competence and, 112–113
  future versus immediate, 64–65
  planning of, 72
Rock climbing group, 253
Role ambiguity, 158
Ruminating, 183–184

School, on-site, 83

Search firms, 11–12
Security
  needs in job burnout, 115–116
  resiliency and, 222
Selection process, 49–50
Self-affirmation, 151–152
Self-awareness, 210
Self-control behavior, 228
Self-defeating beliefs, 28–29
Self-denigration, 166
Self-downing, 30
  with chronic pain, 148–149
  in stress, 163
Self-efficacy, 227
Self-esteem, 70–71
Self-indulgent absenteeism, 135
Self-knowledge, 143
Self-managing teams, 200
Self-pity, 230
The 7 Habits of Successful People (Covey), 191
SF-36 Health Status Questionnaire, 269, 271
Shame, 163
Shared adversity, 253–254
Short-term solutions, 195
Should
  of approval, 61–62
  blocking planning, 67–68
  of demandingness, 62–63
  of prediction, 60–61
  problem of, 60
Sick-child care, 81
Sickness Impact Profile, 269
Simulation assessment, 5–6
  prescreening, 18
Skills training, xiii
Slot machine thinking, 183–184
Social Readjustment Rating Scale, 159
Social support
  to prevent job burnout, 117
  in resiliency, 230
  skills for building, 234

Spiritual techniques, 4, 173–174
　for wellness in workplace, 194–195
Spousal abuse, increase in, xi
Staff development
　by consultant, 51
　programs for, 2
Standards, too high, 73–74
Stress
　activating event in, 162, 167
　belief system and, 162–163, 167–169
　burnout and, 103–104, 105–106
　causes of, 159–161
　definition of, 157
　disorders related to, 4
　mastering, 157–169
Stressors
　negative effects of, 106
　occupational, 158–159
　in workplace, 4, 157–169
Structured conversations, 229–230
　skills of, 234
Subjective monotony, 132
Substance abuse/use
　increase in, xii
　reducing, 192–193
Supervision, candidate selection, 9
Systems
　freedom in, 214
　response to change in, 215

Team
　communication in experiential training, 241
　promotion of, 245–248
Team learning, 259. *See also* Group development
　levels of, 242–252
Technology, improvement in, xii
Technology of Patient Experience (TyPE) questionnaires, 267, 270
Telephone interview inventories,
　standardized, 17
Temp work, xv
Temporal myopia, 64–65
Thinking
　ability to change, 179–180
　deconditioning knee-jerk, 181
　manipulation of, 180
　patterns of, with chronic pain, 147–149
　slot machine, 183–184
　taking responsibility for, 178–186
　videotape analogy for, 182–183
Thriving on Chaos (Peters), 207
Time management, 191–192
Training
　for change, 204–205
　costs of, with candidate selection, 8–9
Transformational change interventions, 211–214
Transformative learning
　catalyst for, 248–249
　connecting to EBTD outcomes, 249–252
　process of, 250–252
Trusting environment, establishing, 256–257
Turnover
　with candidate selection, 9
　costs of, 9

Uncertainty, 207–208
Underemoters, 187–188
Unplanned, planning of, 72
Unrealistic expectations, 107–108
Unschedule, 58–59
　to overcome busyness and bingeing phenomenon, 65–66
Upsizing, pressures of, 1

Values
　conflicting, 108

deeply held, 210–211
differences in, 1–2
Vigor, 231
in resiliency, 234
Vulnerability
biological underpinnings of, 232
mental frameworks creating, 233
versus resiliency, 232

Weekend retreats, 194
Well-being, interventions to promote, 1–4
Wellness
behavioral techniques for, 189–193
cognitive approaches to, 178–186
emotive approaches to, 186–189
fourfold path to, 173–196
future of, 195–196
individual vs. organized group efforts toward, 176–178
spiritual techniques for, 4, 194–195
"What if?" scenarios, 270
Wilderness-based programs, 253–254
Work
adjustment study of, 24–25
outmoded attitudes toward, 90–91
stressors of, 4
Work adjustment theory, 25
Work overload, 158
Work-at-home options, 81
Workers' Compensation Boards, chronic pain syndrome definition of, 139
Work-family conflicts, 81
costs of, 85–87

initiatives to resolve, 83–84
Work-family connections, 3, 81–85, 92–94
models of, 82
organizational benefits of improving, 94–95
scarcity model versus expansion model of, 92–93
Work-family programs, 79–81, 81–85
barriers to, 85–91
changes promoting, 91–98
effective marketing of, 95–97
organizational benefits of, 94–95
Work-family surveys, 80
Working conditions, adjustment to, xvi
Working partnerships, 223
Working "smarter," xi
Workload, 104
Workplace
in burnout, 103
change in, 203–215
changing concepts of, xvi
conditions causing stress in, 6–7
family friendly, 79–98
identifying belief systems in, 27–29
impact of, on family, 93
irrational thinking styles in, 30–31
reducing procrastination in, 55–75
stressors of, xvii, 6–7
wellness in, 173–196
Workshops, wellness, 193
Work-vocation based beliefs, 25
Worthlessness, disputing, 168

Yin-yang energy cycle, 206